Managing the Brief for Better Design

Managing the Brief for Better Design

Alastair Blyth and John Worthington

London and New York

First published 2001 by Spon Press
11 New Fetter Lane, London EC4P 4EE

Simultaneously published in the USA and Canada
by Spon Press
29 West 35th Street, New York, NY 10001

Spon Press is an imprint of the Taylor & Francis Group

Typeset in Gill Sans Light by Wearset, Boldon, Tyne and Wear.
Printed and bound in Great Britain by Bell & Bain Ltd, Glasgow.

British Library Cataloguing in Publication Data
A catalogue record for this book is available from the British Library

Library of Congress Cataloging-in-Publication Data
Blyth, Alastair, 1958–
   Managing the brief for better design / Alastair Blyth & John Worthington.
     p. cm.
   Includes bibliographical references and index.
   1. Architectural services marketing. 2. Architectural design–Decision making. 3. Architects and patrons. I. Worthington, John, 1938– II. Title.

   NA1996 .B59 2000
   720'.68'8–dc21

                                                                00-033908

ISBN 0-419-24470-0

Contents

Acknowledgements

The authors are grateful for the advice and help of the following past and present members of DEGW-Twynstra during the preparation of the book: Mick Bedford, Peter Crouch, Peter Duerks, Frank Duffy, Fiona Duggan, Stephen Greenberg, Andrew Harrison, Stacey Lytton Davis, Nick Morgan, Lora Nicolaou, Tuula Rattue, Susan Stuebing, Tony Thomson, Graham Parsey, Melanie Woolcott, Alison White. The authors would also like to thank Emma Dorreen, David Hutton, Nicholas Hare and Gordon Powell for their assistance with the preparation of case studies. They also thank the readers of an early draft for their thoughts and advice: Vic Allison, Ruth Clifton, Geert DeWulf, Adrian Leaman, David Lister and Phil Roberts.

Case Studies for *Part two: Learning from Experience* were received from:

Briefing for rationalisation
Phil Roberts RIBA CFM is an architect and is currently Head of Facilities at Hertfordshire County Council. Before that he worked in the Facilities Group of the British Council, the UK network for cultural and educational co-operation between the UK and other countries.

Briefing the narrative
Christine Hanway was DEGW's project manager for the permanent Holocaust Exhibition at the Imperial War Museum, London.

Briefing for the changing workplace
Turid Horgen is a research associate at the MIT School of Architecture and Planning. She also runs a workplace design practice in the United States of America and Europe.

Strategic briefing
Despina Katsikakis is Managing Director of DEGW and responsible for the building appraisal, consultancy and research work.

Briefing for adaptable use
Susan Stuebing is a senior consultant to DEGW-The Twynstra Group focussing on information technology and strategic decisions for educational environments.

Figure 6.2, page 80 and figures 8.11 and 8.12, page 134. Source: *Problem Seeking: An Architectural Programming Primer*, Pena, Parshall and Kelly (1987). This is a limited licence for use only as described above and only by the people and entities described above. The referenced items may not be used otherwise nor may the licence to use them be transferred without the express written permission of Helmuth, Obata and Kassabaum, Inc.

Foreword

There will no longer be any excuse for corporate and professional clients and their designers denying their interdependence in developing the brief and carrying out post-occupancy evaluation. Although this raises many questions about who is the client and who is (are) the designer(s), this fascinating book provides the theory, together with a range of practical models as to how to deliver best business practice in the first and last phases of the procurement process.

When Egan's *Rethinking Construction* (1998) built on Latham's excellent *Constructing the Team* (1994) and challenged the industry to improve its performance dramatically, he also identified the parts of the business cycle that are normally missing in construction – the testing of the brief and feedback after occupation. Egan drew on the theories of 'lean thinking' in demanding the measurement of performance against benchmarks in order to eliminate waste and improve that performance. The extraordinary energy that the leading firms in the construction industry and their clients have put into innovation in the construction part of the cycle to their mutual benefit, has tended to obscure these areas of the greatest potential value – the brief and the feedback; and it is tragic that there is so little understanding, in the body of the industry, that they are both integral parts of the design process.

This book draws on the remarkable body of research and design of John Worthington, Frank Duffy and their colleagues over 25 years, most of which has focused on the demands of leading-edge multinational corporate businesses. The lessons and the examples are clearly laid out for us all to use, in whatever sector, and develop for our own needs, with the help of many elegant diagrams, some familiar and others new.

The authors are clear about the way the responsibilities of the many parties involved in the construction process change as the process evolves and provide illuminating examples of good and bad practice. There can, of course, be little progress or value without client leadership from the top. Although their experience is mainly drawn from the corporate sector, the lessons must be adopted by the public sector if we are, collaboratively, to deliver better value to the public sector and thus to our individual advantage.

It is of continuing amazement to me that so many so-called professional clients, often purchasing space for high value activities, pass their responsibilities to unambitious, poorly educated, risk averse servants. The worst brief we have worked to was a catalogue of building failures from which the institution had suffered over the previous 30 years; interesting but not very helpful! This particular client then proceeded to prevent the design team from meeting the users on the basis that we might be led astray by them!

Blyth and Worthington and their collaborators have laid out the theory, from Handy to Brand, and the practice from BAA Process maps to Eric Langmuir's mountaineering, with 9 case studies and 5 models for briefs, all tempered with much common sense, and good tips about every aspect, from how to write a questionnaire to how to get most value out of value engineering.

The authors start provocatively by stating that 'design is briefing and briefing relies on design. . .'. As a designer, I know they are right.

Robin Nicholson CBE RIBA

Introduction

Alastair Blyth and John Worthington

Briefing is a creative process. Design is briefing, and briefing relies on design. Louis Kahn, the inspirational American architect, suggested that only when the building is completed, do you know what to build. The completed building for a perceptive client and designer becomes the 'sounding board' to learn what the next building should be.

This book aims to provide both an inspiration to clients and a framework for design and construction practitioners. The book focuses on the process of briefing as an iterative, creative process, a journey to support the client, design and construction teams in achieving the user's expectations.

Briefing origins

The public sector dominated the architecture of the 1950s[1] with architects playing an influential role in both Central Government policy making, and in the housing, education and civic building programmes of counties and cities. The strong sociological and socialist rhetoric of the predominantly public sector architectural culture led the profession to search for method in design and a rationale for brief making. Ergonomics and detailed room requirements were meticulously analysed, often to the detriment of a holistic viewpoint. Social housing was high on the construction agenda, with closely observed activity data analysis, which became the foundations of the Parker Morris standards for publicly-funded housing. Well meaning and highly articulate architects at the Ministries of Housing and Education researched usage and educational theories to build precise building forms around organisational patterns. In North America the market economy and private enterprise exposed a more relaxed attitude to the mission slogan that 'form follows function'. American architect Louis Kahn's teaching at Yale and subsequently the University of Pennsylvania exposed young professionals to the opportunity to consider the 'intangibles' in brief making. Kahn's reminder that the Roman portal was not built to its impressive dimensions merely to accommodate the Centurian's spear, was a revelation to students brought up in the narrow functionalist tradition. In parallel at the University of California, Berkeley, Horst Rittel[2] had identified the need to recognise the world of 'wicked problems' and Christopher Alexander was bringing structure to the realm of briefing with his pattern language.[3]

British architect and co-founder of DEGW Frank Duffy, after undertaking his Masters degree at Berkeley with both Rittel and Alexander, moved to Princeton University where he completed his doctoral dissertation[4] which provided the conceptual framework for an approach to briefing, subsequently developed at DEGW, which disengaged the long-term demands of the building shell from the fit-out and space management within.[5] The focus from the mid-1970s onwards on commercial buildings, provided a sharp understanding of issues such as user participation, building adaptability and managing unpredictable change which became central to the architectural dialogue in the 1980s and 1990s.

Managing the Brief for Better Design draws extensively on DEGW experience over the last 25 years, and the more recent research and teaching undertaken at the Institute of Advanced Architectural Studies (IoAAS) at the University of York.[6] The Masters degree course in Design Brief Management established in 1996 at the IoAAS, by John Worthington and Adrian Leaman, set a conceptual framework for briefing (see Chapter 11), whilst the research programme and consultancy helped to underpin the theory.

Changes

In the 1970s, briefing was conceived as a process of discrete steps, where design could not begin until the briefing stage was completed. The architect for a large building was often confronted with many volumes of detailed technical requirements – the brief, to which he had to respond. Activity data sheets were a methodology for capturing data, and checking design performance. They were seen as a critical requisite to the success of complex projects. Today the brief is recognised to be less concerned at an early stage with detail, and more with articulating the aspirations of the client, and stimulating the design team. An acceptance that the process of briefing is often more important than the brief as product, is hard to accept for those managing projects. Management succeeds by taking fuzzy situations,[7] and bringing order, by breaking a complex set of roles into their constituent parts. Briefs with clear, quantifiable requirements, and checklists are a joy for project managers. Walker[8] summarises the role of the project manager as 'the planning, control and co-ordination of a project from conception to completion (including commission) on behalf of a client. It is concerned with the identification of the client's objectives in terms of utility, function, quality, time and cost, and in the establishment of relationships between resources'.

The reductionist approach of simplifying problems to their quantifiable constituents is being increasingly challenged. In a world of paradox it's clear that 'the creative fusion of ideas can occur by holding seemingly conflicting thoughts in the mind simultaneously, so creative collaboration between people can occur by an effort to retain conflicting cultural and disciplinary viewpoints in the mind without discarding or allowing either to dominate.'[9] Peter Barrett and Catherine Stanley in their recent book, *Better Construction Briefing*,[10] argue that the most perfect brief can often result in poor solutions and vice versa. They argue that success is less about the right checklists, and more about the appropriate process. The research showed that success was a combination of five key solution areas:

- empowering the client;
- managing the project dynamics;

- achieving appropriate user involvement;
- using understandable visualisation techniques;
- building appropriate teams.

Our understanding of the underlying subtleties of briefing, with communications at its core, has moved a long way from the mechanistic, sequential approach of activity data sheets, which isolated design thinking from user studies and brief making.

Challenges

If successful briefing, as Barrett and Stanley suggest, is about client involvement through an interactive process, managing disparate interests, involving all parties, communicating with all the tools we have available, and building appropriate relationships between designers and users, and within the design and implementation teams, what are the opportunities ahead?

Managing the project splits into two distinct roles. The building project manager charged with achieving success by delivering the client's expectations on time and at cost, and the client's project manager who is concerned to manage the client's needs, and achieve his expectations. We have termed this client role the Design Brief Manager, whose role is conciliatory compared to the hard booted construction manager, continuously listening, teasing out user demands, a good communicator and 'soft slippered' in approach. The emerging role of the design brief manager is invariably within the corporate real estate department or in local authority user departments. They have a critical role in monitoring building usage, identifying shortfalls, helping user departments articulate needs, establishing a strategy for action, choosing the appropriate procurement route and managing client expectations. The function starts long before and continues long after the building project, seeing briefing, design, delivery and facility management as one continuous process. At the heart of success is the ability to learn and improve through continuous evaluation and feedback. Much of the recent research and discussion on briefing suggest that the simpler the process, thus allowing maximum time for constructive dialogue, the more likelihood there is of success.

In a rapidly changing world, perhaps we no longer have the luxury to start with a white sheet of paper for each project and painstakingly build up the brief. If, as Louis Kahn suggested, we only have the brief when the building is completed, why can we not begin with proposing a built prototype, evaluate its shortcomings and adapt the model to the specific requirements? Like 'reverse engineering' in the automotive industry. This process might be termed 'reverse briefing'. The process would begin with a form, and through dialogue, testing, evaluating and adjusting, arrive at a statement of requirements.

Futures

Ubiquitous computing has the opportunity to change our perceptions of briefing. Feedback from experience can be stored and assimilated into the next brief. Information technology allows the brief to be evaluated, and added to by all parties instantaneously via inter- or intranets. Add to this the opportunities for computer visualisation, and we are close to the reality of briefing and design becoming a continuous process, where a high percentage of the product could be standardised while key elements are specified for innovation to adjust to specific needs, and improve from feedback.

Format

The book is organised into three parts. Part one sets out the characteristics of briefing, and describes the process of identifying needs, managing change, communicating expectations, learning from experience and managing the process. Part two uses personal case studies to explore aspects of briefing for different client and building types, and the techniques available. Part three is a succinct summary in flow chart form, which, whilst recognising the danger of describing an iterative process in a sequential format, affords a framework with key activities to develop the appropriate approach.

Notes

1 Saint, A., *Towards a Social Architecture: The Role of School Building in Post-War England*, Yale University Press, New Haven and London 1987.
2 Rittel, H., Planen Entwerten Design – Ausgew–ahlte Schriften zu Theorie und Methodik, Verlag W Kohlhammer, Stuttgart, 1992..
3 Alexander, C. *et al.*, *A Pattern Language*, Oxford University Press, New York 1977. See also the companion volume, *The Timeless Way of Building*, which provides the theory and instruction for use of the language.
4 Duffy, F., Office interiors and organisations – A comparative study of the relation between organisational structure and the use of interior space in sixteen office organisations, A dissertation presented to the Faculty of Princeton University, January 1974.
5 DEGW, *Design for Change: The Architecture of DEGW*, Watermark/Birkhauser, Basel 1997.
6 Subsequent research and consultancy included (Research for the Latham Working Party on Briefing (Briefing the Team) consultancy to Hertfordshire County Council on a Briefing and Feedback process) and the EPSRC Innovative Manufacturing Initiative research on 35 years of briefing and design at the University of York, IoAAS, York 1998.
7 Russell Ackoff identified the importance of recognising a period of uncertainty at the beginning of every project, when space and time should be allowed for conflicts and uncertainties to be aired and explored.
8 Walker, A., *Project Management in Construction*, B.S.P. Professional 1984.
9 Hirschberg, J., *The Creative Priority*, Penguin Books, London 1998.
10 Barrett, P. and Stanley, C., *Better Construction Briefing*, Blackwell Science, Oxford 1999.

Part One
Briefing explained

Part one describes a process (briefing) and a product (the brief). The initial two chapters set the context of briefing with a summary of critical issues and key factors to address in achieving success.

The briefing process is sub-divided into three distinct stages. **Pre-project stage**, when the client's needs are identified, options assessed, and a Strategic Brief prepared. The **Project stage**, when the chosen design team validates and acknowledges the client's expectations, and sets out the requirements, and performance criteria in the terminology of building. The **Post-project stage**, on project completion and after move-in when the process, product and performance in meeting the users expectations are evaluated.

Subsequent chapters provide detailed guidance on identifying needs; briefing for growth and change; communicating expectations both within the design teams, and from client to design teams; achieving effective feedback; and managing the process.

1 The nature of briefing

Process and product

Briefing is one of those words with a variety of meanings. In the context of this book, briefing is an evolutionary process of understanding an organisation's needs and resources, and matching these to its objectives and its mission. It is about problem formulation and problem solving. It is also about managing change. Ideas evolve, are analysed, tested and gradually refined into specific sets of requirements. Sometimes these involve modifying the built environment and other times not. Effective briefing begins without pre-conceived solutions.

Briefing is the process by which options are reviewed and requirements articulated, whereas a brief is a product of that process. It is produced at key points in the project formalising decisions and instructions.

The definition may appear far wider than many people are used to. Often, briefing is taken as a short meeting at which someone is given an instruction (the brief) and a bit of background on a project and asked to deliver a solution. Whilst this 'go do it and let me know when you've finished' approach seems an easy way of delegating a chunk of work, it potentially constrains the client. It does not allow options to be kept open so that changing circumstances can be reflected in the project. Instead, clients are often harried into decisions, with the warning by the designers or suppliers that making changes will be costly and delay completion of the project. They also find that assumptions have been made about critical issues such as how they work and what their priorities are. Clients may also find that they are expected to have a far greater knowledge and understanding of, for example, construction and the implications of what will be built, than they really do. The clients' expertise is their business not delivering buildings, they rely on the designers and contractors to provide a delivery service that will support their business needs.

The chapters that follow map out the briefing process to establish a framework on which to hang different activities and tools which will assist clients through the briefing process. Sticking to a process in itself does not guarantee success. However, it does show the importance of sequence and the necessary progression from identifying the organisational needs before identifying the appropriate kind of project and the need to be clear about objectives and priorities before detailed design. And, once the building has been delivered, testing it to see whether it meets with expectations. This process is relevant to all involved in any potential kind of building project, regardless of scale.

Value of briefing

Briefing has risen on the construction client's agenda as users have become more demanding, accommodation more critical to business success and clients have increasingly found that the buildings they procure are often inappropriate for their needs. Although briefing has always been recognised, it has tended to be treated as a 'black art' carried out by 'professionals' and applied to clients with the promise of the perfect solution. Recent Government reviews[1,2] into the construction industry place briefing high on the priority list for improvement. Research[3] into building use shows how important it is that the building and organisation have a matching 'fit'. Issues such as culture and management strategies radically affect the kind of building solution adopted. For example, the level of maturity of the organisation will affect the relationship between the amount and sophistication of technology used in buildings and the intensity of resource an organisation is able to devote to managing it. The research shows that the more complex technology used, the more intense the management has to be to keep it running effectively. This implies that where it is not in an organisation's nature to devote a lot of manpower to running a building then it should steer clear of saddling itself with complex hi-tech solutions. But, in practice, what often happens is that a particular piece of technology is seen as a panacea and used on the assumption that it will make management easier, in the hope that you are relieving the user of some responsibility. This sort of potential problem can be avoided by a clear understanding of the culture and sophistication of the user organisation.

In this era of rapid change, up-front briefing is recognised as a means of achieving greater clarity and more predictability. For clients an assurance that their buildings can respond to change in a reasonably predictable way is important, whether it is to enable individual staff to change from working in individual offices to working in groups or to enable the organisation to lease part of the building to someone else.

Lisanne Bainbridge[4] pointed to the 'ironies of automation' that are central to the difficult relationship between 'man and machine'. She points out that many systems designers see human operators as unreliable and inefficient and so try to supplant them with automatic devices. Here, of course, she is not particularly talking about buildings, it could be automated machine plant. One of the two ironies that she identifies is that designers' errors make a significant contribution to accidents and events. The second irony is that although the designer seeks to eliminate people, the operator is still left to do the things that the designer cannot think how to automate.

This raises the broader question of who should have control over what. Briefing can establish this and return control to the client/user over those things that matter to them. Often what seems to happen is that control over a problem is lost to someone else who has a different agenda or vested interest in a particular solution. Clients lose control because briefing is often perceived as a one-stop event with only one solution promoted by a construction industry with an attitude 'that knows best'. Not enough time is spent in the beginning identifying the issues surrounding the project; it seems easier to hand over the problem to someone who has a ready-to-fit solution. The trouble with this is that often the contractual routes adopted deny clients and users much of a say in what goes on. As Bainbridge pointed out the irony is frequently designers do not quite solve all the problems that are theirs to resolve and the users are left to carry on as best they can.

The nature of the project is perceived quite differently by the client organisation and the design and construction team. The client organisation is focused on the success of its business. A big supermarket chain will see itself as a grocer. Its business is about satisfying customer needs. Buildings are one of the resources along with staff and information technology. For them a building project is part of its overall business project.

For the designers and builders, building is very often perceived as one of a series of projects to be delivered on time and within budget.

Perspectives vary within the client organisation too. Management is concerned with long-term flexibility, while from the individual user's point of view the built environment must respond immediately to changing need whether it is being able to turn the lights on, or at a more complex level, responding to organisational change. Facility managers are very often interested in the financial performance of the building for cost in use and energy consumption. Developers and managing agents are interested in rental values and the market perception of a building.

Already one can see how complex the web of expectations can become, without including specific specialist requirements or the broader interests of customers and the local community.

During the briefing process these issues can be identified and, where relevant, fed into the project.

Reflecting cultural values

There are clear relationships between an organisation and its culture, and between the culture and the building. The importance of culture to organisations has been recognised since the earliest management literature. Early business pioneers saw their role as creating an environment – in effect a culture – in their companies where employees could be secure and thereby do the work necessary to make the business a success. Culture has a powerful influence throughout an organisation, affecting almost everything from the way that people are managed, the look of the environment and how buildings are used. It shapes the organisation's value system and is a framework around which staff operate, are managed and organised. The environment reflects the culture and can reinforce and communicate it through the way that space is designed, allocated, subdivided and managed. An organisation's values provide a framework around which it can be explicit about its objectives and priorities. A company with a strong culture can gain as much as one or two hours of productive work per employee per day[5]. To enable this to happen the physical setting, technology, work processes, management style, philosophy and values should be in harmony. Organisations with strong cultures such as the Body Shop, or even the Church, remove uncertainty for people because they provide structure, standards and value systems in which to operate.

RECOGNISING THE INFLUENCE OF DIFFERENT PARADIGMS AND PERSPECTIVES

The early stages of identifying needs, alternatives and establishing the decision to build is inevitably a 'fuzzy' process. At the early stage of problem definition, a mismatch has been identified, but neither the scope, the solutions nor the resources required are clearly articulated.

Dr Roy Woodhead in his doctorate thesis identified the origins of a proposal to build and explored its evolution to a point where it could be called a project. The research found that at the pre-project stage the decision to build is subjected to a wide range of different viewpoints, reflecting the interests, experience and discipline cultures of the varying decision makers. These viewpoints were described as paradigms – 'collection of rules, codes of practice and peer expectations that can be identified as belonging to a particular school, social institute or profession'. Within paradigms, different perspectives exist and fight for dominance. During decision making, paradigms and perspectives are influencing either the 'process' or the 'content' of the decision, or a mixture of the two, and can be either predominantly 'internally' or 'externally' focused, or be imposed by an 'outside agent'.

With experienced client organisations, Woodhead identified four clear roles:

* decision approver (e.g. the main board);
* decision taker (e.g. senior executives);
* decision shaper (e.g. the internal real estate department);
* decision influencer (e.g. external stakeholders and consultants).

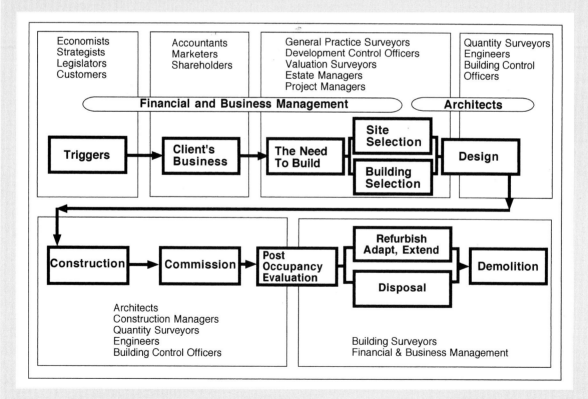

At the ill-defined pre-project stage, the design shapers–project managers will often be pulling the decision approvers and takers to make decisions whilst they are balancing the alternative viewpoints and options. The construction paradigm 'may cause client-teams (i.e. decision shapers) to pursue project efficiency at the expense of organisational effectiveness'.

The decision to build involves a wider spectrum of professionals, each reflecting their respective professional value systems, rules and expectations. Successful strategic briefing at the pre-project stage should recognise these different viewpoints, and allow the time and space for the differences to be voiced.

Source: Woodhead, R. M. The influence of Paradigms and Perspectives on the Decision to Build Undertaken by Large Experienced Clients of the UK Construction Industry, PhD Thesis, School of Civil Engineering University of Leeds, UK (1999).

The shared values and beliefs play a key role in communicating to the outside world what it can expect from the firm. Identifying the 'culture' is difficult. Culture is intangible, often inexplicit and taken for granted because it is hidden in the codes and norms of the organisation, only becoming apparent if rules are broken. It is easy to assume that culture can be designed into a building as an applied finish. When this happens it is from a misunderstanding that, by applying visual images, the culture will follow.

Projects for organisations are about specific priorities which matter deeply to them. These priorities are incorporated in the values and beliefs of the organisation. It is important to identify the essential elements that make the culture unique and will help it flourish. Successful briefing is as much about identifying and communicating these intangible needs, as it is about specifying the measurable.

Critical issues in briefing

CASE STUDY: ARTICULATING PRIORITIES

Two years ago a biotechnology company began building a new facility which included a small and large laboratory space. It was one of a growing number of firms working in the area of genetics, and like most such companies it relied not only on people but also on expensive technology that was sensitive to its environment. Without the equipment the business could not function and given the high capital investment needed to keep up with the state-of-the-art technology such businesses have to be sure that they can recoup the cost fairly quickly.

During construction the designers issued a number of instructions to the contractors changing the route of pipework as well as amending the position of some windows and doors. It emerged that although the client was going to have to pay for these alterations they were not essential to the effective operation of the building so far as his business was concerned. When he questioned the designers about whether the environment in the building would enable the technology to operate effectively they seemed to dismiss it rather casually, giving him some sleepless nights. A review of the brief to the designers showed that although they had information about the business and its activities, the importance of the technology was understated.

Later the client said that he thought it was obvious that if the equipment did not work he would not have a business.

Clearly defining and articulating the goals and priorities for the project is essential. This may seem obvious but in reality people make different assumptions wherever there are ambiguities. When seen from different perspectives the relative importance of different requirements in a project change. In the example above the client quite reasonably assumed that the designers would have understood the nature of his business and that the technology was critical. But clearly they did not and had created a different set of priorities. It emerged later that although there had been interaction between the client and design team most of that focused on the building and its construction, with very little interrogation of the client's business.

In some cases the client may not be clear about priorities and how to communicate them. This may happen where, in the flurry of activity to get things rolling, too little time has been spent early on teasing out the reasons for doing it. The early stage of the briefing process is critical in ensuring that objectives are clearly defined. The project can then be tested against these objectives both throughout its development and once it has been completed. Clearly defined priorities will help the client get what it wants from the project and not only what a designer thinks they should have. Not only will defined objectives provide a basis for appraisal but they will also help identify available building and organisational options.

Many projects suffer from poor definition due to inadequate time and thought being given at an early stage. The amount of time it takes to develop a brief is frequently underestimated due to a sense of urgency fuelled by the desire for an immediate solution. Though time might be set aside, it is the undivided attention of the right decision maker that is critical, rather than 'hours spent'. This quality time may only last a day, so it is important to decide who should be involved and what input is expected from them.

Building projects often emerge from an ether of vague decisions and assumptions about an organisation's future. Sometimes they are the result of the personal aspirations of a senior manager or just a solution that is assumed to be correct. It is too easy to jump straight to what appears to be the obvious solution and post-rationalise the reasons for adopting it.

The biotechnology company already had a building from which it was operating, but it was old, not big enough and difficult to adapt to meet the company's emerging needs. Information on how the previous facility worked is invaluable when looking at modifying an existing or constructing a new building. The biotechnology company was lucky, the old building provided a benchmark which it could use to identify what did and did not work well. However, the firm did not build it originally and so had no experience of procuring a new building. Most clients are in a similar position and they have to rely on experience gleaned by other organisations and their professional advisers. This feedback is crucial to the success of the project and critical to the briefing process.

Briefing involves learning from failures and successes both inside and outside the organisation, whether these are to do with the business, its context or its buildings. Through briefing one can organise and evaluate this feedback to aid decision-making. The value of feedback is relevant to all involved in building projects from the once-in-a-lifetime experience, to those involved in intermittent or continuous building programmes. Organisations constructing buildings on a regular basis have a readily accessible pool of experience to draw upon, and there is the opportunity to incorporate this feedback into the established management systems.

Briefing is a matter of balancing two distinct interests (Figure 1.1): those of the users on the demand side, and those of the delivery team on the supply side. It is important to clearly identify the two because they need to be managed to enable a coherent solution. Difficulties often arise with the demand side speaking a different language from the supply side. Users and others on the demand side will talk in terms of their business and organisation, whereas those on the supply side will speak in terms of construction with a technical language appropriate to their activities. At an operational level design teams will be in the habit of communicating with visual aids, drawings and photographs, whereas the user may be more used to written reports and not familiar with the idiosyncrasies of a designer's drawing. Agendas of the two streams often vary. User interest will continue to change throughout a project so that they keep options open for as long as possible, to ensure maximum business flexibility. Those on the supply side will want to fix everything as soon as possible to reduce risk, particularly as they will be assessed against meeting budgets and achieving the programme. Managers responsible for briefing will need to strike a balance between these two forces, enabling the user to keep options open until the last responsible moment, while giving the project team the relevant information at the appropriate stage of the project (Figure 1.2).

The danger with any iterative process is that a decision is never reached, or that the mist of ideas and information never seems to clear. This often happens when objectives are unclear or seemingly clear but ambiguous, and when there is a poor decision-making strategy.

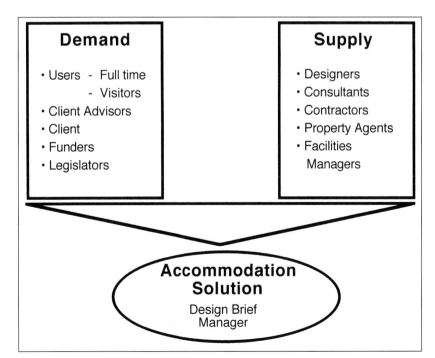

Figure 1.1: Two distinct teams characterised by supply and demand have distinctly different interests in the project. They also communicate using different languages. The job of the design brief manager is to enable the two to communicate effectively. *Source: DEGW*

Figure 1.2: Careful planning at the start can result in major cost benefits later. The potential to save money reduces and the cost of making changes to the project increases as the project progresses.
Source: DEGW

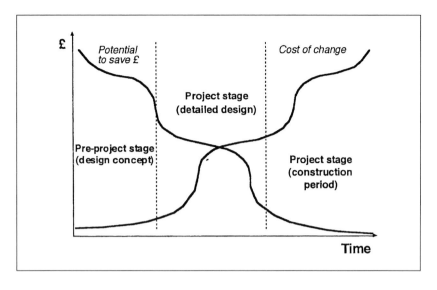

Effective decision making

Effective decision-making processes are the backbone of an effective briefing strategy. Knowing when and what kinds of decisions must be made is crucial to the success of any project. Often, there is a conflict between those who want to freeze the decisions early in the project, and those who want to keep them open for as long as possible. Freezing all the decisions early may affect a client's ability to react to ongoing changes in its business context which may be significant on a long project. Keeping options open may impede design progress because nothing is fixed. A good briefing process is one that provides timely information to meet the needs of the business, the needs of design development and the needs of the construction contract.

Within an organisation, a clear distinction can be drawn between long-term strategic and day-to-day tactical decisions, with a clearly set out programme of who is responsible and how decisions are agreed.

There are three layers of decision making: Corporate, departmental and individual (Figure 1.3). The corporate decision makers are more concerned with the strategic decisions affecting the business such as whether to build and where. Departmental managers and individual managers operate at a more tactical level, whilst the individual looks for maximum freedom of choice without influencing neighbours' quality of environment.

Too often the wrong kinds of decisions are made at the wrong time. Senior managers are often prematurely faced with making decisions about detail at an early stage in the project when strategic decisions are required. During the early stages of briefing, decisions may focus more on the building structure and decisions about furnishing would follow later.

To help order the decision-making process, several levels of design decisions have been identified in a model proposed by DEGW in 1972 (Figure 1.4). These represent different time horizons and stages of permanence[6]. A decision about the shell (cladding and structure) of a building affects the ability

Corporate
• Image, cost
• Size – space standards
• Configurations – type of layout
• Location of department – stacking

Departmental
• Relationships – block plan
• Degree of enclosure
• Space budget

Group
• Style of work
• Detailed layout

Individual
• Workplace

Figure 1.3: Establishing who should make or contribute to which decisions and when enables an effective briefing strategy.
Source: DEGW

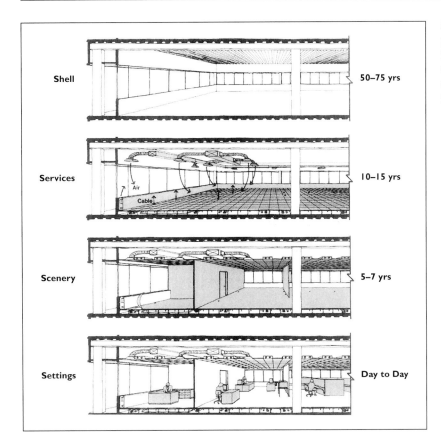

Shell   50–75 yrs

Services   10–15 yrs

Scenery   5–7 yrs

Settings   Day to Day

Figure 1.4: The original diagram proposed by DEGW in 1972 shows four levels of design decisions represent different time horizons and different stages of decision making. *Source: DEGW*

of the building to adapt to organisational change over a long period. A decision about the 'setting' (desks and chairs) affects the ability of the building to reflect daily change.

Effective briefing takes advantage of the most appropriate resources both inside and outside the organisation. When and where the different skills and knowledge bases are used depends on the stage of the project. Consultants engaged during the early stages of project definition may become part of the design team once the project is underway. Such continuity provides familiarity with the organisation and project expectations. However, by using consultants who will be delivering the subsequent project, clients may be concerned about a vested interest in adopting a construction option. To ensure the widest range of options are considered, consultants for the pre-project briefing stage should be independently appointed.

Briefing is a collaborative process between the various parts of the client body, advisers, users and design team. These roles represent different interests in the outcome of the project. The key role is that of the project champion who should 'take ownership' of the project, lead the briefing process and have authority and responsibility to make decisions. It should be someone who can promote the project both within the client organisation as well as outside. A project champion should be nominated within the organisation to take responsibility for the client's role, and particularly to communicate with the project team. The project champion leads the project for the client and sets its parameters.

Achieving briefing success

There are six key areas that are important to appreciate when briefing.

1. Defining the process

First, there is the definition of the process which sets the framework for the briefing work (see Chapter 2). This is not about slavishly following a sequential flow-chart of steps; in reality the process will be interactive, fuzzy and concurrent.

2. Timely decision taking

This is about identifying the value in spending time early on to accurately define the issues to be tackled and of managing the process of making decisions when they are necessary rather than too early when they can become a constraint, or too late when they become expensive (see Chapter 7). It is also about recognising that the briefing process is continuous and looks back on itself as feedback is generated, and looks forward as feedback is used to inform future decisions.

3. Understanding underlying agendas

Property need arises for a host of reasons (see Chapter 3). Sometimes a set of personal or corporate agendas masquerade as real need whether it is why the building is necessary at all or a corporate view about how individuals may use it which is at odds with the reality. A sharp focus on need will lead to a project solution attuned to the organisation and the way that it works today and may work in the future. Change is a substantial driver of organisational life. However, changes in management involves abandoning the old rules, which are all to do with imposing solutions on people. It means getting to know what people need.

4. Planning for future change

The rate at which organisations change seems often to be much faster than the ability of the real estate to keep up (see Chapter 4). 'Futureproofing' is an important element of the briefing process. It enables the organisation to address how change might impact on its built environment whether it be in terms of the location of buildings, work patterns or impact of information and communications technology.

5. Clear and comprehensive communication

Successful briefing demands attention to communication and how information is structured and passed through the system (see Chapter 5). Designers speak different languages to users, yet they must understand the business language of their clients for there to be meaningful communication of needs. Dangers lie in misunderstandings, but also in assumptions where one person interprets something differently from another.

6. *Feedback of experience*

Feedback comes from two places, either learning from within the project, whether it is during the process or from the completed building (see Chapter 6), or it comes from outside the project and organisation such as other companies or the construction industry. Feedback is vital both to the management of the building and the organisation. It is also important for understanding how to carry out such projects in the future as well as managing the briefing process itself.

Notes

1   Latham, M., *Constructing the Team,* HMSO 1994.
2   Rethinking Construction, Construction Task Force 1998.
3   Leaman, A., Bordass, W., Cohen, R. and Standeven, M., *The Probe Occupant Surveys,* Probe Conference, CIBSE February 1997.
4   Bainbridge, L., *The Ironies of Automation,* in Rasmussen, J., Duncan, K. and Leplat, J. (eds), *New Technology and Human Error,* Wiley 1987.
5   Deal, T. and Kennedy, A., *Corporate Cultures: The Rites and Rituals of Corporate Life,* Penguin 1982.
6   Duffy, F. and Worthington, J., *Designing for changing needs.* Built Environment 1972.

2 Articulating the briefing process

Introduction – unravelling the process

Briefing is a process of refinement from a general expression of need to a particular solution. Different types of brief mark the various stages of the process.

The process starts with an examination of the need for a building and extends beyond handover into an evaluation of the building in use (Figure 2.1).

In this chapter the process is unravelled to identify the key components. The extent to which specific projects follow each step depends on their size and complexity. The process presented sets out a framework around which the briefing for specific situations can be built. The process described is linear,

Figure 2.1: The briefing process starts before design and extends beyond building completion.
Source: DEGW

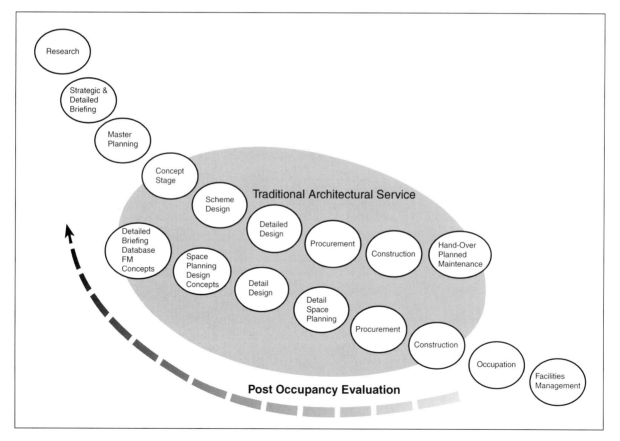

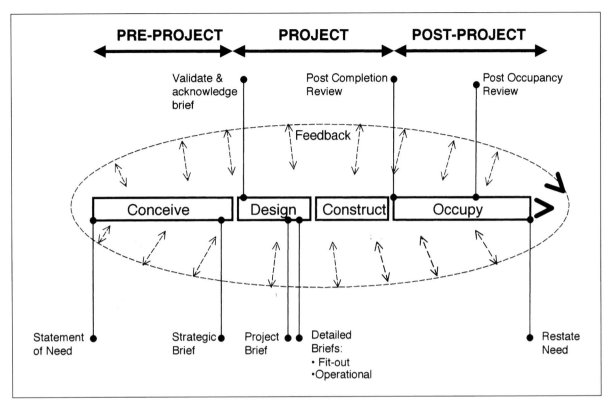

Figure 2.2: There are three principle stages in briefing: Pre-project, Project and Post-project.

though in reality it is not always so simple since some activities might run concurrently.

Three stages to the briefing process delineate different types of activity: the pre-project stage, project stage and post-project stage (Figure 2.2). During the pre-project stage the client defines the need for the project and sets it out in a Strategic Brief. The nature of the business and its objectives are examined and different options are tested, only at the end of this stage is the type of project defined. During the project stage, the design team validates and refor-mulates the Strategic Brief and produces a design which becomes the Project Brief. The project is then delivered. During the post-project stage the result is tested to see whether it meets the need defined in the earlier briefs.

Pre-project stage – setting the strategy

The briefing process starts when a member of the client organisation identifies business objectives which are not being fully met. This represents a need which must be satisfied. A variety of factors may cause this, such as: changes in the operating environment, new legislation, or increasing customer demand for service or products. At this stage there should be no presumption that there will be a 'project', or if there is, that it will be only one project.

Briefing can originate from different primary interests. There may be a financial interest, perhaps driven by the need to reduce costs of space; a human resources interest which is driven by a change in staff numbers or work style; real estate driven; or originated by an information and communications technology need. Briefing could also originate through organisational strategy where the direction of the business is set down but has consequences for its buildings.

The awareness of the 'need' quite often occurs at an operational level in the organisation – for example a production manager trying to meet an increased order book. It may be a 'gut' feeling, based on previous experience rather than through an analytical process. This awareness develops through a period of 'incubation' in which various stimuli enable the manager to build up a picture of the extent to which an organisation's circumstances deviate from what is normally expected. These stimuli are likely to be related to internal performance measures such as turnover or profit, customer reaction to service or quality and changes in the environment such as technological change, the economy or competition.

The role that individuals play in recognising the need is important. Successful business performance often comes down to an organisation's ability to sense its environment either subjectively through feedback from the staff and customers or more objectively through analysis against performance criteria.

Identifying the issues involves gathering enough information to clarify the situation without spending too much time on formal analysis.

To articulate the need, the manager should briefly set out the issues so that the organisation's senior management team can decide whether it is worth pursuing. This statement of need becomes a brief – it is, in effect, asking for someone in the organisation to take action.

Assessing needs, resources and expectations

In response to the statement of need a senior manager reviews the problem and may assemble a 'business case team' of staff and external advisors to assist. The aim is to identify whether the need exists, analyse its causes and assess the extent to which current resources enable it to be met now and in the future (see Chapter 3). The study reviews the 'organisational brief' including business objectives, corporate requirements and policies on property.[1]

The study is wide ranging and may bring into question elements of the business plan that are unclear or may need re-thinking. The research will draw on analysis of documentation and records as well as existing managerial experience. It can be a mixture of desk-based research, surveys and participative workshops which can be used to identify the business expectations and priorities as well as the 'softer' management issues not easily recognised from facts and figures. The process of formulating the issues may bring to the surface different problems and so highlight other needs. Such an analysis can also identify major constraints on the organisation such as the money available to spend on future projects. Focusing the data collected to that which will allow the business case to be formulated, and show physical implications, increases the likelihood of success.

Much of the relevant knowledge will be in written records and reports, and in the experience of the staff in the organisation. Interactive workshops and focus groups can be one way of teasing out such latent knowledge. Also, some of the information will lie outside the organisation which can be effectively accessed by benchmarking, building visits and hiring external experts to provide input at the needs and option appraisal stage. Although information is crucial to making a decision, managers need to balance the effort required to gather this information and its value. Often there is a bottomless pit of interesting information, much of which may only fog the clarity of assessing options and choosing a solution.

To use limited time effectively, this stage needs to ensure that the data collected is relevant to making the appropriate decision. In this 'fuzzy' stage, blind alleys can be easily followed.

The assessment of needs and resources then becomes a springboard for developing and testing different options for meeting the needs.

Generating and assessing options

The process of generating and assessing options is interwoven, with information gathering (see Chapter 3). As the issue or problem is analysed and the information sifted, possible options arise. If one option becomes a preferred route, subsequent analysis of the problem is then affected by whether it fits with the particular solution. For this reason, a distinction must be made between the information gathering phase and option generation phase.

Options should be distinctly different, rather than variations on a theme. Enough options should be provided against which to make a decision, while too many is a recipe for indecision. The range of options might include management changes, a new or extended building, a mixture of these or 'do nothing'. The status quo provides a useful benchmark against which to judge the effect of any changes. It implies that the organisation is not about to embark on change for its own sake.

The aim is to refine the list to a few viable routes each backed by a business case. The choice being made at senior management level.

At this stage a value management review (see Chapter 7) is an effective method of ensuring that there is a shared understanding within the client and user organisations. Value management reviews are structured exercises run generally with the help of an external facilitator to identify underlying goals and reassess opportunities[3]. They also enable those involved to take ownership of problems and are a valuable way of eliciting information and knowledge within the company which can often remain hidden because nobody thought it important. To be really effective these reviews should take place at key decision points throughout the project (Chapter 7), and be facilitated from outside the project team.

Formalising the chosen strategy

Once the decision is made about which type of project to pursue, a Strategic Brief can be used to set out the parameters of the project[2]. The brief is used to instruct the design team, whether it is for a construction, facilities planning, business re-engineering or IT project.

A Strategic Brief is a document that sets out the aims of the project (see Chapter 5 and Chapter 9) (Figure 2.3). It is written in the language of business with clear statements of intent against which later results can be measured. The Strategic Brief should be concerned with 'ends' rather than 'means' (Figure 2.4). But often the reverse happens and briefs at this stage dictate how to achieve the result rather than set out what the result should be.

An inspirational statement:
'The new head office development should provide an attractive, energy efficient building with a quiet, reserved architectural style which motivates and supports the staff of the company, and in which management can plan and reconfigure working groups with minimum disruption.'

Figure 2.3: Mission statement focuses on the project and inspires the participants.

Organisation	Building
• Flatter (less hierarchical)	• *Mixture of open & closed – individual & shared space*
• Faster change	• *Adaptable fit-out*
• More team work	• *Greater variety in settings*
• Greater individual autonomy	• *Flexible environmental control*
• Greater interaction	• *Large contiguous floor plates*
• More effective decision making (speed)	
• Flexible working patterns	• *Adaptable security + environmental systems*
• More effective use of technology	• *Daylight, personal control, natural material*
• Concern for quality for workplace	• *Informal meeting spaces*
• Shared knowledge	• *Open areas – interactive*
• Home based working	• *Support facilities (training area)*

Figure 2.4: Particular organisational attributes matched against building response (language of business, language of building). The organisational attributes are articulated in the Strategic Brief and the building response is developed during the project stage.
Source: DEGW

For example a university department wanted a lecture theatre, where in fact it needed the capacity to hold more lectures, a demand which might have been met by better timetabling and management.

Project stage – validating the strategy

Once appointed, the design team validates the Strategic Brief. Validation involves acknowledging to the client that the design team has understood the brief. It is an opportunity for them to clarify the client's objectives and for the client to ensure that they understand its priorities, particularly those to do with quality, time and cost. It is also an opportunity for the design team to identify the information they need and when they need it. This process reduces the likelihood of disagreements later about the fundamental direction of the project.

Validation is a thoughtful and considered response to the brief. The design team explores the opportunities, constraints and costs arising from the Strategic Brief.

Also, it is an opportunity for them to collect further data as well as to talk to users to better understand the need. It may be appropriate to carry out interviews with the client and users, as well as surveys of the site and existing buildings.

At this stage another value management review will assist the understanding between the client, users and designers.

Developing the project, fit-out and operating briefs

The Project Brief is compiled by the design team and reflects the design process (see Chapter 5). The aim of this is to begin the process of converting the organisational and business language of the Strategic Brief into building terms, fixing functional relationships, giving initial sizes, areas and volumes and establishing quality and image.

On large or complex projects it is useful to divide the project development phase into several iterations (for example, concept, draft final project brief) with milestones for each so that the client can test the proposals and respond before the design has developed too far. Although there would be regular contact between the project team and client, it is useful to establish points during the project when it can be evaluated against the Strategic Brief. Companies like BAA carry this out by having evaluation days where the client and project team spend a day going through every aspect of the project (Figure 2.5). Regular evaluation gives the client confidence in the management of the project and enables decisions to be fixed.

During design, the design team will test and retest ideas. The client should expect alternatives, identifying the cost and benefits of each.

The Draft Project Brief enables the client to review the direction of the project. Value management and risk management techniques (see Chapter 7) enable the brief to be tested against the priorities and objectives set out in the Strategic Brief. The client will then need to agree and sign off the brief.

The Draft Project Brief is refined to a greater level of detail and becomes the Project Brief. This will give dimensions, finishes, colours and a cost plan. As before, it must be evaluated against the Strategic Brief to determine whether it meets the priorities and objectives. The Project Brief is the springboard for producing the detailed construction information to build or extend the building. The client is being asked to confirm the scheme for the project, the cost and the timescale. Again, workshops can be used to test it, agree changes and identify risks. The aim is to minimise the impact of changes and ensure that there is sufficient contingency if change is likely (see Chapter 4). To allow for change, separate briefs may be developed for fit-out and operations which will continue to be central to the management and use of the building long after the new building project is completed.

The fit-out brief for a building project may be a separate or integral part of a Project Brief; although often, in commercial projects, a fit-out is treated as a separate project from producing the structure and envelope of the building. In some situations there may be no other project than a 'fit-out' since the structure, envelope and cores already exist.

The aim of the fit-out brief is to define, in building terms, the client's requirements for the internal building spaces. It responds to the Strategic Brief by setting out the aims of the design and gives detailed information on the dimensions of spaces and elements to be provided.

The operating brief sets out the concept, guidelines and management databases for the project so that it can be used to inform continuing planning and design decisions. The manager who will be responsible for the project after completion should be part of the team developing this brief.

Post-project stage – evaluation and feedback

Feedback can take three forms. Evaluation of the process of design and construction. Evaluation of the product, the building as hardware. Evaluation of performance, which considers how the building supports the organisations performance.

Evaluation of the process which may both occur during and after the delivery of the project. During the briefing process one is trying to progressively fix decisions, moving from broad strategic decisions to the more specific.

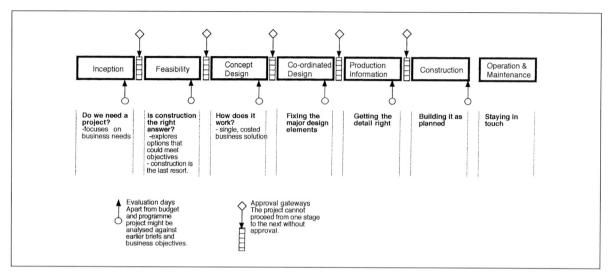

Figure 2.5: Project process at BAA. BAA's project process shows the rigour of evaluation and appraisals throughout. The benefit of constant planning and review is the ability to progressively fix decisions and approve progress throughout the project.
Source: Adapted from BAA's Project Process map[4]

It will be important that everyone involved is clear from the outset about what is to be expected at each evaluation. This should be set out in the Strategic Brief. After each evaluation the client should make the decision to proceed to the next stage and sign off the work completed so far (Figure 2.5).

At the end of the project, a review of the process will identify what worked well or not so well (see Chapter 6). It can give clients a valuable insight into how they may want to change the way that they manage building projects, or if they do not build again, give them information on their management processes. However, such reviews rely on trust. The danger is that they become tools for allocating blame. Where this happens, or is likely to happen, people will not co-operate and a valuable source of data is lost. Developing an atmosphere of trust is hard in our litigious society. But it will be worth it.

Post occupancy evaluation is a review of a building once it has been in occupation for a while, perhaps nine months to a year. A survey is carried out to look at whether the building is meeting the performance measures identified in the early briefs, as well as how the users are using the building. From this information both the building and organisation can be adapted to the new circumstances. It will be worth carrying out similar evaluations periodically afterwards, as this will enable further adjustments to the organisation or building to be made. The information from these reviews becomes a vital ingredient for other projects, even those that do not directly involve building.

Summarising the briefing process

Briefing is a process of understanding an organisation's context, its needs and resources, and matching these to its business objectives. Briefing is iterative, reflective and interactive. Ideas evolve, are tested against different scenarios and some are dismissed whilst others are developed in greater detail. Good briefing implementation is key to providing a systematic and controlled process which avoids expensive mistakes or inferior products. Briefing relies on the interaction between individuals and teams in organisations, and is concerned

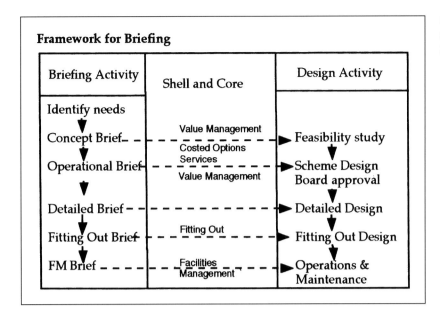

Figure 2.6: Framework for briefing activity.
Source: DEGW

with the communication and management of information within and between these teams.

Design and briefing are integral parts of the same process with much of briefing carried through the process of design (Figure 2.6). During this process the language used by the organisation is converted into the language of building. The Strategic Brief is articulated through words and diagrams, while the Project Brief is articulated through conceptual drawings and workflow diagrams.

SUMMARY OF THE BRIEFING PROCESS

Pre-project stage
Statement of need
* The briefing process begins in response to a statement of need, which provides the initial description of the client organisation's needs to meet a business objective.
* It defines the need, indicates the magnitude and specifies the nature of response and decisions required.
* It is provided by a senior manager.
* The response is to agree to proceed and agree the amount of resources to be allocated.

Assessment of needs and options
* Undertaken by the Business Case Team, supported by the Client Adviser.
* Analyses the client organisation's needs and resources.
* Defines requirements.
* Prepares and tests options.
* Assesses value for money.
* Reviews the needs and requirements against client expectations.

Strategic Brief (see Model Briefs, Chapter 9)
* Prepared by the Business Case Team, and agreed by the Project Sponsor.
* Presents the client organisation's needs and objectives, and outlines assessment of construction requirements.
* Provides an inspirational statement of intent and sets out key objectives, client expectations and method of procurement.
* Reviews statement of requirement against original objectives.

Project stage

Draft Project Brief – acknowledges client requirements and expectations
* Prepared by the design team to validate the client's requirements (Formal Strategic Brief).
* Establishes initial design implications of the outline parameters.
* Contains outline information on the function and configuration of the project.
* Establishes what is expected at next stage.

Enhanced Project Brief
* Undertaken by design team, to establish detailed function, and includes concept scheme design.
* Tests design options.
* Identifies potential risks.
* Assesses value for money, access value for the business case.
* Ensures the brief covers the extent of the project.

Project Brief (see Model Briefs, Chapter 9)
* Sets out functional and operational requirements of the project and includes scheme design.
* Contains information on the size, cost, image and implementation of the project.
* Prepared by the project team and agreed by the users, the client and advisers.
* Assessing value for the business case.
* Assessing risk.
* Encapsulates the performance criteria for the design, and the mechanisms for measuring success and controlling and monitoring change.

Detailed briefs for related topics such as:
* Fit-out (See Case Studies: Model Briefs for example – Chapter 9).
* Furniture (See Case Studies: Model Briefs for example – Chapter 9).
* Information and communications technology requirements.
* Environmental issues.
* Facilities management.

Post-project stage

Post-occupancy evaluation
* Reviews design and construction process, performance of fabric and the facility's use, so that improvements can be made to the project and recommendations made for future building programmes.
* Monitors space performance, records of feedback, measures performance.
* Assesses success of design and construction process in meeting client objectives, and make recommendations for future building programmes.
* Assesses building use against proposals and evaluates client/user satisfaction.
* Aims to assess whether the facility works; the systems and features operate efficiently; and the use of the facility meets the long term goals of the organisation.

Notes

1   Construction Industry Board, *Briefing the Team,* Thomas Telford 1997.
2   Nutt B., 'The Strategic Brief', *Facilities*, Vol. 11 No. 9, 1993. MCB University Press.
3   Male, S., Kelly, J., *Value Management in Design and Construction*, E & FN Spon 1992.
4   BAA *Project process*, BAA.

3 Identifying needs

People often assume that there is a correct, identifiable need which, once pinned down, leads to the obvious answer. Nothing could be further from reality. Needs are compiled from a collection of different interests which are unique to the organisation at a particular time. Briefing is a matter of balancing these interests so that each is taken into account and given a priority[1].

The needs of the organisation are driven by its business goals, its business environment and its operating context, as well as the culture of the organisation[2]. Different stakeholders, from the main board of a company through to individual staff and users of the buildings, have different perspectives and expectations. Invariably each sees their roles and interests as the more dominant.

STUDYING SPACE USE OVER TIME: AN EXAMPLE

A large UK bluechip company began a project to build a new training centre. The company manufactures and sells a variety of technology for use in offices. As with many such leading-edge companies, training is vital throughout all levels of the organisation. The information for the brief was collected from the managers of the training programmes. The quantity of space needed was based on the total number of training rooms that each department would use at one time. However, according to the training schedule, that peak demand would only occur during two days in the year. The brief also assumed that different sets of spaces would be needed for the three types of training programmes that the company ran: management, technical and sales.

Accordingly the new building was to include classrooms, syndicate rooms and technical laboratory spaces as well as residential accommodation for staff attending courses lasting longer than a day. However, the costed scheme was well in excess of what the company wanted to pay.

Concerned both about the amount of space required and the cost of providing it, the corporate client called in consultants to investigate the spatial demand.

The first task for the consultants was to test how the facility would be used over a period of time. This would show whether there were too many spaces. In many situations it is not easy to project accurately the future use of spaces. However, the annual training plans for each of the programmes provided a model of future use. The consultants assembled a database on the types of courses, when they were to be held, the number of people involved and type of space they needed both for training and residential accommodation. There was to be a range of configurations of classrooms, syndicate rooms and laboratories.

It emerged that during one week of the year, because of the way that the timetable was arranged, 16 classrooms would be in use at once. These classrooms would each have several syndicate rooms attached. Over the rest of the year the average use would be much less and during some weeks they would not be used at all.

The brief did not take account of the fact that while the three training programmes were different, the classrooms, laboratories and syndicate rooms they used were identical. Since the training programmes were conceived as weekly programmes, the required spaces would be booked for the week. However, the courses tended to run only for one or two days.

The most expensive element in the proposed building was the residential accommodation, particularly the cost of providing serviced bedrooms. Again, this element of the brief was based on peak demand and assumed that everyone booked on the course would stay there, without taking into account the extent to which people dropped out of courses, or stayed elsewhere.

The consultants' research suggested that with better co-ordination of training programmes by the respective managers, more efficient use could be made of the facilities by evening-out the peaks and troughs in demand. It also suggested that the programme should be conceived in terms of half-weekly slots which equated with the length of most of the courses.

A building would still be needed but not one as large as the scheme proposed. Three of the classrooms were unnecessary and when the associated 12 syndicate rooms were taken into account, removing them amounted to a significant saving in space.

This example demonstrates how accurately identifying a need may lead to a management solution rather than just a building solution, but a management solution may incur other management costs. To maximise the efficiency of the space, the technical equipment would need to be in a central repository so that it could be pulled out and used as necessary. However, this becomes expensive in staff time. But on the other hand, spreading the technical equipment among the laboratories would mean that technical spaces would be unoccupied when staff were not being trained on the specific piece of equipment. In this case, it was more economic to keep the space than to employ staff to move these large pieces of equipment.

Empowering users

Research into the spatial needs of an organisation is a demanding process and involves more than a cursory question to a senior director or facilities manager. The chief executive of an organisation may hold one view and the facilities manager another, but both are expected to represent the 'corporate viewpoint'[3]. This may bear little resemblance to the views of the staff or individual users. They tend to take a personal viewpoint, sensitive to everything that hinders and supports their activities. They know that their productivity is affected by location and the suitability of the places where they work. But they do not always have a voice. The 'corporate viewpoint' invariably prevails. John Zeisel characterised this by noting that:

"Designers have two clients: clients who pay for what is built and clients who use it. The user client has no choice and no control. This situation

Figure 3.1: The user often has no control illustrated by John Zeisel as the 'user-needs gap'.

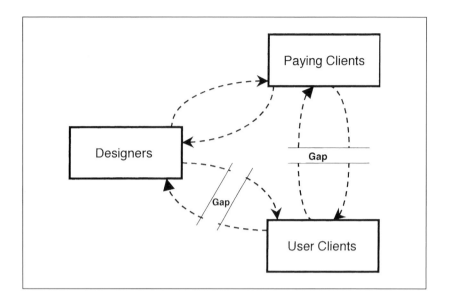

presents designers with a problem: no matter how much they negotiate with paying clients, it is difficult to plan for needs of user clients who are neither well known nor readily available to plan with."[4]

Zeisel illustrated this as the 'User-needs gap' (Figure 3.1).

Productivity in modern business has become more complex, with a close inter-relationship between who is doing the work, how it is done and its location. Solutions to questions about what will best support a business now involve a complex web of people, process and place as an inter-related system (Figure 3.2).

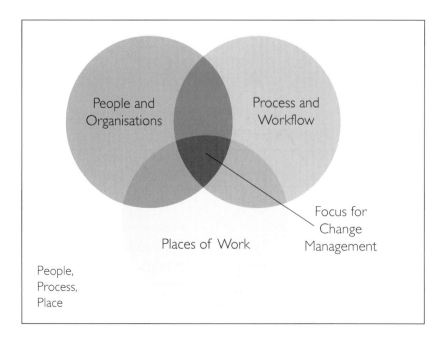

Figure 3.2: Organisations aim to control change at the point where people, process and place interact. *Source: DEGW*

In many organisations those who propose solutions to particular prob-lems tend to do so from the standpoint of their own discipline, whether it is from an information technology, a human resources or a facilities point of view. However, as has been made clear by research, there are links between workers and their environment and the type of work they do.[5] Any solution must be systemic and include as parts of one system the people who carry out the work, the place where it is done and the process used to carry it out.[6]

Empowering users to match their working environment to their work process is essential if effective ways of using space and time are to be intro-duced. Users are closest to the interface between environment and work, and are the first to experience problems (Figure 3.2).

Attempts by the 'corporate user' to superimpose new ways of working, such as hot desking, have not always worked. Organisations who see such solu-tions working for their competitors and copy them often fail to achieve their objectives. Success is achieved by understanding the organisation, consulting the user and finding the appropriate response.

Effective briefing recognises the users' role in identifying needs. When users' needs are unclear or unknown, designers tend to make assumptions as if they were the users. They make assumptions about how a user may interact with the building based on their own intuition or beliefs. Invariably 'real users' think differently and are subject to more subtle pressures exerted by their particular working context.

Identifying the need

Identifying need involves teasing out the myriad of interests in a continually shifting context, then matching this demand with the supply of resources avail-able to meet it (Figure 3.3). Interrogating the demand side of the equation will reveal the extent of homogeneity or separation within the organisation, the number and type of staff, the pattern of work, assimilation of technology and corporate style. Interrogating the supply side will reveal the extent to which

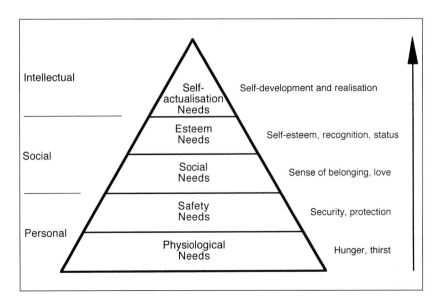

Figure 3.3: As explained by Maslow's 'Hierarchy of Needs', user requirements change constantly and extend from the physiological essentials right up to the level of self-development and realisation. The difficult point is finding out who the users really are.

Figure 3.4: There is a continuous tension between the demand and supply sides.
Source: DEGW

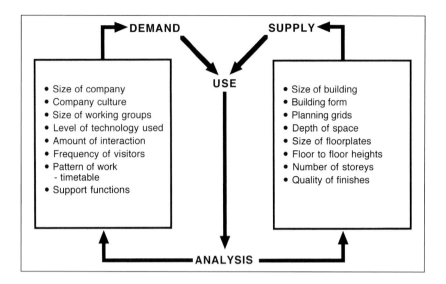

resources such as buildings reflect the demand need. It will show the degree of continuity or dispersal, floor area, depth of space, complexity of servicing, style of design and quality of specification. Matching demand and supply so that user needs are continually reconciled with building capacity is the basis of successful real estate management (Figure 3.4).

Balancing these interests involves understanding where the organisation wants to be and how it intends to get there. Identifying the need may require investigation into areas where people may not want anyone else to look. This resistance is not always due to a Machiavellian desire to be secretive but more often because those people do not realise the importance of the information they hold. It could also be that the organisation is sensitive to particular information reaching either competitors or internal staff. If access is restricted, there is a risk that a vital piece of information can be missed.

The first stage in the process is to:

- understand the need;
- recognise that there may not be a single solution to satisfy the need;
- recognise that there will be several different views of what that need is;
- set the context of the brief;
- recognise the interaction of people, process and place.

To do this, it is important for those preparing the brief to understand:

- the mission of the organisation;
- the operational criteria to enable the organisation to meet their goals;
- what resources are available in the organisation;
- the culture of the organisation. The glue that binds the people together and drives the way that the organisation works;[7]
- what internal factors are driving change – they may be particular departments, individuals or projects and;
- the external factors driving change and which may affect its future, such as market forces, energy, health and safety or government relocation policy.

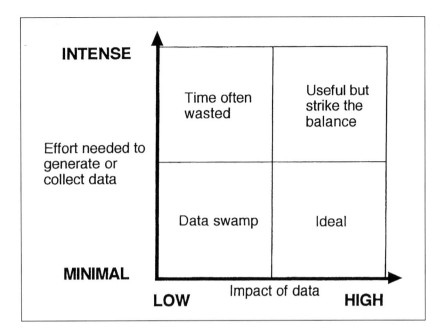

Figure 3.5: A balance must be struck between the effort needed to collect data and the use or value of it. The danger is that too much detailed data is collected too early.

Information needs at each stage

Information is drawn from the raw data that must be structured, assessed and balanced against conflicting interests (Figure 3.5).

Pre-project stage

The objective during the pre-project stage is to define the immediate and future needs and requirements of the organisation, and assess its resources. A range of methods can be used to collect this information. These include: examining records, surveying existing facilities, and interviewing staff. This can be done with or without the help of external advisers. The value of using external experts is that they have experience of other organisations and projects, and can be more objective.

Project stage

At the project stage the aim is to test the key questions asked in the Strategic Brief and translate these needs from the organisational terms of the Strategic Brief into construction terms. This is done through interviews, surveys and by considering design options which are used to test possibilities. It is carried out by the project team supported by expert advisers.

Post-project stage

At post-project stage the need and expectations are verified and tested against the completed project. This is done through: post-project reviews where those involved in the project can feed back much useful information on what did or did not work. Also, they are useful for learning how to approach other projects.

Post-occupancy evaluations, on the other hand, study the performance of buildings in use (Chapter 6). The findings can be matched against the performance measures established in the brief to identify whether the building meets requirements. A study of the organisation and its users will show whether the need has changed and how the building might be tuned to improve the fit. Here again, the approach is to carry out interviews, observe what has happened, and to measure the performance against the standards identified in the brief. The evaluation should be an objective study carried out by an independent group of people who have no vested interest in the outcome. They may be independent by virtue of working for another part of the organisation.[8]

From data to knowledge

In researching the needs of the organisation it is possible to collect a vast amount of data but, in its raw state, it does not contribute much in the way of useful information or knowledge until it has been analysed. The aim is to collect enough data but not waste time collecting too much. A balance has to be struck between the effort needed to collect the data and the impact and relevance of it (Figure 3.5). The framing of the questions behind the investigation will help, as will a programme of information needs so that strategic information is collected first and more detailed information on, say, workspace layouts collected later.

Collecting the information

The approaches listed below can be applied with a 'broad brush', or with great detail. This will depend on the stage of the process and manpower available, the types of decisions required, and scale of project (Figure 3.6).

The **key sources of information** are:

Information from existing sources
* Existing records;
* surveys of existing facilities;
* other organisations;
* published benchmarks.

Sources of new information
* Studies into the use of space and time;
* precedent;
* interviews;
* questionnaire research;
* workshops.

The process of information collection will be made easier by layering the briefing and design process and continuously reminding yourself, the design team,

Methods of collecting information

Pre-project Stage

Method	Information	Resources
Existing Records	Organisation Facilities	Client organisation reviews existing information
Interviews	Key Personnel	Up to 10–14 Interviews
Survey of Existing Facilities	Building Plans and Data	10 man days (Large project) 5 man days (Medium project) >5 man days (Small project)
Visual Survey	Space and Time Usage	20 man days (Large project) 10–15 man days (Medium project) >10 man days (Small project) Use questionnaires
Building Visits	Discussion and Data	4 hours per building visit
Focus Groups	Comparative data from open ended discussion	2–3 hours 8–12 participants

Project Stage

Method	Information	Resources
Activity Surveys	Detailed Requirements	
Workshop	Review Initial Information	
Interviews	Specialist Needs	20–25 Interviews
Questionnaires	Space, time usage Requirements and Verification	
Simulation	Concept and Sketch Design	

and the users, which decisions are appropriate to the site, shell, skin, services, scenery, systems and settings (Figure 3.7).

Existing records

These are an invaluable source of information for external advisers to help them understand the organisation. This source of information is also useful to assist the business case team. They can be easily and rapidly assembled at the early stages. Examples of useful information about an organisation typically include:

- The Annual Report;
- Statement of Accounts;
- business plans, financial and manpower budgets;
- product catalogues or prospectus (if the organisation is a manufacturer);
- organisational chart – which shows the relationship between parts of the client organisation;

Figure 3.6: Methods for collecting information on different sized projects to give an idea of resources needed. The amount of time for different scales of projects is indicative and would depend on the circumstances. A large project = >£5 million Medium-sized project = £1–5 million Small project = <£1 million.

- key job descriptions;
- recent consultant's reports.

In a building, the initial information about the facilities and space use can be found from:

- internal telephone directories – from these one can identify who works in which part of the building;
- security and fire alarm layout plans – these may show an up-to-date configuration of the facility if no other drawings are available;
- layout drawings and furniture inventories;
- visitors' book at reception – indicates the frequency of visitors and which parts of the organisation they visit – may prompt questions about provision of meeting rooms;
- meeting room booking records – indicates whether and how often meeting rooms are used;
- maintenance reports – can indicate problems with the building's fabric or services;
- help line call schedule;
- workflow diagrams.

Firms with established facility and property management departments will normally have key performance data, which can be compared on a year-by-year basis. Continuous changes in interior planning and resource allocation may well be computerised on a Computer Aided Management system.

Surveys of existing facilities and how they are used

Decisions on what might be required begin with understanding the opportunities, and shortfalls of what already exists. The intended original use of some spaces may have changed although the room labels have remained. The study should try to identify how the spaces are actually used; this will give vital information on what may be needed. For example, a corridor may have become an important meeting place.

TIPS FOR CONDUCTING A SUCCESSFUL SURVEY OF THE EXISTING FACILITIES

Steps
* Create a list of existing facilities owned or used by the client organisation;
* identify the extent to which information on the use, physical size, function, performance criteria and physical condition of each is known and recorded;
* identify all areas in which information which is likely to be relevant in relation to meeting the opportunity or solving the problem is absent or inadequate for the existing facilities;
* commission surveys to make up the deficiencies.

Information Sources
Existing drawings and surveys.

A survey can be undertaken by either a desk top analysis using existing drawings, schedules, and records, or a site survey of some or all of the buildings. Information to be collected may focus on the condition of the building fabric, and the potential for adaptation and space utilisation, or both. With limited time and resources, careful sampling of selected buildings or spaces can provide more than adequate results for the early briefing and option study stages.

Data presented in a visual and comparable form helps clients assess need and make decisions of allocation of resources between interest groups.

Interviews

These are a valuable way of collecting information on how users currently use facilities and expect to use them in the future. They can be backed up by questionnaires. Interviews with senior personnel should last no more than one hour and be preceded by a visit to the space with a colleague to identify current usage and potential needs. In addition, before the meeting each interviewee should be given an agenda which explains the purpose of the study and issues to be covered in the interview. An unstructured interview around an agenda of issues, allows for 'hidden agenda' items to be explored, and opens up needs not previously perceived.

TIPS FOR CONDUCTING SUCCESSFUL INTERVIEWS

Steps
* Identify types of staff and stakeholders to be interviewed. These may reflect line-management responsibility, specialist interests, different user functions, status, external interests;
* circulate agenda, with start and finish times;
* once completed prepare and distribute minutes of meeting;
* listen to, and do not contradict the interviewee;
* don't show your own viewpoint, or use the meeting to show off your knowledge.

Information sources
* Personnel lists and organisational charts;
* standard interview agenda, adapted to client requirements;
* knowledge from visual survey.

Typical issues on an agenda for a departmental head of a commercial building
* What are your projected plans for information and communications technology (ICT)? How do you expect this to change your way of working?
* which departments do you most frequently work with on a face-to-face basis? How could ICT change this?
* what image do you wish to present to your customers, suppliers and staff?
* what special needs are to be accommodated now or in the future?

Visiting other organisations

Learning from what others have done well or badly is an invaluable part of the process of understanding need. Visits to other organisations will help to:

- identify features you enjoy and those that won't fit your needs;
- 'benchmark' space standards, procurement routes and management procedures against what is being proposed;
- provide examples of good and bad buildings for opening up discussions with the design team;
- bridge the 'language' gap between users and the design team.

Senior Management should aim to allocate time for visits. The time away is an invaluable period for the client/user team to have time for discussion amongst themselves, review potential design teams and learn from the experience of their peers in other organisations. The range of examples should be as wide as possible (including other countries) to expand expectations and allow lateral thinking.

Comparative 'benchmarks'

Review published experience available within the construction industry (e.g. Cost Indices) and sectoral studies available through organisations.[9] The British Institute of Facilities Management (BIFM) is trying to provide comparative project data, with standard performance indices.[10]

Questionnaires

Questionnaires are used in the brief making process typically at the:

- pre-project stage to collect information about user needs; and,
- post-project (post-completion) stage, to collect comments, ratings and opinions about the facility in use.

At the pre-project stage it is tempting to ask users what they want, rather than what they do. Do not ask leading questions. Concentrate on factual answers to questions about what people do now and what they are likely to do in the foreseeable future. Do not tempt them into 'wish lists', as this will inflate expectations and inevitably lead to disappointment later.

At the post-project stage, questions can be factual, and respondents will be able to relate them to their own experiences of the facility in use.

Studies into the use of space and time

A thorough understanding of how space is being used through time provides invaluable data for reappraising methods of work and assessing how space could be used more effectively. The initial expectation that additional space is required may be refuted by a more in-depth analysis of work processes, which may show how technology or more effective timetabling of space and time could allow for the more intensive use of existing space.

Careful analysis of the use of space and time may result in the decision to replan rather than procure new space.

TIPS FOR SUCCESSFUL VISITS TO OTHER ORGANISATIONS

Steps
* Identify a number of examples of facilities that provide distinct and different approaches to meeting needs which are similar to those of the client;
* obtain permission to visit them and prepare an information pack for each which describes the features of the facility that may be of interest;
* visit each building and discuss its advantages and disadvantages;
* select the best examples and prepare a more detailed information pack based on the discussions;
* the Business Case team visits the best examples and discusses each on site at length to help decide on their own assessment of needs;
* clear objectives for the visit may cover:
  - Facility management
  - Studies of the organisation
  - Performance of the facility
  - Use of space.

Information sources
These can include:

* published copies of reviews of the facility;
* organisation's brochure and annual report;
* internal building measures;
* staff 'welcome pack' and relocation newsletters.

Increasingly, project websites will be a key source of information.

TIPS FOR QUESTIONNAIRE DESIGN AND USE

* Never ask unanswerable questions;
* keep the questionnaire as short as possible, so that it takes no more than ten minutes to fill in;
* use multi-choice tick boxes or tickable scales, always giving people a full range of possible options to fill in;
* allow enough, but not too much, space for comment. One short sentence will often suffice for most topics, but leave a paragraph for general comments;
* use a sample which is large enough to cover sub-groups representatively;
* use standard questions (so data are comparable with benchmarks);
* consider how data are to be analysed when the questionnaire is being designed;
* never underestimate the time taken to prepare a tight, well-structured questionnaire or time spent on data entry into a computer and data analysis;
* when handing out questionnaires, always state that you will personally collect them. Leave half an hour to an hour between distribution and collection.

Source: Better Briefing, Blyth, Leaman, Worthington

For example, studies[11] have identified that in a typical professional or marketing office the workspace is empty for 40–50 per cent of the working day (8 hours) and temporarily unoccupied for another 20–30 per cent of the time 'in use' (Figure 3.7).

A similar analysis of space use invariably shows only 30 per cent of the space being used for individual work stations, the most being allocated to local filing and project areas; centrally-shared conference and amenity areas; circulation and core.

One method of analysis that might be used by a consultant is to define a route through a building so as to collect data on how many people are in each particular space and what they are doing, e.g. working, meeting and so on. This may be repeated at perhaps half-hourly intervals throughout the day to build a profile of how the spaces are being used and at what intensity.

Focus groups

These provide the means to bring a cross-section of interested parties together to respond to pre-defined interview questions. This technique is most valuable for speculative projects, large populations of users or ascertaining community interests.

For neighbourhood planning problems, an extremely effective way of defining goals and assessing options is the action planning event. Action planning brings together a cross-section of stakeholders and through a combination of stakeholder input and working groups, identifies needs, and assesses opportunities.

Workshops

These are an invaluable means of articulating issues, defining problems and balancing the interests of different groups. Using an independent facilitator, they can be focused to explore particular issues, and articulate requirements and solution areas.

Figure 3.7: Mapping the occupancy of different spaces can be done to show use throughout a typical day. However, care must be taken to analyse the data within the context of the organisation. For example, the low level of telephone work may suggest that not much cellular office space is needed. But in a legal practice it is vital for client confidentiality, whereas in a sales environment the 'buzz' from telephone sales activity in an open plan environment may be important. *Source: DEGW*

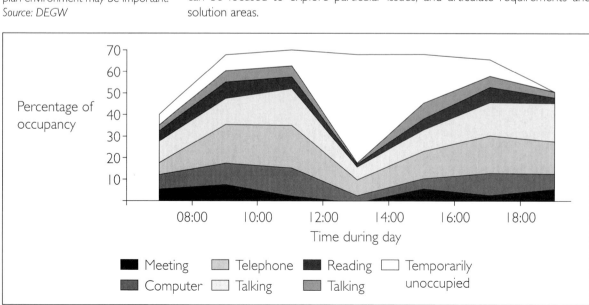

Value management reviews

Value management is a technique used to elicit an understanding of what factors are critical to the different interest groups (values) which then generates a list of priorities of things that are important to the organisation[12] (Chapter 7). Much of a value management review is workshop based. These can be one or two days long with members of the client and project teams present. They identify and evaluate needs and help maintain a strategic focus on the strategic issues during design and construction. Value management reviews should be followed up to ensure that any recommendations have been acted upon.

Simulation and gaming

The presentation of designs is a potent means of understanding what the user requires. When presented with a design or a direction for a design solution, a client can envisage the impact and conflicts which may result from the requirements. Methods of simulation can vary from sketch designs, computer modelling exercises, and role playing to test options, and full scale mock-ups. Briefing is an iterative process, and no more so than at the early stage of needs identification. The use of precedent, or images of what might be achieved, are effective means of helping clients and users articulate needs by envisioning opportunities.

Option appraisals

These are used to test different approaches to meeting the need but can also be used to identify other needs or even eliminate some (see Chapter 2).

The main stages of option appraisals are to:

- identify the business aim and define the objectives which will satisfy it;
- consider which options will achieve these objectives – often construction will not be the only option;

TIPS FOR CONDUCTING A SUCCESSFUL VALUE MANAGEMENT WORKSHOP

Steps
* Appoint a value management facilitator if the necessary skills do not exist in-house;
* assemble a description of the current stage of development of the brief and design;
* bring together senior representatives of all the interest groups involved for a value management workshop;
* use the workshop to identify and clarify the overall objectives, define the client's values, use creative techniques to search for answers that provide better value and then evaluate them to identify those which provide value improvement;
* implement the agreed value improvements.

Information sources
* Company reports;
* business plan;
* descriptions of current brief and design;
* general cost and value data;
* project cost and value data.

- undertake investigations into their feasibility;
- evaluate the costs and benefits of each option;
- put onto a comparable monetary basis the costs and benefits which can be quantified;
- weigh up the uncertainties of each option;
- assess the balance between options.

From the option appraisal a business case can be assembled for each option. The more thorough the investigations the less the risk of inaccurate assessment and inadequate selection.

Option appraisals for construction

In the case of construction options, appraisals could involve survey, design risk analysis, costing work and discussions on planning and other statutory requirements. This may require the assistance of designers and other professional consultants, chosen and managed by the client adviser. Value management techniques should also be used to ensure that the options have been adequately defined and that there is a consensus on the choice made.

Choosing a construction option

The key decisions to be made in choosing an appropriate construction approach are:

- an initial budget taking into consideration all broad costs, including life cycle costs if relevant;
- the outline programme which must allow realistic periods for essential activities;
- the significant elements of risk, contingency allowances and preliminary decisions on how they can be managed.

Conclusion

Defining a need in terms of requirements rather than as solutions is critical for successfully integrating people, place and process. For example, a 'perceived' requirement for an additional building may in reality be a requirement to accommodate 300 student hours a week of teaching. The pressure often from clients is that they are convinced they know what they require. The case study on the training space for the blue chip company at the beginning of the chapter shows how wrong they can be. Of course, a readily-defined solution presented to the design and construction teams makes life easier in rapidly achieving 'implementable solutions'. However, time spent at the start identifying the problem will achieve long-term success.

Time spent at the pre-project stage reflecting on the alternatives and articulating objectives, is invaluable for the subsequent success of a project. Ill-conceived goals, poorly articulated and not believed in by all stakeholders, can lead to redesign, delays and additional expense later. Quality information is the key to this and not the amount of data which tends to do no more than swamp and confuse people.

Notes

1 DEGW, *Design for Change: The Architecture of DEGW*, Watermark/Birkhauser, Basel 1997.
2 Becker, F. and Steele, F., *Workplace by design: Mapping the high-performance workscape*, Jossey-Bass 1994.
3 DEGW, *Design for Change: The Architecture of DEGW*, Watermark/Birkhauser, Basel 1997.
4 Zeisel, J., *Inquiry by design*, Cambridge University Press, Cambridge 1984.
5 Leaman A., *From feedback to strategy*, PROBE Conference, 1997 also Vischer J., *Workplace strategies*, Chapman and Hall 1996.
6 DEGW, *Design for Change: The Architecture of DEGW*, Watermark/Birkhauser, Basel 1997.
7 Cassells, S. and McAulay, T., *Organisations and obsessions: the culture of facilities*, New Realities.
8 PROBE Occupant Surveys. A series of post-occupancy evaluations carried out on a range of buildings including offices, further education buildings and a health centre. So far 17 have been visited. The PROBE project is a collaborative research project conducted by Building Services Journal co-funded by the DETR Partners in Innovation Initiative and managed by ESD with Building Use Studies and William Bordass Associates.
9 The Royal Institution of Chartered Surveyors (RICS tel: 020 7222 7000; www.rics.org.uk) publishes sectoral guides on different building types.
10 BIFM (British Institute of Facilities Management, tel: 01799 508608; www.bifm.org.uk).
11 DEGW has studied many organisations and how space is used through time.
12 Kelly, J., Male, S. and McPherson, S., *Value Management – A Proposed Practice Manual for the Briefing process*, Paper Number 34, RICS.

4 Reflecting on growth and change

Briefing for change

It is often argued that in today's world the one trend we can predict with certainty is change. We live in a world where the speed of change is increasing exponentially with product life cycles measured in months rather than years. To place change in the context of the last thousand years of civilisation, four phases of economic development can be identified with the time between each dramatically reducing. The pre-industrial agricultural economy lasted for over 2000 years. The commodities were natural resources; the assets were land and the institutions were towns or villages. The next wave was the industrial economy spanning 250 years, where the commodities were products; assets were machinery, and the institutions were companies. The third wave was the service economy, already in decline with a foreseeable span of 80 years. The commodities are services, the assets data, and the institutions are bureaucracies. We are currently entering into a knowledge economy which arguably may have a span of no more than 40 years. The commodity is 'know-how'; assets are networks (the world-wide-web) and the institutions are communities of interest, often in dispersed locations.

Information technology (IT) is ubiquitous, having a major impact on the way we organise work.[1] Since 1980, IT has both changed the way we organise functions and use buildings as well as changing the nature of its own technology (Figure 4.1). The IBM desk-top personal computer was brought to market in 1980, and led to the democratisation of computer usage, and for office planners a jungle of cables, heat gain, clutter at the desk and a proliferation of support equipment. Ten years later, mobile communications, lap-top computers and flat screens have reduced space usage, minimised cabling and reduced heating loads. During the 1990s, the internet has enabled faster communication, so as we enter the next millennium, work can be undertaken anyplace, anytime and anywhere. Such speed of change is easy to see; what is harder to predict is the impact that these technological and organisational changes will have on the built environment. What is certain is that, to survive, organisations will need to be dynamic[2] and buildings will need to be supportive.[3] The challenge for briefing and design is to integrate the management of organisational change and building design.

Faced with uncertainty, a variety, of building strategies exist, namely:

- *Short-life, precise-fit*, where the building and its use are tightly coupled, on the assumption that it will be discarded or dismantled over a short period

	IT Developments	Organisational Impact	Real Estate Implications
1980	• IBM Personal Computer (PC)	• Non hierarchical accessible information • Flat organisations	• Heat and wire management • User focus • Business buildings
1990	• Lap-top, palm-top, mobile phone	• Cross building organisation • Project focus • Knowledge worker • Out-sourcing	• Structural wiring • Personal control • Support space • Out-sourced building management
1999	• Internet (WWW) • Wire-less communication • Groupware		• New locations • Serviced offices • Flexible layouts

Figure 4.1: IT developments and their organisational and real estate implications.
Source: DEGW

of time. Such strategies include exhibition installations or prefabricated short-life containers.

- *Long-life, loose-fit*, where the precise activities to be housed are disengaged from the shell that houses them. Alex Gordon in his Presidential RIBA address was an early proponent of such an approach.[4] At the same time, to master the changing and complex demands of hospital users, John Weeks advocated the 'Duffle Coat'[5] principle of loose-fit adaptability.
- *The Virtual Organisation*, IT is opening up opportunities of linking between sites and individuals to function where they choose. With this freedom, organisations are recognising the opportunity not to tie themselves to fixed buildings, but to take short leases on buildings managed by others and move as requirements change. Buildings become a serviced commodity around which organisations grow, change and adapt.

Though organisations are increasingly recognising that buildings can become a millstone rather than an asset, the majority of them still view buildings as an asset and symbol of their culture and heritage. To meet these demands, the building shell should be perceived as a long-term asset that can reflect the inevitable change of functions within. In the 1950s Louis Kahn,[6] the eminent American architect, proposed the making of spaces 'without names', that their form suggested the appropriate use. Adaptability arose from a building providing a range of spaces that through their quality and relationship stimulated use and commitment. Stuart Brand, in *How Buildings Learn*[7] takes the argument further in proposing that, as organisations develop and change, so their needs are reflected in the continuous adaptation of the buildings. Christopher Alexander[8] refers to this process as the 'building memory', where, over time, those adaptations that add to the functionality of the building get built into the permanent structure, while others that are more ethereal are erased and disappear. Briefing for change should aim to disengage the design of the building shell from the short-term uses within. DEGW, with its concern for time as a critical dimension of architectural design,[9] proposed the model in the early

1970s of 'Shell, services, scenery and settings'. Each of these elements has a different life-span and each needs to be designed with a high degree of independence from the other so that different cycles of intervention and replacement can be more easily reconciled.

To cope with unpredictability and change, organisations at the initial strategic briefing stage should aim to:

- predict their speed of growth and nature of change;
- find a balance between meeting current uses and future investment value;
- separate site and building shell decisions from servicing fit-out and management.

A clear understanding of these three issues at the strategic briefing stage will set the agenda, and help to select the appropriate development options for the subsequent project.

Patterns of change

Organisations can be type-cast by the perceived speed that they are changing, and the type of activities they undertake. DEGW, in the Orbit Two study[10] undertaken with Harbinger, Davies, Becker and Simms in North America, showed how office organisations could be classified by their speed of change and nature of work, and the likely movement from one sector to another predicted (Figure 4.2). For those organisations changing slowly and undertaking routine work, a specific design strategy might be selected in contrast to the rapidly changing organisation undertaking non-routine functions. The nature

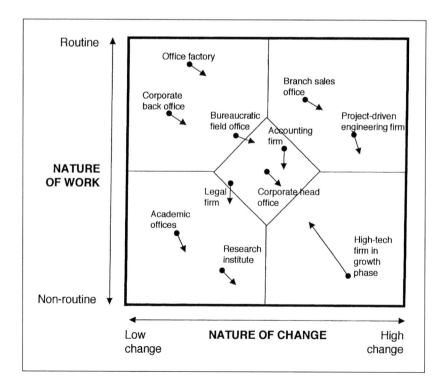

Figure 4.2: Model showing classification of organisations by speed of change.
Source: Orbit Two

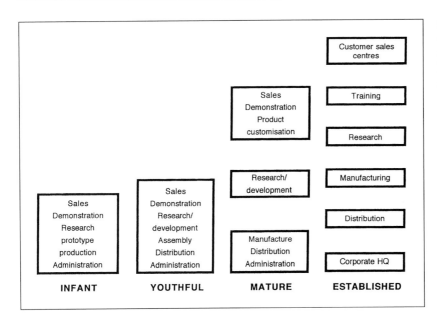

Figure 4.3: Stages of organisational development and the impact on the degree of specialization of the buildings required.
Source: DEGW

and speed of change is also dependent on the maturity of the organisation and their expectations (Figure 4.3). Youthful firms with an entrepreneurial flare will be, by definition, growing and changing rapidly compared with the mature, craft-focused, conservative organisation whose ambitions may be to minimise change but improve in quality. Each organisational type requires a different strategy in planning for change at the briefing stage. Infant organisations will have one unit of accomodation housing a range of functions, whilst established organisations have specialized premises for individual functions.

Predicting future demand

Compared with the speed that many organisations change today, buildings take a long time to procure. For a 5000 m² building from inception of need to completion the process may take five years, the time equivalent of at least two complete product life cycles in today's electronics industry. Few organisations with any confidence can afford to build only to meet today's needs. Looking five years ahead, questions should be posed as to:

- the future size and shape of the organisations;
- how technology might develop and the impact this could have on the organisational structure;
- changing market demand, and staff and customer expectations;
- social, economic, political and social development and their impact on quality and image.

At the strategic briefing stage, two key issues should be addressed:

1. What is the nature of the organisation in respect of its speed and type of change?
2. What will be the impact of change on the building, fit-out and facilities management provided?

Assessing the future

Projecting the future has become an art much sought after by individuals and corporations[11] but which still remains imprecise. Strides have been made in the worlds of meteorology,[12] macro-economic forecasting and the financial markets,[13] where a clearer and more certain understanding of what lies ahead can reap rich rewards. Massive computing power has been marshalled to build predictive models, to support organisations in managing risk and making better-informed judgements. However, even with such intellectual capacity, forecasts are found wanting and the world continues to be faced with major natural, technological or economic catastrophes.

In the world of building, a variety of methods are used to understand the future. They include:

1. *Projecting from past experience.* The most commonly used method for identifying future needs is to review past performance and extrapolate forward, against an educated assessment of what might influence change from what has happened in the past. To answer the question of how big the building will need to be in the future, the statistics can be collected on how staff numbers have changed over the last five years; and in discussions with senior management of their expectations for future growth, numbers can be projected forward with a high and a low scenario reflecting the impact of different factors that could change the projection. Projections can provide relatively accurate predictions in a stable environment, but recent changes in technology and increased mobility have proved many projections all but worthless.

2. *Predicting.* The technique of bringing together groups of users or experts to build a picture of the future based on past experiences. DEGW in association with Steelcase Corporation have developed a software-based tool, to support organisations in envisioning the future.[14] A series of issues concerning organisational structure, style and technology are discussed on a ten-point scale, and, through consensus, the group decides where the organisation was in the past (five years back), where it is now and where it will be in the future (Figure 4.4). Workshops are composed of homogeneous groups either of the same status or within the same function. Questions may be answered either as to what the future will be if trends continue or against their aspiration for the future. Such an interactive approach builds a consensus, and can be a valuable tool in managing the process of change.

3. *Trend spotting.* For many, the future is here today and being acted out by other leading-edge organisations. The skill is to provide the antennae to seek out the relevant sightings from today that will influence the direction and success of the company tomorrow. In deciding on the future requirements of your building, visiting best practise examples, evaluating newspaper clippings of what is happening elsewhere and assessing trends, can be invaluable in focusing on new building requirements.

4. *Scenario building.* In a world of uncertainty, the strategy for a future building should be sufficiently robust to cope with a variety of directions the organisation might go. To test the resilience of a building strategy, alternative scenarios can be proposed. Typical scenario variables may include:

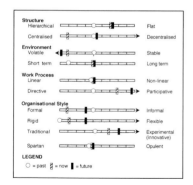

Figure 4.4: An example of the different characteristics that might be tested in an organisation in an envisioning exercise. It looks at where staff believe the organisation is at present, where it was and where they think it should be. *Source: DEGW for Steelcase*

- speed of growth and change;
- mix of staff and alternative patterns of work;
- alternative mix and balance of functions;
- changes in use and take up of technology;
- change of ownership, political agenda, or cultural expectations.

International airport facilities might use this approach, by envisioning a range of different passenger profiles to test the functionality of designs. The number and mix of passenger types at different times of the day can be varied to assess the robustness of the design solution.

Alternative scenarios can be composed through panels of experts or focus groups of users.

5. Back casting. Deciding on the future one would like to achieve, and working backwards to understand what decisions and actions would be required to achieve the end state. An aspirational approach often followed for arts, institutional and cultural projects e.g. The Parisian 'Grand Projet' where the symbolism of the outcome has a high value.

Even the best projections can be affected by the unforeseen, such as mergers, takeovers, political coups or economic recession. Projections are an aspiration against which actuality should be reviewed, and adjusted as the project progresses.

Briefing for flexibility and adaptability

The words flexibility and adaptability are frequently used interchangeably when discussing building change. Flexibility defines change that can be made quickly and with relatively little effort or cost (short-term and tactical) whilst adaptability is concerned with larger scale changes over longer periods of time (long-term and strategic). Adaptability implies the ability to change, whilst still leaving options open and not being unnecessarily costly or complicated. Flexibility is afforded by being able to remove windows or reconfigure furniture, whilst adaptability is afforded by the shape and size of a room which allows it to accommodate a variety of different functions over time. The lack of short-term flexibility can be frustrating and reduce performance, but can normally be changed through retrofit (e.g. a different furniture system or alternative glazing). Lack of adaptability is more serious, resulting in premature obsolescence. In the mid 1980s many of the 1960s office buildings, though flexible in their construction, lacked adaptability. They lacked the capacity to absorb the demands of IT due to insufficient floor-to-floor height to accommodate raised floors, and air handling ducting.

Most buildings outlive the organisations who initiate them. Today we are building for future generations. To remain an asset they need to be built with adaptability in mind. Why have old buildings lasted? Generally they were not built with change in mind, yet often they have been able to accept new uses. Perhaps they are robust enough to withstand people knocking holes in them, or they have sufficient capacity and space to accommodate a variety of demands. Research shows that many buildings have survived because they have become loved and stimulate innovation in use. Their constraints have provided freedom. Research[15] suggests that the 'look' or 'image' of a building might be one of the factors behind old buildings which are successfully adapted. Not only might something that looks stimulating find a sympathetic user, but local authorities may insist on keeping a building for its image.

Achieving adaptability

In Europe three distinct development approaches have emerged:[16]

- custom-designed buildings, conceived to maximise the use value for individual organisations;
- the developer's speculative building conceived to maximise exchange value for selling or leasing; and
- the aesthetically or technology driven solution, which aims to maximise image value.

The challenge for the future is to reflect all three approaches and to exploit technology to create a building which expands the range of options for the user as well as maximising business value.

Making a building adaptable involves overcoming the problems of over-specific design. Part of the answer lies in the modularity of the design within which a menu of furniture settings can be accommodated. A strategy for an adaptable building involves anticipating the quality of space that will be required. Can the building accept both cellular and open-plan office space and absorb restaurant or conference facilities by changing the fit out and services within a standard shell? Managers will have to match demand and supply so that user needs are continually reconciled with building capacity. This can be done on a daily as well as more long-term basis.

To achieve this involves recognising the different life cycles inherent within the building of shell, services, scenery and setting. These different cycles provide a framework against which to make decisions and analyse the impact of organisational change:

- *The building shell.* The skin and structure will last for the lifetime of the building, 50 years or more. The key design decisions concern the shape, size and the ability to adapt to organisational and technical change. These are long-term decisions which are difficult to change throughout the life of the building, and will have major impact on the future adaptability.
- *Building services.* These include heating, ventilation, lighting and cable distribution and may last for 15–20 years. The challenge here is to provide adequate cooling, cabling and power capacity for accommodating increasing levels of technology. The capacity of the building shell should provide sufficient capacity to allow for changes in the provision and technology of services over time.
- *Scenery.* This is the fitting out of the internal elements such as ceilings, partitions and finishes and normally has a shorter life cycle than services (seven to ten years). The scenery and services provide match the detailed user requirements, addressing issues of organisational change, personal identity and corporate identity. The brief for the fit-out can be assembled independently of the building shell.

- *Settings.* The day-to-day management of the furniture and equipment within the building shell. The partitions and furniture layout can be reconfigured to meet the changing needs of the organisation.

The four S's proposed in the original model for designing with time[17] in 1972 (Chapter 1) of shell, services, scenery and settings have subsequently been joined by Site, Skin and Systems (Figure 4.5). The Site, which is timeless, provides context. The Skin, with a 25-year life span, provides the ability to upgrade the image and adjust to surrounding changes. Systems for information and communications technology (ICT), with a 3-year life cycle, are an increasingly costly part of the installations. The ICT for a call centre can now cost several times as much as the short-life shed which houses the function.

A key factor in determining the adaptability of a building is the building shell:

- Floor-to-floor heights are key to determining the adaptability of a building. They affect the servicing strategy – air conditioning, cabling distribution, and the ability to take advantage of natural ventilation and light. Insufficient height will limit the options available to the user. However, excessive provision is not only expensive to build but also to maintain.
- The shape and configuration of the building affects the depth of the building and, in turn, how the building can be used and subdivided. The patterns of work employed by users may vary; they could lead to offices for individuals, open-plan areas for group work, or a combination of the two.

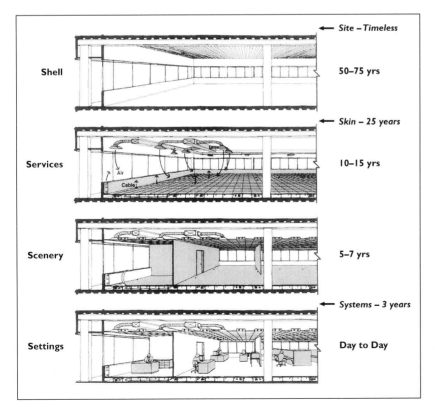

Figure 4.5: The original model for designing with time (1972) has been updated to include site, skin and systems. A building is designed so that one element can be altered without affecting another to any significant extent.
Source: DEGW

- Different floor depths allow different space planning options. For example, in an office environment, the floor area within 6 m of an external or atrium wall would be suitable for enclosed offices. Spaces greater than 6 m from a window can be used for open-plan workstations, internal rooms, ancillary and support functions (Figure 4.6).
- The building's structural (column) grid is an important consideration, since the grid should be a multiple of the internal planning grid to tie in with ceiling, partition and other components. The planning grid is used to lay out a range of components and building systems such as partitions, raised floors and lighting. It is also used to determine the position of offices and other enclosed spaces.

The most adaptable buildings are those with loosely coupled systems. Adapt-ability is impaired by close linkages between one element and another, such as services depending on the skin or IT cabling being integral with furniture systems. In such situations, making a simple adaptation ripples through other elements which otherwise need not be affected.

Building in flexibility

The flexibility of individual components, like furniture systems or partitions, determines an organisation's ability to change its environment on a daily basis. Effective space planning and management rely on a clear vision of how the available floor space may be planned to ensure the efficient use of space. However, this strategy may lead to greater complexity than an organisation can cope with. Such systems need to be managed if users are to benefit rather than become constrained. Built-in flexibility such as automatic controls which are difficult to comprehend or take too much time to operate effectively, and bespoke furniture systems where components cannot be replaced, become constrainers rather than serving to increase options.

Spatial constraints can create physical obstacles such as walls being in the way, or they can create managerial obstacles where the organisation's facilities managers have to spend time carefully planning a change in spatial layout. Users want their buildings to respond to change in a fast and predictable way. On a day-to-day level, simple robust systems are more manageable.

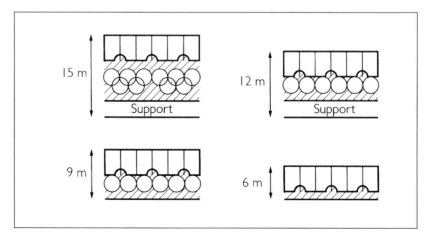

Figure 4.6: Typical glass to core depths in a commercial building showing different space planning options.
Source: Intelligent Buildings South East Asia

Evaluating adaptability

At the design stage, plans can be evaluated to appraise adaptability to different user needs, and their performance against utilisation measures set down in the brief (Figure 4.7 sets out typical performance measures for a business park building).

Building appraisal techniques can be used to analyse and compare the configuration of buildings, floorplates and servicing systems with regard to specific user requirements. It can be used to draw comparisons between buildings. Simple data should be collected so as not to overwhelm (see Chapter 3).

Structured building appraisals are valuable tools for evaluating buildings against current and future user needs. A number of rating methods[23] have been developed to achieve this. Although each one is different, such methods help users to ask sensible questions about their buildings and systems and assess which buildings best suit their needs.

Establishing a briefing process to meet the demands of growth and change

Recognising the inevitability of change is crucial to enabling the briefing process to incorporate this change. Briefs that are viewed as a tool to control the client's ability to change are doomed to failure. The starting point for a flexible briefing process is an attitude of mind where both the consultants and users recognise change, and respond with a management structure that manages the process.

Strategic Briefing

At the pre-project stage, recognise the type of organisation to be accommodated, the speed of change, and the drivers of the change process. The Orbit

Figure 4.7: Performance measures for a business park building. *Source: DEGW*

Business Buildings Compared

Type	Building	Overall Accessibility	Landscape Quality	Site Amenities	Overall Parking	Area Efficiency — For Landlord	Area Efficiency — For Tenant	Potential Flexibility	Company requirements — Hardware Production Cost	Hardware Production Parking	Software House Cost	Software House Parking
Industrial	A	◉	○	○	◉	●	○	◉	◯	●	◯	◉
	B	◯	◯	○	○	●	◯	◯	◯	○	◉	○
	C	◉	◯	◉	◯	◉	○	◯	◯	●	◯	◯
	D	○	◉	◯	◯	◯	○	◯	◯	◉	◯	◉
	E	●	●	●	◉	●	◉	◉	●	●	◉	◯
	F	●	◯	◯	○	◯	◉	◉	Ø		◉	○
	G	●	◯	○	○	○	◉	◯	Ø		◉	○
	H	◯	◉	○	◯	◯	●	◯	Ø		●	◉
Office	I	◯	◉	◉	○	◯	●	○	Ø		●	○

KEY
● Excellent   ◯ Fair   Ø Designed as Office buildings, and are not suitable for production use
◉ Good   ○ Poor

studies[18] undertaken by DEGW in the mid-1980s classified organisations according to their speed of change, and degree of bureaucracy. The location of firms within the model was not static, with mature bureaucratic organisations (e.g. Government Departments) moving to flatter structures, and young volatile organisations (e.g. in the computer sector) becoming more structured. The envisioning process, undertaken with a group of managers answering questions about the speed and characteristics of change (Figure 4.4) is an invaluable tool in establishing the parameters and strategy for change.

The development option and method of procurement selected at the pre-project stage will be dependent on the degree of certainty of the company. Figure 4.8 sets out the development and procurement options for both rapidly changing and static organisations.

Building Project Brief

The broad strategy has been set. As building configurational options are discussed, and plans drawn up, proposals can be tested against alternative use scenarios. To ensure adaptability, a series, of 'what if?' questions can be framed as a checklist in the briefing documentation. Building adaptability can also be regularly checked at the design stage by testing the proposed building plans against alternative user profiles. The Project Brief for a fast changing organisation should aim to layer the information required, so it is available at the last 'responsible' moment, by establishing a process for decision making, and gateways for final agreement.

Interior fit-out (Operational Brief)

The brief for the interior planning of the building may frequently become the framework for the continuous management of the space in use. The brief establishes an interior planning concept, and layout guidelines, with schedules of requirements, which may become the foundations of subsequent space management procedures.

TYPE OF ORGANISATION	DEVELOPMENT OPTION	PROCUREMENT
STATIC • Established markets. • Minimum growth in staff numbers.	• Build to suit. • Custom designed building with ability to adapt to alternative functions or owners.	• Full design and working drawings then select contractor, competitive tender. • Fixed price contracts, against full drawings and specification.
VOLATILE • Rapid growth and change. • Uncertain future technology needs.	• Shell and core separate fit out. • Core requirement of space owned or long lease. Sub let space for growth and change on short leases.	• Construction Management. • Each package tendered separately. • Layered decisions. • Information at last responsible moment

Figure 4.8: Strategies for accommodating change.
Source: DEGW

The facilities manager, in identifying requirements, should recognise the economic, technological and social pressures that are changing the patterns of work and the impact this may have on physical layouts.[19] The office environment is faced with radical change as we move from the processing function to the model of the office as a focus for collaborative work (Figure 4.9). Key organisational questions to be addressed and their layout implications are listed below.

Organisational characteristics

- Amount of interaction required between staff.
- Time staff spend in the office and at the desk.
- Range of functions undertaken, degree of interactive work.
- Degree of interaction with the public, and staff from other locations.
- Speed of organisational change, and sensitivity to technological innovation.
- Importance of status, and degree of hierarchy.

Layout implications

- Proximity of workstations (density of use) and amount of enclosure.
- Allocations of space to shared activities, relative to individual workplaces. Management and sharing of workplaces.
- Range of work settings, and flexibility of environmental systems required.
- Zoning of areas for security, range of meeting spaces provided, varying choice of fit-out and quality.
- Adaptability of building shell and services, degree of uniformity of workstations to allow for interchangeability.
- Staff space standards, number of different workplace types, distribution of fit-out budget.

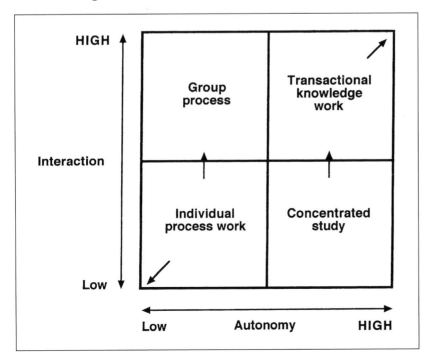

Figure 4.9: The office is becoming a place of collaborative work. *Source: DEGW*

Key issues in briefing for change

In designing for an unpredictable world of change, the expectation that it is possible or even desirable to work to precise practice procedures and fixed performance requirements should be regularly revisited. The brief should perhaps more realistically aim to identify issues and establish expectations.

Experience in designing for the world of work has helped to identify five key issues which may influence the future.

1. *Paradox.* Charles Handy in *The Empty Raincoat*[20] introduced managers to the 'inevitability of paradox, where rather than a perfect predictable world, we must accept conflicting and complex demands working in parallel. We are designing no longer for a world of either this or that, but must reconcile the need for *both this and that*'. Paradox 'confuses because we are asked to live with contradiction and with simultaneous opposites'.

2. *Intensification of the use of space and time.* New organisational and logistical options are emerging that free up the way that we manage time and allocate space. The impact on building specification and usage is profound and needs continuous monitoring.[21]

3. *Continuous process.* The process of managing space and time becomes the product. Evaluation is often now the first step of the process, understanding how work is performed, and identifying areas for improvement which then become the measures for performance, for both the development of the design, and the subsequent space management programme.

4. *Incremental decision taking.* With an increasingly uncertain future, strategic direction is required with a strong, clearly-articulated vision, which is implemented by incremental decisions. Naval gunnery, for example, achieves its accuracy through 'bracketing'. Whilst at a distance the range is identified by firing both closer to and further from the target, within the established target area greater accuracy is achieved by incremental adjustments.

5. *Appropriate responses.* Dramatic improvements in productivity, result from being prepared to reassess established, but now often outdated, work practices and applying lean manufacturing principles[22] and a 'just in time' philosophy. Orbit 2 recognised that solutions were often over specified, with redundant features, inappropriate for the needs of the immediate users. For Services and Scenery (fit-out), build in only that which is required immediately and the flexibility to add in and adapt for subsequent additional or changed requirements.

Notes

1   Worthington, J., *Reinventing the workplace*, Architectural Press 1997.
2   DEGW, *Design for Change: The Architecture of DEGW*, Watermark/Birkhauser, Basel 1997.
3   DEGW, *Design for Change: The Architecture of DEGW*, Watermark/Birkhauser, Basel 1997.
4   Alex Gordon in his Presidential RIBA address in 1972 was an early proponent of such an approach.
5   Weeks, J., *Planning for growth and change,* The Architects' Journal, July 7, 1960.
6   Scully, V., *Louis Khan*, Brazilia.

7   Brand, S., *How Buildings Learn*, Viking 1994.

8   Alexander, C., *The Timeless Way of Building*, Oxford University Press 1979.

9   Duffy, F. and Worthington, J., *Designing for changing needs*, Built Environment 1972.

10 Davis, G., Becker, F., Duffy, F. and Simms, W., *Orbit 2: Organisation, Buildings and Information Technology*, Harbinger 1985.

11 Bernstein, P., *Against the Gods, The Remarkable Story of Risk*, John Wiley, New York 1996.

12 Kelly, K., *Out of control*, Fourth Estate 1995.

13 Kelly, K., *Out of control*, Fourth Estate 1995.

14 DEGW in association with Steelcase Inc. have developed a software-based tool, to support organisation in envisioning the future.

15 Nutt, B., Kincaid, D. and McLennan, P., *Refurbishment for change of use*, University College London: Bartlett Research Project conducted under the LINK Construction Maintenance and Refurbishment Programme 1994–6.

16 DEGW and Teknibank, *The intelligent buildings in Europe*, British Council for offices 1992.

17 Duffy, F. and Worthington, J., *Designing for changing needs*, Built Environment 1972.

18 Davis, G., Becker, F., Duffy, F. and Simms, W., *Orbit 2: Organisation, Buildings and Information Technology*, Harbinger 1985.

19 Worthington, J., *Reinventing the workplace*, Architectural Press 1997.

20 Handy, C., *The Empty Raincoat*, Random House Hutchinson, London 1994.

21 Leaman, A., 'Space intensification and diversification', in *Buildings in the Age of Paradox* (ed. Leaman), The Institute of Advanced Architectural Studies, the University of York 1995.

22 Womack, P. and Jones, D., *Lean Thinking: Banish Waste and Create Wealth in Your Corporation*, Touchstone, London 1997.

23 Baird, G., Gray, J., Isaacs, Kernohan, D. and McIndoe, G., *Building Evaluation Techniques*, McGraw-Hill, New York 1996.

5 Communicating expectations

Briefing is a process of clients and users reaching decisions which are then communicated to the design team through briefs. It involves continuous communication between the user and the design team each of whom have different expectations. Good design arises from well-informed clients who are able to communicate their needs to the design team. In turn, the design team should imaginatively communicate opportunities back to the client in a form that is understandable. The best briefs are succinct and can be tested against the original statement of need.

Patterns of communication

Information continuously moves in four directions: from client to design team and vice versa; between client and users; and within the production team between designers and contractors. Each iteration building on the last.

The overall pattern of communication is straightforward, (Figure 5.1) and is reflected in the various types of brief. There are four principle communication routes – demand to supply; supply to demand; within supply; and, within demand (Figure 5.1). Users' communicate their needs to the design team through the Strategic Brief. This defines the objectives of the project in business terms. The designers respond to this by exploring what this means in terms of building to develop a Project Brief. This conveys what the building will

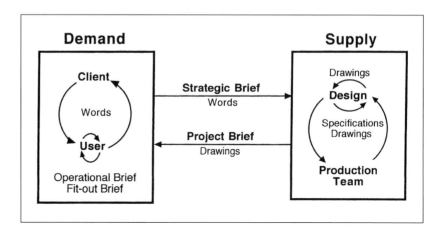

Figure 5.1: Model of the four principal communication routes.

be like. Unlike a Strategic Brief, which primarily consists of text and diagrams, the Project Brief uses diagrams, drawings as the principle medium.

Demand side – communicating within client and user teams

In most organisations, the main board or managing group will be responsible for communicating the organisation's business objectives throughout the business, while the senior managers will be responsible for meeting them. Within this framework on a building project, the board appoints a project champion who is responsible within the client organisation for running the project. In many instances, the communication between these two levels is likely to be strategic, with the project sponsor passing information up the line and calling on the main board for key decisions such as the agreement of budgets. Communication between the project sponsor and user will be on a more operational basis dealing with their needs and communicating the progress of the project through meetings and newsletters.

Supply side – communicating within the design and production teams

Design teams on building projects are generally complex organisational structures. Although the term 'design team' implies a homogenous unit, very often design teams consist of many smaller groups from the various firms representing the different disciplines. The design team may also include the contractors and client representatives depending on the procurement route adopted (Chapter 7).

The design is developed through a process of collective discussions at design team meetings where information and ideas are shared using sketches, photographs, models, literature and perhaps visits to buildings as a means of communication. The quantity surveyor tends to communicate using numeric data to display costs.

As the design develops, drawn information is supplemented with written specifications and data sheets. Both specifications and drawings are used to inform the contractor and specialist suppliers.

Design teams within individual firms tend to be hierarchical with the senior partner or director responsible for representing the firm and often the first person the client contacts. At the next level down might be another partner or director responsible for overseeing the conceptual design and below that an associate or a project architect or engineer responsible for designing the systems to make the concept work. At the lower levels would be technicians responsible for the detail design of specific elements and who will decide how to produce clearly defined drawings that meet the needs of the site and clearly represent the designers' intentions (Figure 5.2).

Joanna Dodd[1] points out that it is important that the connections between the different design firms are compatible and at the same level so that 'individuals approach the problem at a similar level of awareness and decision-making ability'. While a level IV architect might provide the overall direction and framework, the main communication should be between the design contributors at level III because each has specialised input of overall systems and they need to be able to discuss the issues with colleagues working at the same

Figure 5.2 a, b and c: Comparisons between the decision-making involvement during three design stages of a school. The degree of involvement changes during the project, suggesting that in effect the nature of the team changes.
Source: Blyth after Dodd. J [1]

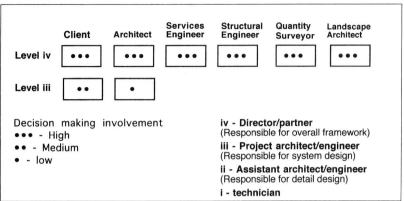

a) Concept Design Stage

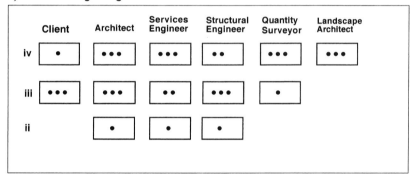

b) Scheme Design Stage

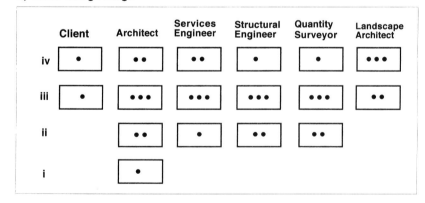

c) Detail Design Stage

level. It is at this level that oversights in the design become clear and that tensions between pragmatic and aesthetic concerns emerge.

The inter-relationships between the people within the design firms can mean that the designers of a specific element of a building may have little or no contact with the client or user. Therefore the effectiveness of the designed solution relies on the communication links between the interface with the client or user and the individual designer.

While there needs to be vertical communication within the system, horizontal communication, particularly across level III, is vital to provide the contractors on-site with fully co-ordinated production information.

Within the complex design scenario, sub-teams often form to resolve particular issues and can involve perhaps two or three of the disciplines, for example, architect, structural and services engineers. Throughout the life of the project different sub-teams form to discuss and resolve a particular issue, and the conclusion is then fed back to each other or the whole design team. The interfaces between these sub-teams need managing to enable effective communication between the groups.

Communicating between supply and demand – project organisation

Communication between the supply and demand sides takes place for various reasons:

- to get information;
- to get a decision;
- to share understanding.

The project organisation is based around communication between the client and users, and the design and construction teams. Effective projects have a clear information distribution and validation structure although it may appear to be relatively complex given the number of people and groups involved. On a project most participants yearn for a relaxed atmosphere avoiding formality. However, while informal communication can enable problems to be smoothed over, when it is not passed through a recognised formal link any decision or reason for a decision may not be recorded and become a source of confusion later.

Communication between designers and clients is characterised by the interchange of different briefs. A variety of forums are used to exchange data

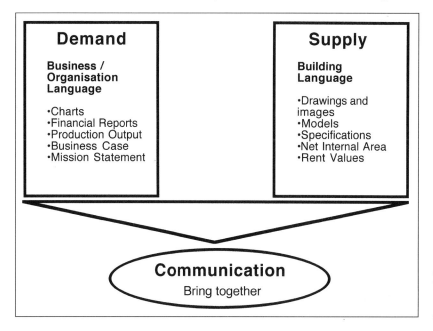

Figure 5.3: Communication between the groups is key. There are two principal languages.
Source: DEGW

and information including design review meetings, design/user interviews and meetings with 'outside' interests such as the planners.

There are several reasons for poor communication between designers and their clients and users during briefing.

Lack of client experience places clients at a disadvantage when dealing with the construction industry. Studies of communication patterns between clients and professionals during the briefing process have shown that where a client had no previous experience of construction, the professionals tended to dominate the discussions.[2] Whereas the opposite was found where clients did have experience.

Defining a common language is key to the briefing process. The lack of a common language often leads to ambiguous statements which are misinterpreted through assumptions made about what is meant.

A shared understanding between users and designers will assist with communication. In their book *Frame reflection: Toward the resolution of intractable policy controversies*,[3] Schön and Rein look at the mutual understanding of problems between people. Problem frames not only exist in the minds of individual designers but also need to be shared within a team. Schön and Rein suggest that 'intractable policy controversies' are caused by a 'frame conflict'. Different 'frames' which are not reconcilable are held by members of the team and they bring different interpretations to the facts. An individual arguing one proposition needs to be aware of the premises, or points of departure, that the evaluating audience accepts as valid. Whilst the audience and arguer may accept some common premises as facts, it is the values held by each that are the yardsticks used to make decisions, and it may be these 'values' that are more likely to conflict.[4] Designers may well be trying to persuade the client to adopt a particular course of action without appreciating that the client does not share the values or viewpoints.

The Strategic Brief sets out the 'problem' and should be a place where common ground is struck. The design team will need to investigate this problem further and test the opportunities. This should enable a deeper understanding of the issues surrounding the problem. The aim is to build a shared understanding from the wider appreciation of the problem set out in the Strategic Brief to the greater detail established in the Project Brief.

Means of information exchange

Giving clear, concise information in a form that the receiver can understand is critical. One of the most divisive features of briefing can be language. Yet language is how briefing is conveyed. Whether it is a 'written brief' or spoken exchange of ideas, briefing conveys meaning and values. Building projects are characterised by there being two languages. For most people the medium for expression is speech and written text; for designers it tends to be images and drawings.

Often, the construction vocabulary is different from that used by many businesses, it ascribes different meanings to familiar terms, it is extensive and, like any vocabulary, it is steeped in hidden meanings. The jargon inflicted upon the unwary leads to confusion. Cynics would doubtless suggest that it provides the perfect opportunity for designers and contractors to seize greater control over the process than they should.

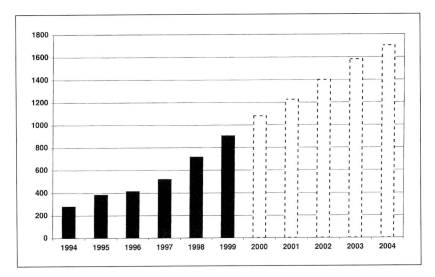

Figure 5.4: Example of personnel projection.
Source: DEGW

Elaborate drawings which are difficult to interpret are often a cause of communication problems. They can hide, perhaps unwittingly, a spatial complexity which will limit users' and clients' ability to respond.

Reflecting user needs

The character, configuration and expectations of the client organisation can typically be described through:

- *Organisation charts.* These can be used to convey important information on the structure of the organisation, roles, external relationships, how the different components are connected and the decision-making mechanisms.

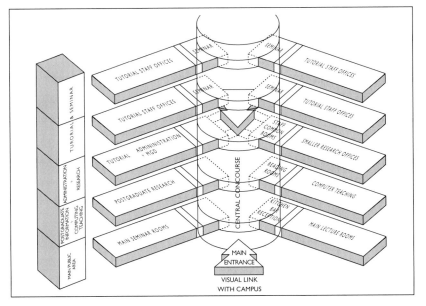

Figure 5.5: Adjacency diagram showing relationships between departments in an organisation.
Source: DEGW

Figure 5.6: Workflow diagram.
Source: DEGW

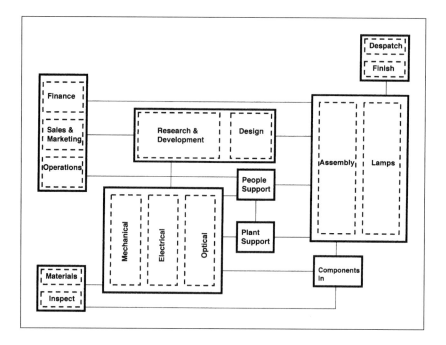

- *Personnel projections.* The extent of change and growth in an organisation (see Chapter 4) can be shown by using personnel projections. Figure 5.4 shows a graph giving previous growth in staff and it charts potential changes 3 to 5 years ahead. Alternative scenarios can be similarly mapped out but the reasoning for the different projections should always be given.
- *Adjacency/relationship diagrams.* Setting out the relationship between different parts of the organisation is invaluable to the designers. The relationships being described may be those of departments, activities or people. Diagrams to show this can be set out in different ways – in two dimensions or three dimensions, for example (Figure 5.5). In adjacency diagrams showing spaces, the relative size or importance of each space can also be shown. However, these diagrams should be used to describe relationships and not try to mimic an outcome. The designer may find different ways of planning the building that match the prerequisites of the diagram.
- *Workflow diagrams* (Figure 5.6). How an organisation 'works' can be demonstrated through the use of work flow diagrams. These can be used to describe the whole activity of an organisation, such as a manufacturing process, or an individual component such as order processing.
- *Visualisation techniques.* A range of visualisation techniques such as abstract images, photographs and sketches can be used to enable the client and user to convey information to a designer in a recognisable form to increase shared understanding.

  Visualisation techniques can be used to convey both tangible as well as intangible ideas, for example perceptions of an organisation's culture. Abstract images can be used to identify how people see their organisation and what they think that it should be like. They can also be used to identify a user's preferences.

Images of particular situations or objects can be used as references to convey more tangible ideas, and visiting existing buildings may provide real examples and helps when discussing options, or identifying particular needs (Chapter 3).

Visualisation techniques can also help clients and users assess the implications of design decision and suggestions. When confronted with a set of dimensions for a room or spaces, it may be helpful to mark out the areas on the floor to get a feel for the sizes of spaces. However, even then this can be deceptive with areas appearing smaller than they would be once the walls are built.

SUMMARY OF THE MEANS OF PRESENTING INFORMATION USED BY DESIGNERS

* *Drawings – plans, elevations, sections.*
  These represent buildings in two dimensions but they show the relationship between rooms and elements such as windows and doors; it can be difficult to appreciate the spatial implications of the design.
* *Perspectives.*
  These can be drawn in different styles with more or less detail and convey an interpretation of what the buildings will be like.
* *Axonometrics, isometrics.*
  These are not the same as perspectives, and in many ways are false representations of three dimensions, although often presented as if they represent reality.
* *Images – photographs, montages, computer-drawn, fly-throughs, virtual reality.*
  Computing software developments enable designers to produce sophisticated images. Montaging a proposed building onto an existing street-scape, for example. Often, high-quality photographs of the existing environment are scanned into a computer and the proposed building is drawn onto it digitally. Again, these seem to represent a reality. However, before the computer is involved, the photograph may have been taken using filters and other photographic tricks. Whilst it may be difficult to say that these images are false, they are only an interpretation of reality.
* *Models and mock-ups.*
  Many designers, users and clients find it easiest to work with models and mock-ups. Basic card models can be a very useful way of discussing a building, giving a feeling for the shape and size of volumes.
* *Computer simulations are often used to simulate 'Fly-throughs' and 'walk-throughs'.*

Applying communication

While the technological revolution provides the advantages of speed in communication, whether it is sending e-mail, faxes or data files, there is a tendency for people to send everyone much more information on a subject than they need. For communication to be effective it is important to distribute just enough for the other person to fulfil his or her function. The adversarial nature of the construction industry seems to encourage everyone to scatter documents widely on the 'You've seen the information, so don't blame us' principle. It is helpful to identify exactly what sorts of information the different people involved need to receive, and to encourage people to ask for more on an 'as needed' basis.

Table 5.1 Typical means of communication

Internal project communications

Meetings	Questions to consider during preparation
• Team meetings	• Who should attend?
– In-house	• How often should they be held?
(including external advisors)	
• User or interest groups	• What is their purpose?
• Interviews – selection	• Who chairs the meeting?
• Discussions	• Who facilitates the workshop?
– Group	• How much time do facilitators
– Individual	need before and after?
• Workshops	• How are conclusions to be recorded?

Internal and external project communications

Presentations	Questions to consider during preparation
• To board	• What is the purpose and how will it be made clear?
• To users	• Where should they be held?
	• Who is involved?
• To external stakeholders	• How many are involved?
• By the design/construction team	• How will questions be handled?
	• Are handouts required?
	• Are record copies needed?
• Phone	
• E-mail	
• Memos	

External project communication

Bulletins	Questions to consider during preparation
• Press releases	• Who should receive them?
• Newsletters	
• Letters	
• Faxes	• Are they formal/informal? – is this clear?
• Web pages	• Does a new address/domain need to be set up?
	• Who has access?
	• What type of information goes on it?
	• Is interaction necessary?
	• Who manages the site?
	• Who will contribute to it?
	• Who will use it?

CASE STUDY: UNCLEAR COMMUNICATION

A manufacturer asked a design team to design a new headquarters building. The building was to have space for old artefacts, including leather and cloth from the sixteenth and seventeenth centuries, books and other objects. This material formed the historical roots of the organisation, but had been locked away in safes. Now the client wanted to display it for the benefit of staff and customers.

During a 'sanity-check', where an external consultant was asked to review the project and test whether the client was getting what it needed, it emerged that the client was worried about whether the 'history space' would work. While the brief identified that cabinets, storage, security and particular environmental conditions would be needed for the artefacts, this information was submerged within a large quantity of material on other matters. What became clear from the discussion with the client was that this historical element was really very important. However, the client felt that the designers had tucked the room away, and paid little attention to how accessible it was. The connection between the company's past and its future were not clearly fed through into the briefing process. The client felt that the design team was concentrating on things that were important to them but not him.

Identifying expectations

In any activity which involves more than one person, there is a variety of expectations which must be managed. The client, users, designers, contractors, local community and regulators all have their own needs and aspirations. However, for a project to be successful, these interests need to be shared. This does not mean that the client or users' interests should be subrogated to those of others; it means being careful to communicate what those interests are, and sharing an understanding with others. It involves listening to different views and consulting with others individually or in groups about the opportunities and implications of the project.

The expectations bound up in a project reach right into the core of the 'business idea'. What is the business there to do? How does it do it? What is its context? What are the operational criteria for meeting the business plan? These not only have to be known to the users and client, but clearly under-stood by the designers and rest of the project team. They are the ultimate test of whether the completed project is a success. When built, clients and users will ask: does this building enable us to deliver our business plan?

These business criteria form the basis for exploring needs discussed in Chapter 3. User needs form the backbone of the project. The expectations of users will be different from those of the client in as much as the client will perhaps think of the project in terms of cost and timeframe, whereas users will be more concerned about the quality of the environment and how it impacts on what they do. However, the scope of individual user's expectations will be moderated by constraints imposed by the client or senior managers in user organisations. Cost is likely to be one such constraint, business goals another. These must be made clear to the individual users so that their expectations are relevant and do not become wish-lists.

False expectations can also be raised merely by someone in authority asking questions. Ask someone how they would improve their working environment and this quickly becomes an expectation that it will be done. Managing expectations is a critical task for anyone managing the briefing process.

During the development of the brief it is easy to raise the hopes of those involved, even if this is accidental. Sometimes this happens because different people make different assumptions or see things in different ways. For one person an airy space might suggest a lot of natural ventilation and to another it might suggest that it will be well lit with natural lighting. Their hopes could be dashed if it does not meet these expectations. Other times, hopes may be raised because there has been a misunderstanding perhaps where something has been changed but no one told. Expectations which are needlessly raised and then dashed could lead people to lose faith in the project.

To understand the expectations, merely asking groups of people what they need is not enough. Nor is collating lists of needs. Even if they are within the context of the business, such lists are likely to be a collection of personal objectives – things that are important to one group of individuals, but not necessarily the whole organisation. However, they must be recognised by the others in order to achieve the shared understanding about what is important to the organisation.

If the objectives are unclear, it becomes difficult to judge whether the project is a success, but also leads to 'mission creep'. The scope of the project may become broader than intended, possibly with much effort spent on solving the wrong problems altogether. Clearly-stated objectives with agreed priorities enable the users to be sure about what they are getting, the client to manage the process, and the design/construction team to know when it is running off track.

Setting levels of performance

Balancing performance and prescription

When specifying what is required, either one can describe in detail how it is to be provided or merely identify the performance expected, leaving it up to the respondent to work out the exact nature of the final product.

Clients which build regularly, such as large retail chains, will specify solutions that have worked well in the past. The brief will be largely prescriptive, focusing the project team's innovative abilities on the elements where performance can be improved and costs reduced (Figure 5.7). Clients who build infrequently or require to fulfil a specialist need, will tend to produce briefs with a higher proportion of performance specification. Briefs that are completely performance related, with no reference to past experience, can be risky. On the other hand, a brief which is totally prescriptive will stifle innovation. The best briefs have a mixture of innovation and past experience.

Performance requirements and measures

The brief should set out performance requirements which are statements about the 'measurable level of function that must be provided for an objective to be met'.[6] There can be more than one performance requirement for each objective.

EXAMPLES OF OBJECTIVES AND SUPPORTING PERFORMANCE REQUIREMENTS

1. Objective:
Provide secure management for the whole organisation and its constituent parts.

1. Performance requirement:
Allow separate security needs for users in buildings in the future (access, reception, goods).

2. Objective:
High levels of information technology to support business needs using PCs and Local Area Networks.

2. Performance requirement:
Slab to slab height must allow variety of servicing strategies within raised floors/ceiling voids, likely to be between 3.6 m–4.0 m.

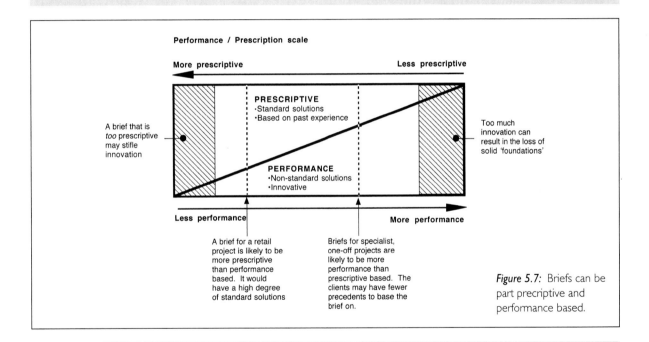

Figure 5.7: Briefs can be part precriptive and performance based.

WRITING A PERFORMANCE REQUIREMENT

A performance requirement should:

* address the outcome of an objective;
* be precise and unambiguous;
* be measurable;
* be operational – be capable of being met; for example it does not contravene legislation;
* be positive and not negative;
* be capable of being used as a yardstick.

Source: From Duerk: *Architectural Programming*

Examples of different types of measures
Process
* Delivery against the programme;
* cost and value;
* timely decisions against milestone deadlines;
* risk against return.

Business
* Return on investment;
* ease of informal communication;
* productivity;
* user satisfaction;
* customers.

Building
* Cost of building per unit floor area;
* utilisation – percentage usable to gross floor area;
* adaptability – number of alternative layouts;
* expansion capacity;
* operating costs.

Each requirement should enable alternative solutions to be generated, but should not be so general as to allow anything to pass. For example, merely stating that space should be provided for a particular activity, would allow any shape or size of space, whereas the user may have some more specific requirements.

In her book *Architectural Programming*, Donna Duerk[5] suggests that a good performance requirement is one that is specific, measurable and operational.

It should be precise, avoiding ambiguities. Its detail may depend on what is appropriate for the scale of the project. For example, in an 'urban brief' (Chapter 9) one might be saying that a commercial area should be easily accessible to a retail area. But one would not be saying that each front door of each house should overlook the road. The detail may also depend on the type of brief. The statement of need may identify a general level of business performance, whereas the Project Brief will identify particular amount of energy use, among other things (see Table 5.2).

An important component of any brief is that it should enable the result to be tested. The measures might include established standards, yardsticks, guidelines, benchmarks or limits. Measures can be absolute so that there is

Table 5.2 Brief example of performance requirement

Statement of Need	To achieve a successful, profitable business that attracts creative staff.
Strategic Brief	Every individual to have direct external aspect.
Project Brief	No workspace is more than 9 m from a window wall.

a 'yes' or 'no' conclusion as to whether a requirement is met. They can be presented as a range of values using measures such as size and energy performance, giving maximum and minimum criteria. They can also be a matter of judgement, where the evaluation is based on values and priorities if it is not possible to be absolute.

To be comparative, key measures should have both a building and a business component. To merely compare the floor area provided per person between buildings says little about the quality of the business, other than its frugality. However, to provide a measure which both presents the floor area provided for staff (15 m² net usable per person) and the productivity of the individual member of staff (£100 000 earning capacity per staff member per annum) gives a clear focus of the performance of the building (Figure 5.8).

Floor area per person (15 m²) related to average earning per member of personnel staff (£100,000 per annum)

Figure 5.8: Measure of space utilisation.

Organising a brief

A brief should provide a coherent story of the project which can be understood by all those likely to use the document. It should clearly identify the objectives and main priorities in the project, and set out expectations. It must also anticipate who is expected to respond to it and how.

Assumptions and their underlying values need to be made explicit. Weak briefs are those that assume what others know and how they will interpret a piece of information. Ambiguities and begged questions in briefs often lead to a design team pursuing a line of thought not intended by the client. Just as assumptions made by the design team will leave clients and users bewildered.

The process of producing a brief may be carried out by developing a series of drafts which the contributors can review and amend.

The audience for the final product should be clearly established before work is begun so that the brief is customised accordingly. The biggest difficulty might be trying to cater for a readership ranging from a reader outside the organisation, such as a customer or visitor, to the chief executive and the design team. In this type of situation the reader from outside might only be interested in the 'headline' statements with perhaps one sentence of explanation, whereas other readers may need more detail. This can be achieved by layering the information and arranging it typographically so that readers can scan over what they do not need to read.

The aim is to make the document clear and concise so that it gives all the appropriate information for the stage without becoming too long and impenetrable. Too much information can obscure the message. It is as important to consider what can be left out as well as what can be included.

The first part of a briefing document sets out the mission and context of the project. Setting out the context is an important component for helping readers understand the background to the project. It should describe the purpose of the briefing document and the period within which the work was undertaken. It should also identify who the client is, who was involved in the development of the brief and who the audience is. The format of the document should also be summarised. An executive summary can be used for setting out the major decisions.

Designing the layout of the brief involves deciding on the hierarchy of information which can then be reflected in the typeface and type size,

---

TIPS FOR WRITING A SUCCESSFUL BRIEF

For each issue:

* set out a simple statement of what is to be achieved;
* explain the argument – why it should be as stated;
* give the evidence. This can be drawn from: existing examples; data collected; facts.

By using this method, if any new evidence comes to light the argument can be refuted or reinforced. It enables everyone – clients, users and designers – to be clear about any area of dispute.

TWELVE TIPS FOR EFFECTIVE BRIEFING COMMUNICATION

1. Clearly state priorities.
2. Be concise and clear.
3. Provide only the relevant information sufficient to make decisions at each stage of the process.
4. Drawings, diagrams and charts can be worth a thousand words.
5. Explain requirements with supporting evidence as they can be accepted, adapted or refuted.
6. Provide a statement of intent that is inspirational, comprehensive and precise.
7. Provide easily applied performance measures, which allow solutions to be assessed.
8. Use the appropriate language for the audience to be addressed.
9. Prescribe previous solutions where they are well-tried, tested and successful.
10. Communicate measures for success in both building and business terms.
11. Check the relevance of information provided by ensuring it allows an appropriate design response.
12. Express a limited number of key objectives.

---

paragraph numbering, indentation and graphics. The most important information must be instantly accessible. Items that are too detailed or interrupt the flow of the story should be put in a separate document of Appendices. A common criticism of briefs is that they can become so involved in minutiae when all the reader needs is a summary. As such they become difficult to absorb.

Types of brief

At each stage of the process, briefing information will be focused at different audiences.

The best briefs are succinct and provide a framework within which to challenge, develop and measure specific needs.

Statement of need (prepared for the board or managing group of the organisation):

- contains information on an aspect of need required to enable senior managers to decide whether there may be a case;
- presented using text;

- concerned with identifying a need and the possible impact of not meeting it.

Strategic Brief (prepared for the project team):

- contains information required to select and brief the design team, and inform user interest groups;
- presented as text, charts and diagrams;
- concerned with establishing the context, user expectations, concepts and issues.

Project Brief (prepared for approval by the client and for use by the production team):

- contains information required to brief the production team and ensure understanding and agreement of scope and specification by the client;
- presented as text, measures, drawings and models;
- concerned with agreeing concepts, performance, and parameters of time and costs.

Essentials of a brief

Every brief should set out:

- the mission;
- objectives;
- performance requirements and measures;
- priorities;
- management of decisions and responsibilities;
- timeframe;
- who is expected to respond.

Mission statement

Set out in 5–6 lines at the beginning of the brief, the mission statement is a statement of intent and should express the reason that a client is undertaking the project. It should be short, sharp and inspirational as well as be a continuous reminder for clients, users and designers of what they have set out to achieve. The statement should focus on the goals of success, and the essential characteristics and qualities expected of the project.

Objectives

The statement of objectives sets out how the mission should be accomplished. Each objective should support the mission and embody the aspiration of the client and users. They should state the level of quality that the solution should achieve. The objectives should focus the designer's search for a solution to a problem without limiting the potential to explore alternative concepts that will meet the objective. They should also provide a clear focus and avoid using ambiguous wording.

EXAMPLES OF PRIORITY STATEMENTS

* Training represents an important part of the culture of this organisation and should be reflected in the location and presence of the training suite within the building.
* The training suite must be capable of responding to a number of different teaching and learning approaches.
* Energy efficiency represents an important ethos of the business and must be reflected in the approach and design of the building.

Priorities

The statement of priorities sets out the issues which are important to the client and users. A priority identified may concern the business and reinforce issues identified in the business case. For example, the operation of a particular piece of equipment may be vital to the success of the business whereas to the designers it might get overlooked as something that is neither more nor less important than something else. Issues surrounding sustainability may be important, this will have far-reaching implications on the design and procurement of the building.

The aim is to get the design team to concentrate on what you think is important rather than waste resources only on what concerns them.

Management and decision-making (see Chapter 7)

The brief should set out who is responsible for making what sorts of decision and when they should be made. It should also clearly indicate who should communicate what to whom.

Conclusion

Effective communication demands attention to the project organisation and developing a common understanding through the definition of the problem and its exploration using a shared language.

Information between the supply and demand sides needs to be structured. This involves identifying *who* should give and receive *what* information, and *when*, and who is responsible for *what* decision (Chapter 7). The transfer of data, requests for information and all decisions should be routed directly between nominated representatives of the client and design team. A project plan should set out a schedule of all the stages which need to be worked through. It will help determine key dates for decisions, for example when to submit for planning approval, ensuring legal possession of the site. The use of value management, risk management and evaluation workshops are part of the communication structure.

Tips for a good brief

Aim to ensure that your brief:

- expresses your goal and inspires the design team;
- doesn't get too detailed too soon;
- only provides the relevant information required to make the relevant decisions at each particular stage of the design process;
- continually refers back to the context established in the Strategic Brief;
- doesn't make promises which cannot be fulfilled;
- presents information in a way that can be acted upon;
- describes requirements so the design response's success in meeting the client expectation can be measured;
- provides performance specification where fresh ideas are called for, and prescriptive solutions where successes from the past can be repeated.

Designers generally communicate using visual imagery and they communicate with contractors and suppliers with a mixture of visual and written media. The organisation of design and construction is complex with many different groups of people involved. It is clear that although vertical lines of communication within each group are important, the horizontal contact across groups matters as much, and needs careful management by the team leader. Clients as members of the design team may well be part of this process.

Notes

1 Dodd, J., 'Organisational Structure of the Design Team', in *The successful management of design*, Gray, C., Hughes, W., Bennett, J., The Centre for Strategic Studies in Construction, The University of Reading 1994.
2 Gameson, R., *Clients and professionals: the interface* in *Practice Management. New Perspectives for the Construction Professional* (eds Barrett, P. and Males, A.,) E & FN Spon, London, pp. 165–74 1991.
3 Schön, D. and Rein, M., *Frame reflection: Toward the Resolution of Intractable Policy Controversies*, Basic Books, New York 1994.
4 Stumpf, S. and McDonnell, J., *Relating Argument to Design Problem Framing*, Proceedings of the 4th International Design Thinking Research Symposium (DTRS '99), Massachusetts Institute of Technology, Cambridge, Mass., USA, 23–25 April 1999.
5 Duerk, D., *Architectural Programming*, Van Nostrand Reinhold, New York 1993.
6 Blyth, A., *Design Team Monitoring*. The Design Council appointed Alastair Blyth to monitor and evaluate the design team on a primary school project designed and built for Essex County Council. A key finding was how the nature of the design team changed during the project because of the extent that different staff across a range of organisations were involved as the project moved from strategic design to detailed design.

6 Learning from experience

It is well recognised in management literature that to manage and improve performance, a company must initially have a clear and explicit set of objectives, against which performance can be measured to establish whether the initial objectives are being met. Edwards Deming[1] one of the founders of total quality management proposed a cycle of planning, doing, checking and action (Figure 6.1) as the foundation of successful problem solving. At the heart of quality management is:[2]

- an awareness of the need for quality and continuous improvement;
- reporting progress (feedback);
- communicating results;
- measurement (keeping score);
- process: 'Do it all over again to emphasise that the quality improvement programme never ends'.[3]

The same is true in design; improvements result in learning from previous experience. Design and briefing is a creative process of proposing, testing, adjusting and reformulating the proposals. To achieve such advances requires well-formulated, measurable objectives that can be reviewed both at the design stage, during construction and at the completion of the project. The concept of measurement, evaluation and feedback is now well established in measuring business success, but it is surprising how the same principles are still relatively

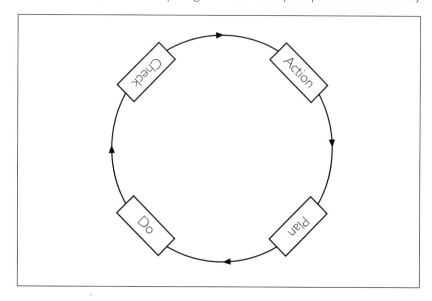

Figure 6.1: The Deming cycle, proposed by Edwards Deming.

poorly implemented in building design and construction. This chapter sets out the focus and objectives for evaluation, the perceived benefits and alternative approaches for establishing a successful programme of feedback.

The focus of evaluation

Traditionally in the construction industry, feedback has been seen as learning once the building is complete and occupied through post-occupancy evaluation (POE) studies. Post-project evaluation originated with studies of buildings in use in the 1960s and 1970s.[4] These early studies were invariably initiated by central government departments (e.g. the Department for Education and Science or Ministry of Housing) and were focused on collecting feedback to influence policy and provide more effective guidance. With the decline of central government control in the 1980s, post-completion studies were initiated by enlightened developers,[5] who recognised the value of feedback to improve their investment policies, or corporate clients, such as the banks and utilities[6] who recognised the cost of building failures and the effect of building performance on the productivity and health of staff. In parallel, enlightened corporate clients and developers with serial building programmes were applying the lessons of continuous feedback, by establishing quantifiable measures at the start of a project, and assessing design options[7] or establishing 'milestones' to review proposals against objectives (BAA Value Management Days[8]). Evaluation is now recognised as being part of the first stages of a project, when a company looks to learn from relevant practice on other projects. Evaluation and feedback continue through design testing, to final feedback at the post-completion evaluation.

In construction, project feedback can be focused on the:

- Product – how well the building kept the water out, and achieved the pre-defined specification of fitness for purpose.
- Process – how well the team integrated to provide the product, measured against the ability to keep within budget, deliver on time and meet the clients' expectations.
- Performance – how well the building supported the company's business goals, and met the users' aspirations.

Post-occupancy evaluation studies tend to focus on performance, reflecting on the way that the product and process support client organisational goals. Construction industry post-completion research tends to focus on product and process, and how to improve construction industry productivity.

Major improvements may be made in cost and performance through feedback.[9] The Chartered Institute of Building Services Engineers (CIBSE) and Building Services Journal have undertaken a series of Post-occupancy evaluations[10] under the PROBE (Post-Occupancy Review of Building Engineering) programme which have placed issues of building performance and design feedback on the construction professionals' agenda. The Construction Round Table,[11] a forum of major corporate clients, has recognised the need to learn from past experience. In its report on post-project audits it suggests:

> "Post-project audit is a key part of learning. However, it demands scarce resources and it can only be justified if it provides tangible benefits … properly managed post-project audit does indeed deliver such benefits."

WORKPLACE OF THE FUTURE AT SCOTTISH ENTERPRISE (WOTFSE)
CONTINUOUS EVALUATION AND FEEDBACK

There are few incentives to evaluate performance at the end of a project. Rather than unearthing many of the shortcomings, it is far more exciting to move on to the challenges of the next assignment. Despite the limited incentives, evaluation is normally expected to happen at the post-project completion stage. The reality is that feedback seldom happens. At the first glimmers of a project, feedback from other experience and evaluation of organisational and building performance to help formulate needs and solutions, is a more attractive proposition. Scottish Enterprise with their pilot project in Glasgow for 'flexible working' began by evaluation, and established a continuous process of feedback.

Scottish Enterprise, Scotland's quango for stimulating inward investment and economic success, undertook a pilot project for approximately 76 staff to assess approaches to flexible working, before a planned consolidation of the headquarters staff to new premises. The project originated by Adryan Bell (Head of internal communications) and was spread over a year with four months for implementation. The initiator and sponsor was the Chief Executive who was aware of the sea-change happening in leading-edge organisations, and recognised that Scottish Enterprise should, in its work processes and space use, be forward looking and give a lead to Scottish businesses. The project which aimed to create an environment 'that was flexible to change as well as conducive to learning and sharing experience', began with a period of assessing what others were doing, and evaluating existing ways of working within Scottish Enterprise. A review of the literature was undertaken. Other projects were visited, a programme of 'networking' with leading-edge organisations both in the UK and abroad was begun, and best practice assimilated. A ground floor, vacant showroom space, of approximately 500 m^2 was identified and the project established. Volunteers who were interested in working in a more flexible manner were canvassed with a good response. The final pilot project provided a base for 70 staff, which has increased to 100, with a wide mix of settings including:

* 14 permanent desks;
* 14 hot desks, allocated on an as-required basis;
* 5 carrels for guest work;
* 3 'hot' offices;
* 3 touch-down work tops.

The project took four months for detailed design and construction, and throughout this period the proposals were fine tuned from feedback from potential users, and experience of others. During this period HR consultants, Coopers Lybrand Hawthorne, were appointed to undertake a post-completion evaluation, and over this period collected information on:

* selected users' expectations and perceptions of their current space and workstyles;
* existing space use.

The evaluation was undertaken over a nine month period, beginning three months before move-in. The final evaluation report was valuable both for stimulating internal improvements and drawing conclusions for external dissemination.

In addition to the formal evaluation programme, there was continuous feedback through the:

* 'ideas board' – where members of staff pointed out improvements;
* 'concierge' – who kept a daily diary of usage (bookings) comments by staff and visitors, and the type of groups visiting;
* staff comment sheets.

Immediate changes implemented were to provide an extra hot-office, adding more art work, and to introduce a goldfish bowl, as a humorous icon of staff feelings.

The implementation group for the Pilot project, which consisted of the five operational groups involved plus representatives from IT facilities, and Personnel, has continued in existence, and become the focus for feedback and input into the new Headquarters building project.

Evaluation and feedback was an integral component of the pilot project, and has provided strong foundations for the major relocation project ahead. Personalities have changed, the original champion has moved on; however, the principle of continuous feedback is established, and individual experiences and knowledge are being transferred to the corporation.

LEARNING FOR THE FUTURE

The level and nature of interest in Workplace of the Future (WOTF) from a wide range of business, academic and educational organisations emphasises the importance of WOTF-style developments and the value of sharing experiences and knowledge.

Some of the key learning points for Scottish Enterprise from the project are:

* People are the most important ingredient, their attitudes and behaviour to support the experimental project has been vital.
* People are not resistant to change – but they are resistant to being changed.
* It's all about choice and flexibility – never assume that everyone wants to work in the same environment or at the same worksetting.
* The extremes of complete open plan or hot desking are not appropriate. Getting the right balance of open and enclosed space, as well as interactive and quiet space is extremely important.
* Induction programmes for new staff are crucial to aid the understanding of the desired culture of the workplace.
* In future, organisations will need to consider offering more than just a salary to retain staff, individuals are now placing a high value on flexibility, empowerment and control in their working lives.
* Sometimes it's the smallest (and often cheapest) details that matter the most!
* There is never a better time to act than now but there will always be an easy excuse not to take control.
* There is never a better time to act than now but there will always be an easy excuse not to take action!
* Once people experience the benefits brought by the new ways of working they will not want to revert back, therefore you must ensure you can deliver to meet their demanding expectations.
* Taking an integrated, holistic approach to a changing workplace environment will reap most rewards; consider your technology, organisation policies and practices, management styles and physical infrastructures in relation to each other and not in isolation.
* Organisation change is aided by the support of senior management – ensure that there is a sponsor appointed who is actively dedicated to supporting and leading the change.

Source: Scottish Enterprise and Adryan Bell, DEGW

The goals of post-project evaluation

Duerk[12] identifies four reasons for undertaking evaluation:

1. To test the success of the project on meeting the goals of the brief.
2. To test how well the project implemented the goals and then fine-tune the buildings and or systems to improve performance.
3. To gather information for future projects.
4. To develop policies, guidance and regulatory controls by reviewing failures.

Each of these objectives has a different time horizon. Testing the ability of a project in meeting its goals (as stated in point 1 above) occurs during the project as well as after the project has been completed. The process of gathering information for future projects and policy (points 3 and 4) can happen years after the completion of a project, and invariably happens on inception of a new project.

Perceived benefits and barriers

The motivation and method of undertaking a programme of evaluation, depends on the type of client. Expectation will vary according to whether the client has:

- a continuity of budget – e.g. Government departments who are funding a continuous building programme, but are disassociated from the day-to-day use;
- a continuity of usage – universities or hospitals, which have a continuous programme of maintaining, adapting or intermittently building a stock of space;
- a focus primarily on investment and return – e.g. property fund, developer or retailer.

The Construction Round Table identifies the following benefits from post-completion evaluation:

- technical feedback;
- process improvement;
- financial/cost gains through: selecting the right tender, life-cycle continuity, cost effective design and cost benchmarks.[11]

Evaluation is based on 'the pressure that we will get better, less costly buildings if we repeat our successes and avoid making the same mistakes over and over again'.[13] The most commonly recognised reason for undertaking evaluation is to 'learn through reflection' and continuous development.

Despite the logic of feedback and learning from experience, the barriers to achieving regular evaluation are formidable. The building project culture means it is more interesting to start on the next new project than to reflect on the uncertain successes and failures of the last. Post occupancy evaluation is seen as an audit to find the failures and distribute blame. Independent evaluations may unearth results that could damage perceptions, and professional reputations. White points out in Prieser, 'Building Evaluations'[14] that undertaking evaluation studies have to respond to 'client concerns such as avoiding embarrassment, defending results, satisfying administrative superiors, boosting morale, minimising disruption, resolving conflicts and obtaining maximum public relations benefit.'

Measuring success

Whether or not a building is successful will depend on the criteria used to judge success. The ability to measure the success of a building project relates to the yardsticks introduced in the brief, against which it can be measured. It is important to set out the factors for success in the formal Strategic Brief covering cost, time and performance. Briefs should identify how outcomes will be measured.

Measures are either quantitative or qualitative. Quantitative measures, such as usable space or energy consumption are easier to understand in terms of success or failure. With qualitative measures such as image, character of an organisation or comfort, success is subjective. Yet, such qualitative judgements are often the criteria by which people measure the success of projects. Users' satisfaction can be hard to identify precisely. The level of satisfaction or dissatisfaction may be to do with the characteristics of the organisation rather with the facilities. Dissatisfaction manifests itself in the level of complaints about the new facility. A high level of complaint suggests a problem.

Project success may be defined in terms of the following criteria:

- The process:
  - delivery against the programme;
  - service from the project team, post-project back up;
  - communication between the various teams of people involved, as well as within the client organisation;
  - cost;
  - risk – either that risks identified did not occur or did so only within the parameters identified.
- The client organisation (performance):
  - business objectives;
  - communication;
  - productivity;
  - flow of products, materials;
  - flow of information;
  - customers/clients, visitors.
- The product:
  - flexibility of the facility;
  - quality – perhaps in term of finishes;
  - safety – in both use and maintenance;
  - maintenance – is easily maintainable within costs predicted;
  - life-cycle cost;
  - operating cost;
  - few or no defects;
  - acoustic performance;
  - environmental criteria;
  - lighting;
  - thermal performance (building);
  - use of space (building).

For most clients there will be two primary criteria by which success is measured, namely: the success of the organisation in relation to the facility; and the success of the facility itself.

In terms of the organisation, the sort of measures might be productivity, financial return, satisfaction within the organisation, adaptability and flexibility in use and image. In brief, measures have to be realistic, attainable and accurately reflect what the client needs. Measures are at the heart of the value management process, where a balance is being explored between costs and benefits.

During the pre-project stage, the objective is to test options against cost, capacity, potential of disruption to the organisation, and consider other constraints such as location/planning, and potential problems on the sites.

During the project stage the objective is to test the design options and define the measures by which the completed facility will be judged.

Typical measures and methods assessment at the project stage may include:

- thermal modelling – a way of analysing the facility on computer to see how it will respond on hot or cold days, at night or during the day time, at different times of the year;
- energy efficiency modelling and analysis – this looks at how much energy, such as electricity or gas, the building might use when it is in operation. It also looks at the energy efficiency of the production process behind the manufacture of the materials and products that are used to build it;
- space – the net to gross and net to usable ratios;
- models – that explain the building
  - physical models
  - computer models
  - visualisations
  - sketches
  - schematics;
- cost models;
- fire safety models which look at how quickly a fire might spread throughout the building or how the smoke will spread;
- health and safety plans for safe construction and maintenance.

Approaches to post-occupancy evaluation

There are a myriad of techniques available for evaluating buildings in use and gaining feedback, including:

- *questionnaires*, which can be provided to staff before and after move-in to assess levels of satisfaction and perceptions of performance;
- *interviews*, (one-to-one feedback) and focus groups with staff from similar interests or status. Such feedback interviews are facilitated by a professional with a loose agenda, so allowing free discussion to pick up issues that may not be initially obvious. Homogeneous groups (e.g. off the same grade or function) allow for more open discussion and feedback;
- *benchmarking*, this enables comparisons to be made between buildings or space performance against recognised leading-edge examples. Benchmarking is a continuous systematic process of measuring relative performance

against relevant comparators. IBM defines benchmarking as 'the continuous process of analysing the best practice in the world for the process goals and objectives leading to world levels of achievement';

- *measurement*, by assessment of environmental conditions against those specified, or measurement of data collection against predictions.
- *walk through*, either by the original design team or an independent professional group. This method can use both observation, reflecting on how space is performing, and informal discussions with users to identify conflicts.

William Pena, in *Problem Seeking*,[15] sets out procedures for undertaking 'walk throughs', which can either be applied at the design stage (on the drawing board) or after building completion. These procedures were subsequently operationalised by CRS – Sirrine.[16] Central to Pena's approach is the desire for the design and development team to reflect and learn by:

- detecting, observing, and reporting on existing conditions and changes from the original intention;
- recommending corrective action, and identify lessons learnt.

The walk through aims to address four issues:

- form;
- function;
- economy;
- time.

Addressing these issues serves the purposes of justifying action and expenditures, measuring quality (performance to requirements), fine-tuning, adjusting to make improvements for future programmes, and testing the application of innovations. The evaluative programme aims to assess both the quantifiable comparative data, and qualitative perceptual responses.

The quantifiable data can be collected through measurement, and regularly assembled data covering:

- functional adequacy – gross area per person;
- space adequacy – gross to net, net to usable;
- construction quality – cost per m^2;
- technical adequacy – cost of equipment related to m^2 cost;
- energy performance;
- user satisfaction – questionnaires.

The qualitative assessment is the balanced feedback from a cross-section of interests e.g. owner, facilities manager, user representative, programmer (brief maker), designer and construction manager, reflecting on goals, concepts, changes, and response to problem statements. The CRS Sirrine model[16] has three internal groups (designers, managers and technologists) who review the building on the drawing board and at post-completion in terms of Form, Function, Economy, and Time (Figure 6.2). Each member of the team gives the project a score in each category, on a five-point scale, against a standard set of criteria. For a post-occupancy evaluation, Pena suggests the need for 25 man days of time (five-person team, including a trained facilitator) spread over four weeks. The process should reflect on the initial briefing goals, and undertake the following sequence of activities:

Function	1 people 2 activities 3 relationships
Form	4 site 5 environment 6 quality
Economy	7 initial budget 8 operating costs 9 life cycle costs
Time	10 past 11 present 12 future

- initiation – set up meeting to agree purpose, themes, measure;
- preparation – collect and analyse measurable data;
- walk through – using eyes, and ears (random interviews);
- discussion – first impressions and conclusions;
- assessment – against pre-decided criteria on 1–5 rating;
- summation – review of key issues as wall display (analysis cards);
- documentation – immediate copy of analysis cards.

The Probe studies similarly rely on an expert panel, both collecting and analysing measurable data, and on-site visits to discuss qualitative aspects from different experts' perspectives.

Feedback during design can be successfully provided by user groups (for certain designed buildings) or tenant profiling for speculative developments.

Factors for successful feedback

The Institute for Advanced Architectural Studies (IoAAS) at the University of York undertook a study for the National Health Executive[17] on the application of post-project evaluation (PPE) in the public and private sector. The objects of the study was to ascertain:

- how far PPE was 'mandatory' and the degree of 'compliance';
- the motivation for undertaking studies and the role of stakeholders;
- the type of projects most successfully subject to evaluation;
- the nature of procedures for collecting, evaluating and acting on feedback;
- the focus of the feedback as process, product or performance;
- impact on future projects.

The study was undertaken with a recognition that there was much rhetoric in support of post-occupancy evaluation and feedback, but few examples. One outcome of the study was a recognition that evaluation and feedback in the private sector was motivated when there was a direct link between building

THE FOLLOWING ARE KEY CLIENT/USER INTERESTS TO BE CONSIDERED IN A POST-OCCUPANCY STUDY

Use of energy
Analysis of energy consumption data is an excellent way of establishing overall performance. Many building systems are energy dependent. Efficient use of energy is often linked to good management practices and comfortable occupants. Often energy consumption is higher in practice than the designers expected.

Use of space
The higher the 'net to gross' the more efficient a building is deemed to be in spatial terms. As well as efficiency, building owners are often interested in occupant density. Often post-occupancy studies show that densities are lower than planned.

Clients are also interested in whether or not the building is being used properly, especially in communal areas such as lecture theatres and meeting rooms. Studies into the use of space are used to monitor the demand for rooms and will show whether they are being used as planned.

Use of time
Changes in the use of space have been driven by changes in work practices such as job sharing or flexible hours. Use of time is often included in post-occupancy studies as a policy aid. Other time-related factors, such as travelling to work, may affect staff performance and productivity. Information on perceived comfort, satisfaction and productivity of the staff is widely used in post-occupancy studies, often in association with other topics such as the health of occupants on environmental controls.

Operating costs
Although much attention is given to construction costs there is surprisingly little information available on operating costs, but this is rapidly changing. Energy costs are one example, others are cleaning, rent and rates, and security.

Image
Image tends not to feature prominently in post-occupancy studies, and there are no standard measures in this subjective area. Often, buildings which present an excellent public image are not as well loved by their occupants.

performance and business success (e.g. retailing) or the building had an investment role (developers).

Successful feedback was a result of:

- the culture and aspirations of the organisation, the most effective evaluation programmes occurring in those organisations:
  - who could recognise strategic and performance benefits;
  - had large capital budgets and repetitive building programmes; and
  - had a defined plan and structure for evaluation;
- firms with buildings which showed a direct business return;
- evaluation programmes that had simple methodologies properly resourced, with measurable performance indicators;
- organisations with a 'learning' culture, not a blame culture. Strong commitment and follow through from the top are essential, so that the culture reinforces the opportunity for learning not auditing;
- a recognition of evaluation as a continuous process. 'Not the end only the beginning', which benefits the long-term investment, rather than merely being an exercise which confirms the delivery of short-term results.

POST OCCUPANCY EVALUATION OF BUILDING USE AND PERFORMANCE (PROBE STUDIES)

Post-occupancy evaluation research shows that the complexity of the inter-relationships between buildings and users are complex. One of the publicly available sources of POE information is from the PROBE investigation. PROBE is a collaborative research project conducted by *Building Services Journal* co-funded by the DETR Partners in Innovation Initiative and managed by ESD with Building Use Studies and William Bordass Associates.

So far, the researchers have carried out post-occupancy evaluations on 18 buildings ranging from offices and further education buildings to a health centre. The buildings are selected on the basis that they have been in operation for more than a year but less than about five.

The buildings are analysed in terms of user satisfaction with the working environment, energy consumption and manageability. User survey questionnaires are circulated and collected on the same day to enable maximum response. These are backed up by focus groups which reflect on staff reactions to the building. Energy data is collected from bills, meter readings and data from building management systems and compared with UK benchmarks.

The research is instructive both for clients, users and designers. The studies show that there are many inter-related causes of dissatisfaction or satisfaction among individual users of buildings. It also shows that there is a positive association between productivity, satisfaction, comfort, control and energy use. The key findings are:

* *Productivity.* If people feel they have control over their environment then they feel more productive;
* *Comfort.* Whether a building is perceived as comfortable depends on how responsive the building is. If a user wants to alter the thermal conditions they expect a fast response either from the heating system or facilities manager;
* *Control.* An individual's level of control affects their perception of both the physical and organisational environment. In buildings where there is a high degree of technology there must be more intensive management. If the user organisation is not able to provide intensive facilities management systems then it should avoid sophisticated technologies in its buildings;
* *Responsiveness.* The speed of response is critical. Individuals become dissatisfied very quickly if they do not get a fast response from the technological systems or facilities management.

Adrian Leaman and Bill Bordass, members of the PROBE team, have characterised four 'killer' variables. They have borrowed the term 'killer'[18] variables from computing language, and it refers to things that have 'critical influence on the overall behaviour of the system'.

The four 'killer' variables are personal control, responsiveness, building depth and workgroups. Building depth affects whether the building can be naturally ventilated, it also determines how close people can sit near a window (people tend to prefer natural ventilation and being near a window). Building depth also impacts on the complexity within the building. 'Buildings become disproportionately more complicated as they get bigger,' suggest Leaman and Bordass. There are likely to be more mechanical services and technology, along with more activities and a greater chance of conflict between them. This operational complexity leads to chronic failure with increasing cost and risk.

Workgroups are important, Leaman and Bordass argue, because the bigger the workgroup the less each member has personal control over the environment. Evidence from Leaman and Bordass' research, including the PROBE studies, suggests that 'well-integrated workgroups of four to five people will probably be acceptable, but the risks of lower productivity in bigger workgroups can increase substantially thereafter.'

This kind of research, based on the real world rather than academic problems, can be carried out by building users and give valuable insight into how their buildings function. Although the post occupancy evaluations in the PROBE project are on relatively recent projects, there is much to be gained from repeating the exercise throughout an occupant's tenure, and perhaps especially when it is about to embark on a new workplace project, whether it is to construct a new building or reorganise the staff.

Notes

1 Edwards Deming, W., *Out of Crisis,* MIT Center for Advanced Educational Services, Cambridge, Mass. 1986.
2 The Economical Intelligence Unit, *Making Quality Work,* London 1992.
3 Crosby, P., *Quality without terms,* McGraw-Hill, New York 1984.
4 Early studies in the United Kingdom include work by the Building Performance Research Unit at Strathclyde (Markus *et al.* 1992).
   In North America Sym Van der Ryns' study of student dormatories at UC Berkley (1967).
   Clare Marcus' Easter Hill Village housing study (1975) and Michael Brill's evaluation of office design with OSTI (1984) were landmark studies.
5 Stanhope Properties plc, Directors and Founders: Stewart Lipton and Peter Rogers. Projects include: Broadgate, London and Stockley Park Consortium Ltd (1985).
6 Lloyds Bank undertook post-occupancy evaluations of user responses and space use for both Hays Galleria, London, and Cannons Marsh, Bristol.
7 DEGW successfully developed a methodology for assessing the effectiveness of space utilisation and planning flexibility of office buildings, e.g. *Eleven Contemporary Office Buildings,* a comparative study prepared by DEGW for Rosehaugh Stanhope Developments 1985.
8 British Airports Authority (BAA), *Project Process Guidelines,* BAA plc 1996.
9 Millman, J. and Phiri, M., *The Organisation and Delivery of Post-Project Evaluation: Lessons from other organisations,* A report on the study on behalf of NHS Executive by NHS Estates in association with the Institute of Advanced Architectural Studies, The University of York, NHS Estates, Department of Health, 1996.
   A further outcome of the study has been a follow-up project at the University of Sheffield to develop and create a Post-Project Evaluation (PPE) toolkit aligned to a standardised methodology for post-project evaluation.
   The project addresses the lack of widely available guidance on the practical evaluation of projects. The best practice implementation guide for PPE is being developed as a code of practice available on the World Wide Web allowing users to download the document or associated forms.
10 PROBE is a collaborative research project conducted by Building Services Journal co-funded by the DETR Partners in Innovation Initiative and managed by ESD with Building Use Studies and William Bordass Associates.
11 Construction Round Table, 'Post-Project Audit: A route to continuous improvement in construction', February 1996.
12 Duerk, D., *Architectural programming: Information management for design,* Van Nostrand Reinhold, New York 1993.
13 Worthington, J., Leaman, A. and Blyth, A., *Better Briefing,* IoAAS, The University of York 1996.
14 Preiser, W., *Building Evaluation,* Plenum Press, New York 1989.
15 Pena, W., Parshall, S. and Kelly, K., *Problem Seeking: An architectural programming primer,* AIA Press, Washington 1987.
16 Duerk *ibid.*
17 Millman, J. and Phiri, M., *ibid.*
18 Leaman, A. and Bordass, W., *The 'killer' variables,* in Clements-Croome D. (ed.), *Creating the productive workplace,* E & FN Spon 2000.

7 Managing the process

Introduction

Much of the success of briefing will depend on the management of the process. With the pace of change, managing decisions so that they are made at the right time and by the right people is critical. Although identifying who plays what role is important, much of the activity happens through teamwork. But managing teams is complex. One of the problems with managing teams during briefing is that they are composed of individuals representing different organisations. They have different agendas and priorities. During a project, the make-up of the team can subtly change. For example, during its early stages the design team consists of senior managers from each firm and as the project progresses, more junior staff have a greater level of involvement (see Chapter 5). If that is not managed, there is a danger of ending up with a team with quite different perceptions and objectives to the client.

Briefing involves managing risk. As individuals we tend to manage risk intuitively – for example, when crossing a busy road. However, when managing projects there are advantages in more explicit risk management. One of these advantages is that it throws up opportunity. By addressing the risk of whether or not to build, a better solution may become apparent. Risk management therefore should not be seen as a negative, it is a tool to help identify the critical issues to be addressed within the project.

Roles and responsibilities

Simple characterisations of client, user and design team belie the complexity behind the organisational system. Within each of these groups there are many sub-groups and layers, all with their own agendas and interests in particular project outcomes. Uncertainty in who is playing what role leads to ambiguity and unfulfilled expectations. Unfortunately different titles are used by different organisations when referring to similar roles. Below we review the key roles in the briefing process and how they fit into the project organisation.

Defining the roles

There are four key roles in the briefing process which represent different interests in the outcome of the project. They are:

- *corporate* or senior decision makers and their professional support team who are concerned with the business goals and mission;
- *users* and occupants who are concerned with getting their work done with the minimum of disruption;
- *facilities managers* who want to provide a service to enable users to get their jobs done; and
- *the project team* which is responsible for the delivery of the project and includes consultants, designers, contractors, evaluators and managers.[1]

Responsibilities of the client

The client is responsible for deciding whether there is a project and how it is to be delivered, as well as ensuring an effective management structure for the project.

A client may be one person or be a body that includes several different people. The client may be the owner/manager of a small business who

---

RESPONSIBILITIES OF A CLIENT

Pre-project stage
* Identifying and setting objectives and priorities for the project. Achieved through assessing the need and options to meet it. Deciding which option to pursue and identifying risk and value, preparing a business case and Strategic Brief;
* ensuring that the Strategic Brief is clear and unambiguous;
* ensuring that critical assumptions made in preparing the brief are valid, realistic, achievable and made clear to everybody involved;
* arbitrating between conflicting demands – user groups, specialist groups, facilities managers, finance departments;
* establishing and implementing a plan to meet the objectives – including defining the procurement route and selecting the project team (designers, contractors);
* ensuring decision-making criteria are made explicit and that systems are in place for controlling time, cost and quality and change.

Project stage
* Appointing the project team;
* establishing reporting and decision-making criteria;
* making decisions;
* providing in-house support and access as appropriate;
* reviewing the direction, approving and signing off at each stage;
* giving go-ahead to proceed with next stage;
* paying the project team as agreed in the appointment;
* meeting specific terms of contracts;
* accepting handover of project on completion.

Post-project stage
* Reviewing the project process;
* evaluating the completed project against objectives;
* evaluating the performance of the building through post-occupancy evaluation.

exercises a lot of direct control, or may consist of several departments in a large conglomerate or public authority with many divisions, where control is dissipated. The owner/manager of a small firm is likely to be the decision maker and fulfil several different roles, whereas in larger firms, much of the authority is likely to be delegated (see Table 7.1 – Client roles). Larger firms are more likely to draw upon in-house expertise and experience of other projects, whereas smaller organisations will need to rely more upon external advisers for both expertise and experience.

Chief executive

The chief executive should be responsible for approving a major project or programme of projects and then maintain a visible senior management commitment to its delivery. In large organisations, reporting to this level would be the exception. When the need for a project is raised, the chief executive should appoint a 'project champion' who has the authority to provide the necessary leadership. A project board could also be appointed to offer support to the project champion as well as bring together interests at senior management level.

Project champion

A central role is that of someone who takes responsibility for the whole project's ability to meet the client's expectations and has authority to make decisions on behalf of the organisation. This role should not be confused with project managers who look after the day-to-day running of a project and its delivery on time at cost.

Appointed as soon as the project is conceived, the project champion drives the project, making decisions as they are needed. He or she may be appointed either from within the organisation or externally for the duration of the project. This ensures continuity both in decision making and understanding; it also means that there is some stability. Experience has shown that many projects fail through lack of continuity of the project manager or lead architect. The project champion is then responsible for assembling the team of people from within the organisation and professional advisers outside. In some organisations, the role may be known as a project sponsor or project executive.

The person in this role must have the authority to make decisions on behalf of the client organisation and get others to make relevant decisions as necessary.

The project champion should be accessible to people within the organisation as well as managers of other firms working on the project. He or she should be committed to encouraging good team-working practices within the project. The project champion will, in effect, be trying to balance the interests of the client and users on the demand side, and those of the project team on the supply side.

Table 7.1

The role of the senior decision makers in the client's organisation can be subdivided. This table shows how they are often identified, although different terms may be used.

Role	Definition	Responsibility and Authority
Executive Client	Most senior individual or collective decision makers in the client organisation such as: – main board – owner of client organisation	* Makes strategic decisions on policy and spending. * Appoints the Project Champion.
Funder	Provides some, or all, of the finance for the project from within the client organisation such as, Finance Director; or from outside such as a Bank.	* Providing the finance. * May impose conditions on how the project is carried out.
Project Champion	Leads the project for the client organisation.	* Answerable to the executive client. * Has authority and responsibility for making decisions on behalf of the client organisation.
Business Case Team	People with an understanding of the business objectives of the client organisation – may be internal and include departmental heads or representatives; may include external client advisers; for smaller projects may be one person. Identified by Project Sponsor.	* Analyses the needs and resources of the organisation. * Prepares the Assessment of Need. * Assists the project champion prepare Strategic Brief
Client Advisers	External consultants appointed with a knowledge of construction able to understand the client's needs and business objectives. Must be free from a vested interest in whether a construction option is chosen. May be appointed as a member of the project team later in the process.	* Assists the project sponsor and business case team test the options and develop the requirements.

PROJECT CHAMPION

The responsibilities of the project champion should be to:

* co-ordinate the preparation of the assessment of need and options, prepare the business case and budget for the project if it is decided to go ahead and submit them to the project board and/or chief executive;
* set up an appropriate structure for managing the project, including a structure for reporting and making decisions;
* ensure that users and other stakeholders are involved;
* ensure that the briefs reflect the project objectives;
* ensure that any changes in circumstances affecting the project are evaluated and that appropriate action is taken;
* arbitrate in disputes on the client side;
* approve any changes to the scope of the project, ensuring that any changes which impact on time, cost or the objectives are assessed and reported to the project board or senior management team as necessary;
* ensure that a post-completion evaluation is carried out and considered by all parties;
* co-ordinate and foster teamwork;
* ensure effective delivery of the project;
* ensure effective feedback from the project by carrying out a post-project evaluation and an occupancy evaluation aimed at informing the different client interests of:
  − how far the project met the client's interests and objectives; and
  − what lessons of good and bad practice need to be learned for the future.

Users

Users cannot be summed up as one entity. They are a complex collection of people and groups with varied interests and perspectives. They might be part of the client organisation, be tenants or they may be a mixture of both; or they may be people upon whom the organisation relies, for example, its customers, clients or visitors.

The view of users is important to the functioning of buildings. In most organisations the business of being evermore productive is a complex problem bound up in the relationship between the people involved, their environment and their work processes. To provide a context in which an organisation can achieve its objectives means that people, process and place must be tackled together. Users have a prime role to play in this: how they organise themselves, how they use buildings and what matters to them.

Managing user involvement is partly about listening (see Chapter 3) and partly about communication (see Chapter 5).

Facilities managers

Facilities managers are responsible for ensuring cost efficient management of the building and associated facilities, and creating an environment that supports the activities of the building user. Facilities management varies considerably from one organisation to another.[1] At one end of the scale is the office manager, which is not a distinct facilities function within an organisation but part of someone's general duties. Other variants range from dedicated managers of a single building to departments that manage facilities across different countries. Depending on the particular situation, a facilities manager may have little authority within an organisation, be detached from key decision makers and handed down decisions made with little or no reference to them. Yet their experience and knowledge would provide vital background to building-related decisions.

Client advisers

During the pre-project stage, the client may need to appoint an external adviser with the necessary expertise to help carry out organisational studies, option appraisals, prepare the Strategic Brief and advise on the procurement route and appointment of the project team. Some organisations retain this adviser during the project to act as a watchdog to see if the team is performing as anticipated or to give strategic advice. Other advisers, perhaps designers, can be appointed during the pre-project stage to carry out option feasibility studies to see if building is an appropriate option. This appointment should be independent of any appointment made during the project stage so that the designer is not seen to be working to 'get the job'. At this stage it is important to feel that you are getting an objective view. Some clients make it clear that whoever carries out initial feasibility work will not be appointed as part of the design team.

For the Project Stage a team which delivers the project is assembled and includes the designers, project manager, and construction professionals, who may be part of the design team and contractors.

Design team

Traditionally the design team includes architects, structural and services engineers, quantity surveyors, landscape architects and a range of specialists such as lighting designers. It is now common to find contractors as part of the team offering advice on buildability. The quantity surveyor, or cost consultant, advises the team on cost matters although on small projects the architect might take on this role.

From within the design team a design team leader is appointed. Often this is the architect, but may be one of the other consultants. The leader manages the work of the design team and ensures there are sufficient resources available. Members of the team can be appointed separately or be part of a multi-disciplinary organisation.

Project manager

The complexity of the building process and the large number of organisations that may be involved in the process may mean that the client might wish to appoint a project manager who pulls the whole process together. This person may come from within the client's own organisation or be appointed from an external consultancy. Project managers may be either process project managers, working directly on the client's behalf or transmitting expectations to the building team, and ensuring objectives are met; or construction managers who organise the building work on the client's behalf.

Roles and actors

Culture and tradition in the construction industry often suggests that individuals with particular titles always play particular roles. It need not be so. For example on a construction project an architect may, or may not be, a project manager. What matters more is the individual's attributes and skills at performing their role.

What also matters is the expectations of the particular role. Charles Handy notes that role incompatibility and role conflict are crucial issues to consider, as they influence an individual's ability to perform the role effectively. Incompatibility occurs when there is a clash between an individual's concept of a role and other people's expectations of it. Role conflict results from someone carrying out more than one role in the same situation. Senior managers making decisions about the direction of a project whilst at the same time representing the 'user view' may find themselves in conflict.

Although we have listed activities of some roles (above), job descriptions themselves are not enough.[2] What does need to be made clear are the scope of responsibility, expectations about performance and how the work will be evaluated, or, in effect, measures of success. This is necessary if there is to be meaningful dialogue during and at the end of the project about how well the process worked and whether individuals are doing what is expected of them.

Managing the decisions

An effective decision-making process is the backbone of an effective briefing strategy. Too often the wrong kinds of decision are made at the wrong time. Managers may be spending too much time making decisions about detail too

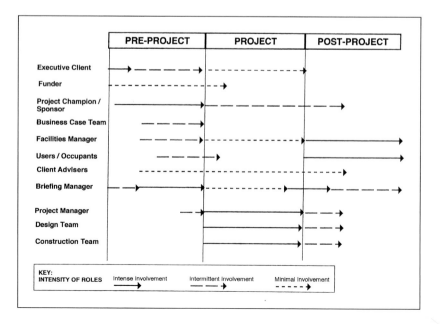

Figure 7.1: Diagram identifying involvement of key players during each stage.

EFFECTIVE DECISION MAKING

Managing decision making effectively is a matter of:

* clearly defining objectives which are consistently referred back to project goals whenever a design decision is made;
* articulating assumptions and ensuring that everyone makes their expectations explicit;
* establishing records which log decisions taken and those outstanding;
* balancing different interests and expectations.

Setting out the framework:

* define in each brief what decisions are expected at the next stage;
* set out project milestones and programme;
* identifying the gateways – what is fixed and what is not – evaluation of decisions.

---

early in the project, when it is important that the decision with broader implications should be made.

Last responsible moment

Not all decisions need to be made at once. A good briefing process is one that provides information and decisions at the last responsible moment to meet the needs of the business and demands of the procurement process. Users and clients want to keep their options open for as long as possible to enable them to react to change, whereas designers and contractors want decisions frozen at the earliest possible opportunity.

Fixing decisions

Design involves synthesising and resynthesising as new information becomes available, and this could be an infinite process. A designer's inclination is to leave everything open and continuously rework things seemingly never to finish. On the other hand, managers will think in terms of definite steps, setting up procedures to meet goals. This leads managers to accuse designers of never making a decision and never wanting to hit targets, whilst designers see managers as being too quick to make the imperfect decision. The reality is that both views have elements of truth. Design does involve re-evaluation of ideas yet this must be done within the context of meeting project deadlines. Making all decisions immediately might stifle innovation or adequate exploration of alternatives, but not making any early on will lead to chaos.

A project programme should include a strategy for fixing decisions progressively throughout the project, but enable clients to keep options open on those matters which cannot be decided early. If there are no clear decision points then there is confusion about what 'decisions' might change, with some members of the team reluctant to do too much work in case things change.

Sign-off gateways

The concept of approval gateways throughout the project provides a frame-work within which decisions can be fixed and stages of the project approved and signed off. Ken Allinson, in *Getting there by design*,[3] suggests that 'gateways' are both entry or exit points but that different criteria are applied depending on whether a stage is being exited or entered: *Have we achieved what we intended to?* and, *Are we prepared for the coming stage?* He cites four sets of criteria that should be applied at each gateway:

- *Fit with strategic aims and ambitions.* Are the objectives about the coming stage clear? Do they fit with the overall objectives of the project? Has anything changed?
- *Specific deliverables.* Have they been identified? Are they clear? How will they be measured?
- *The project plan.* Is there a plan? What are the risks and success factors?
- *Responsibilities and accountabilities.* Are the necessary resources available? Who is accountable for which aspects of the work? Can the team deliver?

As Allinson points out, the concept of gateways is applicable at all levels of a project from discrete parts such as roofing to whole stages such as design to construction. From the overall project perspective, gateways should occur at key project stages to ensure that risks, value, cost and programme are being managed. Before approval is given for what has been achieved in the previous stage, and for moving on to the next stage, a project evaluation should look at whether:

- the objectives in the brief are being met;
- decisions made at the previous stage have been incorporated;
- risks have been identified, evaluated and allocated; and,
- all design and procurement options have been evaluated and the recommended option justified.

Layering decisions

Decisions tend to be layered. Initially a general decision is made about an issue and later on a more detailed one follows. This layering can be seen in terms of the decision makers (Figure 7.2) and what they make decisions about. It can also be seen in the hierarchy from those relevant to the site through to those about the setting.

The concept of layering is important because it suggests when certain types of decisions should be made and who should make them.

An implication of this layering is that decisions not made, or properly considered, by the top level decision makers get passed down as constraints to the lower level decision makers. For example, the climate of the site location might affect the design of the building's skin and whether the building needs to be highly serviced or not, which will impact on the users and how they are able to control the internal environment. Decisions about planning, design and management, and use of buildings will need to be integrated with an understanding of how expectations and needs within this hierarchy will interconnect and change over time.

The Board
- Location
- Culture
- Image
- Capital
- Life costs
- Allocation of resources

Divisional Management
- Workstyle
- Relationships
- Management of space and time
- Range of settings

Individual
- Use of space and time
- Workplace

Figure 7.2: Different levels of decision makers.
Source: DEGW

Clarifying expectations

Unclear expectations about the extent of involvement in decision making leads to confusion and conflict. For each type of decision, involvement will vary from those who will:

- make the decision;
- participate and share some responsibility for it;
- be consulted about the issues surrounding it; and
- be informed but are not involved in making it.

There is a clear distinction between who decides on long-term issues affecting the organisation and the level of participation in day-to-day issues (Figure 7.2). This is reflected in decisions about buildings – decisions about the building site and its location and those about the workplace.

Corporate decision makers are more concerned with strategy. For example, in the pre-project stage they are concerned with whether the building option is most appropriate, and if so, where the site should be, how much space different departments should be given, and how much the organisation can afford to spend. Departmental managers would be more interested in relationships between teams of people and the allocation of space between individuals and ancillary functions. Individuals may have flexibility to vary the planning of their workspace and selection of furniture accessories.

However, managers must be aware of which hat they are wearing when they make a decision. Too easily things become muddled, and what turns out to be an individual type of decision is made under the guise of a strategic one and perhaps too early; more dangerously a strategic one tries to masquerade as an individual one later in the project. Once a strategic decision has been made, the impact changing it must be thoroughly investigated to avoid the project descending into aimlessness and confusion.

To make a decision the person must have the authority, resources and skill to do so. There is a tendency for decisions to be off-loaded by one person onto others. Conversely there is also a tendency for some to try to gain more control by taking decisions that others should make.

Who leads and when

Different groups need to predominate throughout a project[4] (Figure 7.3). This springs from the different knowledge bases within the project. During the early stages the client will be leading the decision making, during the design stages the design team becomes predominant and during construction the contractors are leading, and then back to the client during occupation. The client must still remain in control and be ultimately responsible, but the lead role is being delegated to those best able to perform it.

Team working

Building a successful team goes deeper than merely selecting the most brilliant experts in each field, putting them into a room and hoping that they can work

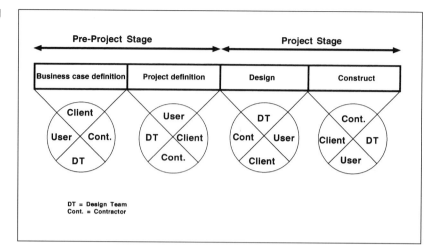

together. A common complaint about the construction industry is that members of design teams act independently of each other, become isolated and may even act against each other. This leads to the contractor being thrown a bag of barely integrated bits where the services, structure and fabric do not correspond to each other.

On many occasions project teams behave as though they are a collection of people who merely contribute to the extent of their expertise. A team where the members can cross the boundaries of their professional discipline will enhance the value and effort of the team. They will be able to offer quite different perspectives on the problem definition, and this involvement will promote a greater sense of shared ownership. In the early days of a project where the design direction is being set and the team is exploring ideas, the variety of perspectives will enable a more rounded project to evolve. Members of the team also have other expertise than just their professional discipline[5]. Some might be good at persuasive argument, or at organising technology. These strengths can be used by the team throughout the project just as some team members may be able to take other responsibilities. This approach will enhance the value of the team and improve the integration and shared ownership of the project. However, for many within the construction industry and outside, working this way will require a 'sea change' in attitude and approach.

Synergy

In management theory on team working, a great deal is spoken about the chemistry between team members. Various researchers have suggested that ideal teams should be made up of people fulfilling roles with particular characteristics. Famous for this are Meredith Belbin[6] who identified eight team roles, and Kolb who characterised four types: divergers, assimilators, convergers and accommodator/executers. The practicalities of getting together a group of people from different firms makes it very difficult to precisely put together the 'perfect' team. The right mix of team roles may mean the wrong mix of experts. However, the synergy between team members and the mix of characteristics between them is important.

BELBIN'S TEAM ROLES

Chairman – disciplined/focused
Shaper – highly-strung, dominant, driven, passionate
Plant – thinker
Monitor–evaluator – introverted, analytic
Resource–investigator – sociable, extrovert
Company worker – practical organiser, methodical
Team worker – supportive, steady
Finisher – worries about deadlines

Source: Belbin

KOLB'S TEAM CHARACTERISTICS

Diverger – good at interpersonal relations and generating alternatives
Assimilator – logical and reflective
Converger – goal-oriented, seeks single answers
Accommodator/executor – action-oriented

Cutting across agendas

At the heart of working as a team is understanding each other's agenda, and accepting each other's differences and expertise. Often, a disparate group of people is brought together, each with their own objectives which may conflict with each other, as well as with the group goals. If all members of the team share the same objectives and values it will be more effective, therefore building common goals becomes an important aspect of team work.

In the beginning, individual agendas will be unclear and may take time to tease out. It is not always going to be possible to satisfy both individual and team objectives simultaneously. To achieve the best combined result, individuals will need to be able to express their own objectives, understand those of others and develop a level of trust. They will need to share ownership of the group objectives. Unless common objectives are agreed and team members trust each other, they will tend to put their own interests first. This does not mean that the client's objectives should be changed or compromised to suit the team, but it does suggest that members of the team should find ways of accommodating each other.

Continuity

Continuity of key personnel is vital to team success. The timeframe on many construction projects can be relatively long and see a turnover in people.[7] The severity of the break in continuity within the project when staff changes might vary depending on the seniority and involvement of the person, but it has been demonstrated that there is a detrimental effect on the project when this continuity of staff is broken. The team will have to be re-built with the new member to develop the trust and working relationship. With the departing member goes some of the knowledge and understanding of the project which may never be regained by those left. Commitment from the beginning that the key personnel will be able to see the project through is important. In practice, it is difficult to get individuals to work on this basis, especially if the client is relying on this commitment from staff employed by others. It may be possible to provide some incentives through a reward scheme so that, the longer people stay, the greater the benefits.

Building the team

The first meeting of a new team predetermines the success of the team working together. The aim of this meeting is to build relationships and enable people to understand the project. A danger with teams is that there could be one member in difficulty, but the others think that someone else is managing it. A workshop based approach is a successful method of avoiding this. Often teambuilding exercises are used and can be based on a substitute task or based on the actual project. For most teams, the actual project may be the more appropriate option since the other exercises can seem irrelevant, whereas the actual project is more immediate and real.

This workshop should be held away from the workplace. This reinforces the importance of the task, avoids distractions and enables people to concentrate on the project.

This workshop clearly set out how the project will be run so that everyone understands what is expected of them. It should address the 'etiquette' of the project, who should make what decisions and when, and what the modes of communication are.

However, the opening meeting is not enough by itself. A danger is that the team works well to begin with, then encounters difficulties which test their relationships. Or, subtle changes occur where one member tries to resolve another's problems. When things go wrong on a project and finding a resolution becomes tough, it is easier for the members of the team to retreat to their discipline since, for many, cross-disciplinary working is not the norm. Regular reviews throughout the project will ensure that it is on track and that the team is still working together.

It may seem a paradox but a team can work too well, it can become too comfortable with its solutions and it needs an external 'wild card' to challenge it. This is a role that the outside health check can perform.

Appointing the design team

When appointing a design team, the client can appoint each member of the team separately, choosing one to be the design team leader. An alternative is a single appointment with either a multidisciplinary firm which can provide the full range of architectural and engineering services, or with a lead consultant.

TEAM-BUILDING OBJECTIVES

Team building has the following objectives:

* breaking down the barriers to effective communication, encouraging listening and understanding;
* understanding of the goals and aspirations of all parties;
* developing an atmosphere of trust and respect in which everybody is encouraged and supported to achieve their highest performance;
* understanding the styles and culture of the various organisations involved in or affected by the project;
* promoting the understanding of the culture and value system of the project organisation itself;
* examining and developing new ways of working together to identify and solve problems;
* developing common goals to achieve win/win situations for all concerned.

Source: BAA

Separate appointment offers the opportunity of selecting the best firm in each discipline. However, there is a risk. The client is responsible to each consultant if another does not perform and this exposes the client to the risk of greater fees. A client may choose to manage the risk through careful selection of the project manager. A good project manager will be able to reduce the likelihood of problems.

The benefit of the single appointment lies in its administrative simplicity and single point of responsibility for the design. The lead consultant appoints the complete design team and takes responsibility for their performance. The lead consultant may be an architect, cost consultant, project manager, or services consultant, depending on the emphasis that the building requires. For many projects it may be the architect who is the lead consultant but it need not be. For example, the bulk of the budget in complex manufacturing plants or laboratories may be engineering focused, suggesting that an engineer should be the lead consultant with architectural and other inputs brought in as required.

When to appoint

Designers may be appointed during the pre-project stage to test design feasibility but these appointments should be independent of any future design work. This gives the client the choice of whether to appoint the same designers if a 'building' project is chosen – enabling continuity – or, using different designers who may have more appropriate resources to carry out the work needed for the particular type of project. A separate appointment also means that the designers' role is independent of there being a lucrative design project.

The design team as part of the project delivery team should be appointed once the client has agreed the Strategic Brief. There are benefits in appointing all members of the team at the beginning so that all aspects of the project can be developed together from the start. The report 'Rethinking Construction' notes that:

The efficiency of project delivery is presently constrained by the largely separated process through which they are generally planned, designed and constructed. These processes reflect the fragmented structure of the industry and sustain a contractual and confrontational culture.

Selecting the design team

Selecting the appropriate design team is the key to project success, it is perhaps the most important design decision and will influence subsequent style and approach.

Consultants can be selected by:

- open, limited or invited competition;
- pre-selected panel, where a list of accepted consultants is drawn up by a combination of referral, interview and past experience;
- referral, from trusted colleagues or other consultants.

Sophisticated clients with a rolling programme should aim to establish in advance a preferred list of consultants based on past success and a continuous review of the most suitable consultants in the market place. For clients with one-off projects, who are unfamiliar with the options available, the selection route can be as limited as looking at what other clients in similar situations have used and seeking referrals.

The selection of the consultants requires a careful balancing of the following attributes:

- *Capability*. The experience of the firm in projects of similar size and function. Also, the availability of sufficient, uncommitted resources within the firm;
- *Competence*. Experience on past projects can be ascertained by detailed references from past clients;
- *Staff*. The experience and capability of the key staff the firm intends to use on the project, as well as whether those staff are likely to remain for the duration.

Competitions

Three possible competition routes are:

- an ideas competition to select a concept;
- project design competition to select a building design; or
- competitive interview to select a designer or design team with whom the client can work.

The selection of participants can be through:

- open competition: with response from public invitation;
- limited competition where certain types of firm, such as those with particular experience, are invited to participate; or
- invited competitions where the client chooses a short-list of participants.

Increasingly, open competitions are being used to find design teams rather than designs. This has been encouraged by EU Directives, and the need for transparency in appointing designers by public bodies and lottery funded projects,

DESIGN TEAM SELECTION PROCESS: LARGE PROJECTS – £10 MILLION OR ABOVE

The selection of the team can be open to participants through public advertising, asking for easily-provided practice data, approaching the professional institutes and then selecting a shortlist. To ensure a balanced selection appropriate to the project, the list of practices can be enhanced by inviting practices onto a shortlist. The six step process below sets out how to select a design team/practice.

Step 1
Review experience of wide range of practices (30–60) who are asked to submit practice brochures. This step can be by open invitation in the construction and architectural press, or by the client adviser selecting a cross-section of practices. The brochures will give a flavour and help to focus on the next level of criteria. The range of practices may cover:

* small/large;
* commercial/business – artistic/studio;
* traditional/modern;
* young/innovative – mature/repetitive;
* design oriented – delivery oriented.

This list of practices should be reduced to a list of between 12 and 20 practices for further consideration in a half-day workshop with the client and adviser. It is still important to keep the range as wide as possible.

Step 2
Selected practices to submit practice information and relevant work.

The information should be requested against a standard form (The information should include size of practice, number of professionals, range of skills, size and type of completed projects). Photographs of work will also be useful as well as contact details for those clients.

From this list the client draws up a short-list of between six and eight practices.

Step 3
Visits to offices and buildings of practices on shortlist.

The client and advisers may visit relevant buildings by each of the selected practices, and the practices' offices. At this stage the list may be reduced to three or four firms who will be asked to attend an interview.

Step 4
Short-listed design teams submit statements of approach.

The final list of practices is given a summary of the Strategic Brief and are invited to visit the site and meet client members in their offices. They are given an opportunity to respond to the brief with a short written statement. The client is not looking for a design but a team, therefore the response might include a description of their approach and include sketches and diagrams. They should also be asked to explain how they will resource the project in the timetable given. The time given to the practices to respond from being selected for interview should be kept short (two to three weeks) so that the firms cannot prepare elaborate presentations.

Step 5
Interview (3–4 firms).

Each practice is then invited to an interview (1 to 1.5 hours long) to discuss their approach and to enable the client to assess whether they can work with the practice concerned. The practices will want to investigate the brief and will also want to establish the scope and terms of the appointment.

Step 6
Final selection.

The final choice of the design team should not be confirmed until the client has agreed the terms and scope of appointment.

DESIGN TEAM SELECTION PROCESS: SMALL PROJECTS – UP TO £500 000

Step 1   Identify practices
Identification of practices can be done by talking to colleagues or contacts who have recently built, identifying buildings recently built and their designers or by contacting the professional institutes such as the RIBA Clients Advisory Service. As with the larger projects it is useful to have a range of practices.

Step 2   Select list of practices
Contact six to ten practices and ask them to submit brochures and practice information against a standard form (see box for large projects).

The list can be refined to between four and six practices.

Step 3   Short-list visits
The client and advisers may visit relevant buildings by each of the selected practices, and the practices' offices. At this stage the list may be reduced to two or three firms who will be asked to submit a statement on their approach and attend an interview.

Step 4   Interview
Each practice is then invited to an interview (1 to 1.5 hours long) to discuss their approach. The client is not looking for a building but an approach and a team it can work with.

Step 5   Final selection
The final choice of the design team should not be confirmed until the client has agreed the terms and scope of appointment.

where competitions are used as a way of achieving quality. As it becomes more widely recognised that the design of a project is an iterative process and requires input from many people, which cannot be achieved easily during a design competition, clients have recognised the value in trying to find a team based on whether they can work with it rather than whether it has an immediate design response. Also, design competitions are expensive on resources for designers.

A successful competition requires a clear set of objectives, sufficient resources, time and commitment. In an effort to balance quality with cost in the selection of design teams through various types of competition, clients are using the 'double envelope' system. Under this arrangement the candidates are first judged on quality to weed out those not meeting the client's standards, with fees being the secondary factor.

Experience has shown that successful selection processes are founded on:

- investing in a clear statement of requirements – the Strategic Brief;
- differentiating between the role of client manager (who helps the client establish the brief and choose the appropriate design team) and project manager who is concerned to deliver a good building on time at cost;
- investing adequate time and money into this early stage to remunerate advisers, and cover the expenses of short-listed practices. Experience of undertaking competitions suggests that between one and two per cent of the total construction costs should be set aside to cover brief writing, management and selection costs.

Managing risk

A construction project represents a major investment which will have a profound effect on most businesses. The success or failure of a project and business depends on the organisation's approach to risk. Risk management is a process for evaluating the impact of risks and developing a strategy for minimising their effects. It is most beneficial when it is systematic and part of the overall management philosophy of the project and business rather than an isolated set of applied exercises.

Benefits of risk management

Risk management is a tool which enables organisations to move towards greater certainty over business deliverables. It can help identify objectives and priorities. Risk management on a building project should be considered within the wider corporate picture. The building project is one part of the 'business project' so risks to the organisation as well as to the building need to be assessed. A systematic approach makes risks easier to manage although good risk management does not mean merely reducing risk.

Systematic risk management helps to:

- deal with unforeseen circumstances;
- minimise damage caused by identified problems;
- identify objectives and priorities;
- identify constraints on the project;
- inform decisions;
- enable more effective cost management;
- improve accountability.

During the pre-project stage, uncertainty is very high, yet paradoxically, that is when many major decisions that will have the greatest impact on the project are taken. It is at this time that the information on which to base decisions is most likely to be incomplete or inaccurate.

Whilst rigorous risk assessment and management has its greatest impact during the pre-project period prior to project approval, like design, risk management is an iterative process and offers greater overall benefit when applied throughout the project life cycle.[8]

It is not possible to remove every uncertainty. However, it is possible to improve the chances of the project being completed on time, within budget and to the required quality.

Table 7.2 Typical areas which may increase exposure to risk

Pre-project	Project
* Stakeholder expectations;	* Participants' priorities;
* Poorly-defined objectives;	* Unclear responsibilities;
* Procurement selection.	* Poor communication between organisations;
	* Poor co-ordination;
	* Design changes.

The risk management process

Risk management relies on experience especially when it comes to setting up an independent team of individuals. These may include senior managers from inside the organisation, members of the project team and external advisers who can draw on a wide range of experience and ensure evaluation from several different perspectives. An external facilitator will be impartial and have greater credibility among the risk management team members.

Initially, clients will need to consider whether risk management is applicable to the business situation and the project. This involves identifying the significant risks to the business which may stem from the need not being met, or not being met within a particular timeframe or budget.

Once a project has been identified, the risk management process will involve identifying the risks related to the specific project. However, the relative importance of risks change as the project progresses and new risks emerge. Regular reviews of risk exposure during the project will identify these. The stages at which a formal risk analysis is carried out might depend on the complexity of the project. However, it should occur at the approval gateways:

- Option appraisal stage – to identify the risks with each option;
- Strategic Brief stage – to identify targets and milestones, cost, time and procurement routes;
- Draft project stage – to identify risks with design proposals;
- Brief – the final go-ahead to allocate resources;
- Pre-tender;
- Post-tender – to identify where there may be 'hidden' risks such as design changes;
- Handover.

Responding to risk

There is a balance between the threat or cost of a risk and the opportunity of an outcome that represents better value for money.[9] A risk response might take the form of:

- *Avoidance.* Where the consequences of the risk are totally unacceptable. This might lead to reviewing project objectives or perhaps cancelling altogether.
- *Reduction* through:
  - re-design;
  - reviewing methods of procurement or construction;
  - more detailed design to improve information on which assessments are based.
- *Transfer.* To pass the risk on to someone better able to control it.
- *Risk retention.* Balancing the benefits to be gained from accepting the risk against the costs.
- *Risk removal.* Eliminating the risk by removing the hazard.

Allocating risk

Factors which should be considered when allocating risk are:

- who is best able to control the events which may lead to the risk occurring?
- who can control the risk if it occurs?
- should the client be involved in the control of the risk?
- who should be responsible for a risk if it cannot be controlled? and
- can that person or firm bear the consequences if it occurs?

The procurement strategy for the project is one of the most important factors in allocating risk during a project. A number of issues will affect the procurement strategy:

- how well the project can be defined at the outset. How much will need to be developed as information emerges during design, construction and operation of the building;
- compromises that result from decisions being frozen. Flexibility to change at a later date;
- number of different specialists needed;
- size of project in relation to the resources of the organisations to be involved;
- relative importance of the programme and importance of cost certainty.

However, while some contractual methods enable the client to allocate more risk to a contractor, it is important to remember that with the allocation of risk goes the authority and responsibility for controlling it. Therefore the desire to transfer all of the risk should not be the sole driver of the contract strategy.

Allocating contingency

Once action has been taken to reduce risk, whatever is left needs to be covered by a contingency. Contingencies can be in the form of extra money, float in the programme or a tolerance in the specification. The contingencies should be reviewed during the project to ensure that there is adequate cover. The size of this contingency should reduce as the project is defined.

Procurement strategy

Rarely do clients have all the resources in-house to carry out a project. The procurement of external resources such as advisers, designers and construction skills is essential. The different procurement strategies available affect briefing in various ways. They affect:

- what information and decisions are communicated and when;
- the extent to which the client has to make decisions earlier or later in the process;
- the extent to which the client can make changes without incurring a large cost penalty;
- the relationship between the client and advisers, whether the design team can report directly to the client;
- certainty over whether the project can be finished on time, within budget and to the required quality.

Within the construction industry, procurement is generally tied up with different forms of construction contract. These contracts enable different relationships between the designers, contractors, construction and project managers so that they are more or less directly responsible to the client depending on the contract type. This may eventually change as new thinking about procurement (Rethinking Construction) is developed and clients, designers and constructors set up different types of relationships, such as partnering.

Principally, there are five basic procurement models with additional variants.

The traditional route

In the 'traditional' construction route the contractor constructs the building for a lump sum cost to a design supplied by the client. The design should be completed before contractors are invited to tender and the main contract is let. The design team is appointed by the client to produce the design and construction information and may also advise the client on the selection and appointment of the contractor, and act as contract administrator between client and contractor.

Under this strategy, the contractor assumes responsibility and takes on the financial risk for the construction work. The client assumes responsibility for, and takes the risk for, the performance of the design team. If the contractor is delayed by failure of the design team he can make a claim against the client for extra cost and/or time to complete the project.

Decisions and information affecting the design of the buildings must be made before construction. Late changes will affect the cost and programme. It is possible to phase the project so that part of it is started later.

Construction management

The client employs a design team and separately engages a construction manager who co-ordinates the design and construction activities. Under this strategy, the construction work is carried out by trade contractors through direct contracts with the client. The work is divided into packages for which a particular contractor is responsible. Separate contracts between the client and contractors exposes the client to greater risk than if there was a contract with only one contractor. The client is responsible to the other contractors if one of them causes delay. The construction manager does not have contractual links with the design team or contractors, but is able to inject construction expertise from the beginning and improve the buildability of the design.

With this system the design and construction activities can overlap which will speed the project up. However, there is no certainty of price until all of the construction work packages have been let.

Management contracting

A management contractor is appointed by the client to manage the building process and is paid a fee. There are separate contracts between the design team and client. The management contractor is responsible for all of the construction work and has direct contractual links with the trade contractors and so bears the financial risk and responsibility for the construction work. The management contractor can give construction advice to the design team. Under this system, not all of the design work will be complete before the first trade contractors start work.

Overlapping design and construction leads to earlier completion. There is no certainty of price until all of the construction work packages have been let.

Design and build

This is a package deal where the client is able to unload more risk. The contractor assumes the risk and responsibility for designing and building the project in return for a fixed price lump sum. By transferring this risk to the contractor, the client loses some control over the project.

Under a variant of design and build, known as 'develop and construct', the client appoints designers to prepare the concept design before the contractor assumes responsibility for completing the detailed design and construction. By separating the role of building concept design from detailed design and implementation, the client may continue to keep control of the briefing and strategic design stages, while shifting the responsibility and liability to the contractor at the later stages. To ensure continuity of design, the design team can be novated to the contractor.

BOOT

Under the build-own-operate-transfer (BOOT) route a contracting organisation offers a package to provide and run a building for a number of years in exchange for 'rent'. At the end of the period, the ownership of the building reverts to the client.

Partnering

Partnering is a way of managing business relationships across contractual boundaries. It relies on the partners being committed to agreed mutual

Figure 7.4: The cost of change for different procurement routes. a: Traditional where construction starts once design has been completed; b: where design and construction activities happen together; c: Design and build, where design and construction are handed over to the contractor who has agreed to provide the building for an overall cost.

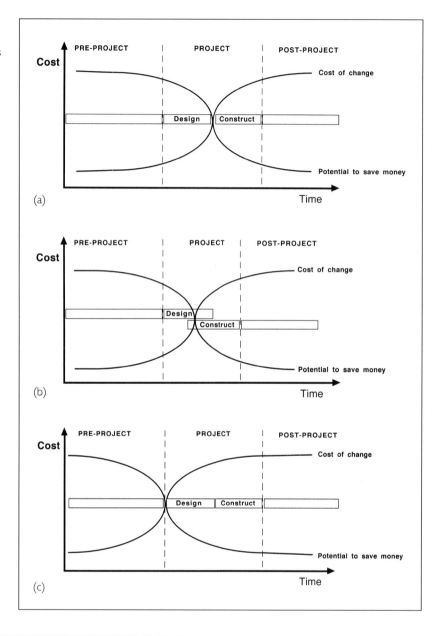

VALUE MANAGEMENT REVIEWS – WHEN THEY MIGHT OCCUR

* option appraisal – identifying the need for a project and the key project objectives and constraints;
* Strategic Brief – concerned with the means of achieving the project objectives;
* Project Brief – reviewing key design decisions to ensure that the design is in line with the Strategic Brief, that the needs and objectives are being achieved;
* end of detailed design – check that decisions made at previous VM exercise have been implemented. Review project objectives and priorities;
* handover – evaluate whether the project has achieved the objectives set out in the Strategic Brief.

objectives, agreed methods of problem resolution and continuous improvement throughout the relationship. The aim is to build long-standing relationships throughout the supply chain with the benefit of continuous improvement. There is greater benefit if partnering is applied throughout the supply chain rather than just between the contractor and client. Within the construction industry, partnering throughout the supply chain is still in its infancy. However, attitudes are changing and Sir John Egan[5] identified it as a key to the future for construction projects.

Managing value

Value management is a structured approach to problem seeking and problem solving.[10] It is about understanding what value is rather than applying arbitrary cost cutting, as is so often thought. It is a way of identifying priorities – those things that are most important to the organisation. In fact, you may redistribute and add cost.

The terms 'value management' and 'value engineering' are often used interchangeably. However, a distinction can be made between the two. Value engineering is a disciplined procedure for achieving a particular function for minimum cost but without detriment to quality, reliability, performance or delivery.

Value management is carried out as workshop exercises generally over one or two days using the staff of the organisation as the main resource. Such exercises can be useful for looking at individual elements or every aspect of a project.

HOW A VM WORKSHOP WORKS

Pre-workshop
2 days
* Facilitator reads background information on organisation and project;
* facilitator holds individual interviews with key participants to flush out key issues which need to be explored in the workshop.

Workshop
2 days, divided into several sessions
* Facilitator brings the team together;
* information sharing, might include: brainstorming, SWOT analyses;
* analyse and understand project drivers;
* explore options/alternatives/solutions;
* criteria weighting exercise;
* action plan.

Post-workshop
1.5 days
* Detailed workshop report;
* feedback/follow up.

The facilitator is the key to a value management workshop. That person must be independent and objective with no axe to grind. Such a person can come from within the organisation; this is easier in a large organisation where the person with both the skills and the necessary objectivity might exist. Otherwise, it is someone from outside who is perhaps best placed to provide the necessary skills.

Value management reviews can be held throughout the project. The number of reviews may depend on the size and complexity of the project.

Value management reviews are carried out as workshops and involve members of the organisation and project team. An external facilitator will be impartial and be more credible to the participants.

When the workshop starts, in many ways the group of people may be quite disparate – there will be personal agenda, positions to defend, as well as knowledge that is known to some but not to all. The idea is that by the end, everyone should be sharing the same objectives and understanding of the project. Essentially value management is about establishing a framework around which participants can communicate and make decisions rather than providing all the answers.

All reviews and studies should end with recommendations for modifications or design development.

Conclusion

Best briefing practice involves careful management of the process. The roles of the participants need to be clearly identified, with a project champion as the central figure who has the authority to make decisions.

Developing a project, building or otherwise, is a risky business. Cost and time over-run, as well as whether the project is appropriate, could have a significant impact on the profitability of the organisation. To be effective, risk management needs to be systemic, taking into account all of the activities of both the organisation and the project. Assessing risks helps a client make key decisions about the direction of a project, particularly its procurement.

Notes

1   Barrett, P., *Facilities Management: Towards best practice*, Blackwell Science 1995.
2   Handy, C., *Understanding Organisations*, 4th Edition, Penguin 1993.
3   Allinson, K., *Getting there by design*, Architectural Press 1997.
4   Gray, C., Hughes, W. and Bennet, J., *The Successful Management of Design*, Department of Construction Management and Engineering, University of Reading.
5   Katzenbach, J. and Smith, D., *The Wisdom of Teams*, McGraw-Hill 1993.
6   Belbin, R. M., *Management Teams: Why they succeed or fail*, Butterworth-Heinemann 1981.
7   Blyth A., *Design Team Monitoring*. The Design Council appointed Alastair Blyth to monitor and evaluate the design team on a primary school project designed and built for Essex County Council. A key finding was how the nature of the design team changed during the project because of the extent that different staff across a range of organisations were involved as the project moved from strategic design to detailed design.
8   Chapman, C. and Ward, S., *Project Risk Management*, Wiley 1997.
9   CIRIA, *Control of risk: A guide to the Systematic Management of risk*, CIRIA 1996.
10 Kelly, J. and Male, S., *Value Management – A proposed practice manual for the briefing process*, RICS Paper, No. 34.

Part Two
Learning from experience

The process of briefing in practice takes many forms depending on the characteristics of the client, and the time and resources available. The series of case studies that follow present personal perspectives of approaches to briefing. The final chapter analyses five generic briefing types:

- an *Urban Brief* where the briefing process established for buildings is shown to be equally as relevant for urban areas;
- a *Strategic Brief* which sets out the goals, objectives and case for a project based on an organisation's needs;
- a *Project Brief* which operationalises the Strategic Brief into a programme of building requirements;
- a *Fit-out Brief* which defines, in building terms, the client's requirements for internal building spaces; and
- a *Furniture Brief* which establishes the furniture attributes to meet the requirements of the Fit-out Brief.

For each briefing type the key issues are presented, with an annotated case study example, drawn from DEGW experience.

The case study chapters present the personal reflections of the authors, each of whom have been involved with the briefing process. Phil Roberts, in-house professional representative for the British Council, describes a process of briefing closely integrated with a programme of organisational change. The case study for the University of York describes research that looked at 35 years of continuous building, and aims to identify the triggers for successfully achieving feedback and continuous improvement. Work in North America, more recently applied by German architect Gunter Henn, has successfully used visualisation as a tool to focus on conflicting demands, and visualise opportunities. Susan Stuebing from Twinstra, a firm of Dutch management consultants, describes the process of preparing the brief for Shell's International Learning Centre, when no site existed, and the client's requirements were ill-defined. Lend Lease's Bluewater Shopping Centre on the outskirts of London is an inspiring example of how well-focused market research, linked to a clear vision, can be articulated as a direct Strategic Brief for innovative design thinking. Alastair Blyth describes his experience for the Design Council of monitoring the briefing and design process for a primary school, with clear goals for innovation. Christine Hanway and Stephen Greenberg from DEGW reflect on their recent experience of museum and exhibition design, and draw conclusions on managing a process where briefing, design, and implementation become overlapped and entwined in meeting the goal of communicating a developing and continuously changing story. Turid Horgen, a research fellow at the Department of Architecture at MIT, describes a series of action–research projects that culminated in a programme for 'Process Architecture'. The process provides an interplay between the workplace and work processes by engaging the users and the designers in a joint undertaking of design inquiry that spills over into work practice and sometimes changes the work culture. Despina Katsikakis (DEGW) describes ongoing consultancy for Andersen Worldwide, which has resulted in workplace guidelines, and a process of implementation, change management and continuous learning for the partnership globally.

8 Case studies

I *Briefing for rationalisation*

Phil Roberts, Facilities Adviser

Is the designer always right? This study explores a project carried out by the British Council which illustrates the need to create strategic space in order to allow design skills to flourish. It suggests that strategic space is created by the client through rhetoric, negotiation and political management, and is a precondition to deploying professional skills most effectively. It describes the briefing process for a headquarters rationalisation project that began in 1993 and was completed in 1996 to a modest budget within tight time and cost constraints. Despite these constraints, the consultancy team were able to create imaginative and innovative improvements to the workplace, whilst at the same time setting down a framework for future adaptation and improvement.

Strategic background

The British Council is a registered charity and the United Kingdom's international network for education, culture and development services. It operates in over 100 countries around the world. Peter Drucker has characterised organisations like the British Council as third-sector organisations. They share a number of common characteristics including a:

- not-for-profit ethos;
- strong business focus in the planning and management of operations;
- constraint on capital;
- programmes focused on short-to-medium-term benefits.

Over the past ten years, the British Council has set aggressive targets for expanding its overseas network. The growth was supported partly by increasing Enterprise activities overseas but also through redeploying resources from the UK. The introduction of new technology and telecommunications enabled more work to be managed effectively overseas, leading to corresponding reductions in the need for a substantial UK headquarters operation. However, the Council was locked into a number of leasehold premises of about 17 000 m^2 in London and 11 000 m^2 in Manchester whose facilities costs accounted for about half of total world-wide facilities expenditure. If the Council was to achieve its expansion objectives, a headquarters rationalisation programme was essential.

Around 1992, discussions opened with the landlord of the Council's Spring Gardens building to explore the shared benefits that could be achieved from a lease restructuring. The proposal involved the Council surrendering

Location	Building	Utilisation	Description
London	Spring Gardens, East Block	Medium	Medium–shallow plan, air-conditioned, restricted floor-to-floor heights, 1960s specification. Long lease period.
	Spring Gardens, West Block	Low	Shallow plan, air-conditioned, restricted floor-to-floor heights, 1960s specification. Long lease period.
	Portland Place	Low	Shallow plan, inefficient circulation. Naturally ventilated. Medium lease period.
	Seymour Mews	Medium to high	Shallow plan, naturally ventilated. Lease ending.
Manchester	Medlock Street	Medium to low	Deep plan, VAV air-conditioning, 1980s specification. Long lease with break point.

about half its office space in exchange for a new lease on the remainder on improved terms.

The briefing process

The briefing process divided into four iterative stages (Figure 8.1) which can best be described as:

- finding the venue;
- designing the set, Step 1: a proper job;
- designing the set, Step 2: best value;
- setting the stage.

Each stage formed a layered process that enabled a controlled progression from an outward-looking, benefit-driven business case to a managed design brief. It was successful in providing a context for the design team that met business objectives whilst at the same time providing the opportunity for innovative design thinking.

Pre-project stage

Finding the venue

In early 1993, a small Workplace Planning Team (WPT) was established to take ownership of the project. It was mandated by the Council's Board of

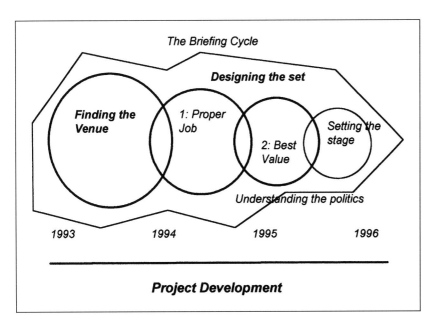

Figure 8.1: Four iterative stages of the briefing process.
Source: Phil Roberts

Management in accordance with PRINCE, the Council's project management standard. Under the leadership of a full-time Project Manager, it drew on part-time membership from Human Resources Group, IT Group, Facilities Group, Management Consultancy and Corporate Communications. At the outset, to ensure tight control of the real estate negotiation, it was decided that the WPT would be independent of the negotiating team, which was managed directly by the Facilities Group (Figure 8.2). The WPT was asked to review the Council's Headquarters Accommodation Strategy, and consider the options for rational-isation. These options included major relocation within London and between London and Manchester. At an early stage, strategic advisers were appointed[1] to support the team in achieving the most appropriate match of facilities resources to business needs. The WPT set out to develop the business case

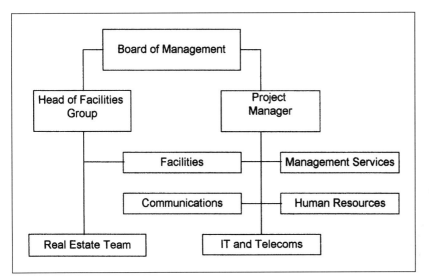

Figure 8.2: The Workplace Planning Team led by a project manager drew on part-time membership from human resources, IT, facilities, management consultancy, and corporate communications groups.
Source: Phil Roberts

from both internal and external sources. Internally, it drew upon Facilities Group information about the performance of the estate, and externally drew upon information from a number of sources, including the consultancy team.

Strategic briefing: internal sources

Working with the senior management group, the WPT analysed the business drivers of each of the Council's Strategic Business Units to identify:

- *location constraints;*
- *business objectives;*
- *workplace operational needs.*

Working with the Corporate Planning Department and business unit managers, the team analysed forecast staff numbers.

Strategic briefing: external sources

Working with Facilities Group, the WPT:

- *reviewed space utilisation across the estate;*
- *benchmarked costs for improvement and adaptation;*
- *considered options for improved space utilisation, including new methods of working;*
- *reviewed condition assessments of the headquarters estate.*

Working with the real estate team, the WPT:

- *reviewed alternative letting options for the existing estate;*
- *carried out a market survey of alternative premises;*
- *visited a range of potential alternative premises.*

At the outset of the project, there was no clear senior management view, other than that further benefits from headquarters rationalisation were essential to meet the Council's overall business objectives. However, towards the end of this phase of the project, the WPT had succeeded in establishing a strategic dialogue with the Board of Management and the Council's sponsors that showed a clear political consensus for a solution that retained the Council's Spring Gardens location for the long term, provided that the capital cost of adaptations could be managed within targets that maximised the business case benefits.

Designing the set: a proper job

The focus of the briefing work then shifted onto the evaluation of options for the rationalisation of the headquarters accommodation on the Spring Gardens site. Progress on the real estate negotiation required:

- agreement on the technical split of the building, in particular in relation to mechanical and electrical services;
- specific agreement on areas to which the landlord would contribute to the tenant's additional costs in restructuring access, goods delivery, and waste management.

An agreed accommodation strategy which identified Spring Gardens as the Council's medium-to-long-term location raised further questions about the scale and scope of the adaptation work required. Consultants[2] were appointed to carry out a detailed cost and programme review, and competitive interviews were held for design and space planning consultants to support a detailed feasibility study. The first stage evaluation had shown that there was a tight match between workspace supply following rationalisation and forecast demand, and a preliminary report was prepared by the consultancy team to validate:

- space budget and utilisation targets;
- condition of the Spring Gardens building;
- options for renewing the IT infrastructure within the building;
- programme constraints;
- cost constraints.

The report explored both a minimum and a maximum scheme with the overall time constraints. However, the maximum scheme required substantially greater capital investment than the minimum scheme on which the business case had been based. In order to address these issues, a value management workshop was undertaken with a group of key middle managers. The workshop suggested that users were concerned about the extent of resources allocated to:

- planned adaptability of the workplace, particularly to support team space;
- objectives for the public and common spaces within the building;
- environmental and air quality of the workplace;
- wayfinding into and around the building.

The design team argued that the rationalisation project provided a unique opportunity to improve the working environment and recommended a floor-by-floor phased refit based on a maximum scheme. However, this conclusion not only challenged the viability of the business case approvals but also presented a number of difficulties to a heavily capital-constrained organisation.

In order to prepare the PRINCE end-stage report, the WPT decided to put both the business case and the design team's report through an external review procedure. Coopers and Lybrand had acted as critical friend to the Council in the development of its accommodation strategy over a number of years, and had a good understanding of the organisation and its business objectives. The presentation to the external reviewers was made jointly by the WPT and the consultant team. The review re-established the fundamentals of the business case benefits, and supported its conclusions, but argued for an enhanced minimum scheme rather than the proposed maximum scheme. Crucially, it also suggested that more work should be done to show how a programme of continuous improvement to the building and its facilities could meet the needs of users and business managers as expressed in the value management workshop.

Project stage

Like the pre-project stage, briefing for the project also consisted of two iterative cycles. The start of the project stage was marked by signature to the agreement to surrender which bought benefits but also imposed critical time constraints.

Designing the set: best value

The WPT re-evaluated the consultancy skills requirement and negotiated the final scope of services. Working collaboratively with corporate service departments, a Strategic Brief was developed under a number of headings:

- *Design management strategy.* Design management objectives were set for the workplace, wayfinding, public and common areas. The strategy envisaged key objectives for the project, but also a process of future continuous improvement by the Facilities Group.
- *Facilities strategy.* The facilities strategy set down key targets for the type and quality of support services required, including public and common spaces, catering, and office support. In order to take advantage of the rationalisation programme, the Facilities Group launched a parallel project to review the management of the in-house and contracted facilities service throughout the rationalised headquarters estate.
- *IT strategy.* IT Group also launched a parallel project to rationalise and upgrade the headquarter's IT and telecommunications infrastructure, linking the rationalised headquarters estate to the Council's world-wide network.
- *Quality strategy.* Project targets for time, cost, quality and space utilisation.
- *Communications strategy.* Dedicated project resources were allocated to identifying internal and external stakeholders, their objectives, and the means of providing each of them with key information.

User involvement and communication had been limited during the pre-project stages in order not to prejudice the Council's negotiating position. However, user involvement at this stage substantially increased through:

- village hall meetings;
- team briefings;
- newsletter and notice board flyers;
- meetings between the consultancy team and business unit managers to confirm their requirements;
- detail surveys and discussions with users over space planning, storage and other facilities;
- establishment of a help line to resolve particular problems.

Setting the stage

The final briefing stage consisted of technical specification for specific areas such as mail and waste handling areas, catering, and IT and communication equipment areas. The feasibility study had shown that to minimise risk to the tight deadlines, a partnering approach should be taken towards the fitting out of the project. Following a two-stage tender, a fit-out contractor[3] was selected in early 1995. Their appointment allowed for the development of further detailed briefing and user consultation during construction. The project was completed on time to allow the Council to hand back West Block to the agreed schedule. The final adaptation cost was a modest £850/m^2 of which about 40 per cent was spent on essential fabric improvements and IT networks.

Putting the client in control

The experience of this project highlights a number of critical success factors that are needed to create the strategic space within which projects deliver assured business benefits, whilst at the same time providing the design team creative opportunities to contribute to the effectiveness of the workplace as a whole.

Strategic ownership

From the outset, the client side took possession of the strategic framework and business benefits. It is often said that no final consultancy appointments should be made until at least 10 per cent of the project resources have been committed. This project illustrates the importance of careful preparation to provide a foundation on which the consultancy relationship can be built.

Strategic dialogue

At each stage of the process, the WPT facilitated dialogue and exchange of information through collaborative working with sponsors, business managers and end users. It also sought to create the opportunities for the professional skills of the consultancy team to contribute in an open and inclusive way, not only to the development of design solutions but also to the briefing process.

Strategic management

Effective briefing would not have been possible without a project management framework that provided clear lines of reporting, authority and responsibility.

Strategic briefing

The briefing process was managed as a series of layers, each of which allowed for the structured exploration of options and benefits whilst at the same time remaining adaptable to the uncertainties and opportunities of the real estate negotiation.

Strategic partnerships

The consulting and construction team were selected not only on their ability to bring specialised skills and resources to the project, but also on their willingness to challenge, be challenged, and share in the Council's aspirations and objectives.

Each of these factors contributed towards creating the strategic space between sponsors, managers, users and the project team that enabled design to contribute effectively to the Council's objectives.

Whole life briefing

The experience of this project suggests that effective briefing takes place at three levels:

Level	Focus	Briefing level	Communication forums
Programme	Primarily an outward-looking process	Establishing fundamental business case. Establishing philosophy and approach to workplace planning. Establishing targets for the workplace through benchmarking and evaluation. Establishing workplace selection and evaluation criteria. Programme risk assessment.	Strategic dialogue with key stakeholders. Management of expectations and concerns. Senior manager workshops. Comparative building evaluations. Occupancy reviews. Space audit.
Planning	Both an inward- and outward-looking process	Establishing targets and interdependencies for projects needed to achieve business case objectives. Project risk assessment. Establishing project briefing for time, cost and quality objectives.	Communication programmes providing information and feedback opportunities. Value management workshops. End-user needs and requirements assessments. Village hall meetings. Mock up and experimental zones.
Project	Primarily an inward-looking process.	Managing project delivery within targets. Quality management of design products.	Extension of communication programmes. Design presentations. Space planning consultations. User team briefings.

At each of these levels, the briefing process allows for re-evaluation and testing of the assumptions in the business case against design options and objectives. However, the experience of the external scrutiny also showed that there was a critical balance between the project objectives, and the opportunities for continuous improvement through effective facilities management. Clients generally employ design consultants on terms that encourage solutions that tend towards the grand project, and which underestimate the opportunity

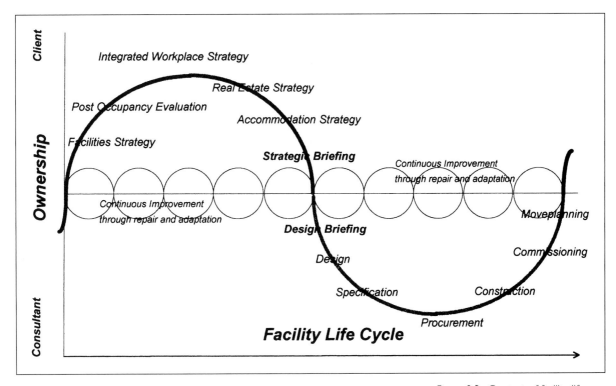

Client

Ownership

Consultant

Integrated Workplace Strategy

Real Estate Strategy

Post Occupancy Evaluation

Accommodation Strategy

Facilities Strategy

Strategic Briefing

Continuous Improvement
through repair and adaptation

Continuous Improvement
through repair and adaptation

Design Briefing

Move planning

Design

Commissioning

Specification

Construction

Procurement

Facility Life Cycle

Figure 8.3: Context of facility life cycle.
Source: Phil Roberts

for continuous improvement through creative adaptation. In reality, projects need to be seen in a wider context (Figure 8.3) to ensure not only that they achieve benefits at the outset, but that they provide opportunities for future improvement. Institutional clients have a key role in understanding these inter-relationships.

Is the designer always right? The designer is given the opportunity to be right when the client is prepared to take responsibility for managing projects within this wider facilities context. The Strategic Brief is positioned at a crucial point in the life cycle of a building. It provides the opportunity to integrate the knowledge and learning from continuous improvement into a renewed strategic vision for the next phase of the relationship of the building and its users.

References

1   Projects In a Controlled Environment, a standard developed by the CCTA.
2   Acknowledgement is made to Duhig Berry Ltd: *Programme Management* 1995.

Notes

1   Strategic Advisers: DEGW.
2   Cost and programme review: Davis Langdon Management.
3   Fit-out contractor: Interiors plc.

2   *Briefing for continuous building*

35 years of briefing and design at the University of York

John Worthington

Briefing for organisations with a continuous building programme has the potential advantages of building relationships, learning from experience and improving performance whilst driving down costs. Of the total annual construction budget, it has been estimated that 80 per cent of the spend is with 20 per cent of clients, the majority of whom have permanent estate professionals on their staff and a continuous building programme. It is ironic that many of these clients still do not see briefing as the cornerstone for construction success, nor do they have any formal processes of evaluation and feedback.

Briefing for a continuous building programme

The case study that follows presents the conclusions of an EPSRC/IMI-funded research project undertaken at the Institute of Advanced Architectural Studies (IoAAS) at the University of York.[1] The study focused on the 35 years of building at the University of York and sought to test the hypothesis that 'with continuity (of key personnel, etc.) there ought to be learning and feedback leading to improvements in quality and performance, added value, elimination of waste, reduction in costs, reduced defects and maximisation of benefits including better management of risks for the client.' The study assessed this experience from the perspectives of the clients, their management (Estates) and user (university academic departments) representatives. It addressed the following questions:

- were the university's expectations as a client and user met by the building programme?
- what was the impact of the briefing process on the building outcome?
- with a continuous building programme, did the university, its advisers and contractors:
  - learn and improve from past experience?
  - improve performance and reduce real costs?
- could the benefits of the design brief be measured as part of a programme of quality improvement?
- could the benefits of building programmes be attributed to clearly set out strategic objectives?

The study concluded that whilst the university's building programme did not decline in quality, it did not see a step change improvement, and costs were neither better nor worse than others in the sector. Learning was through mistakes, rather than a positive programme of evaluating past performance. The over-riding lesson was that the university, like the majority of its counterparts, despite having a continuous building programme and robust estates strategy in the early (1962–72) and recent (1992–present) stages, did not have a formal programme of learning from past experience. The longitudinal study of building briefing over the life of the university provides valuable insights into the importance of a continuously maturing Strategic Brief, and feedback through both in-project feedback and post-project evaluation in order to repeat successes and avoid making the same mistakes.

Thirty-five years of development

Over the 35 years of its life, the University of York has represented the characteristics of a professional client with a:

- *continuous building programme*, with an average annual building programme of £3.5 million and phased developments providing opportunities for repeat commissions and learning by accumulation of past experiences. Over its life, the total University of York Estate has grown to cover 90.2 hectares, the majority being at one out-of-town campus. The total building stock now comprises 1 480 079 m² of teaching, administration and residential accommodation.
- *repetitive functional requirements*, comprising teaching, research, administration and residential activities, each providing opportunities for both innovation and improved performance.

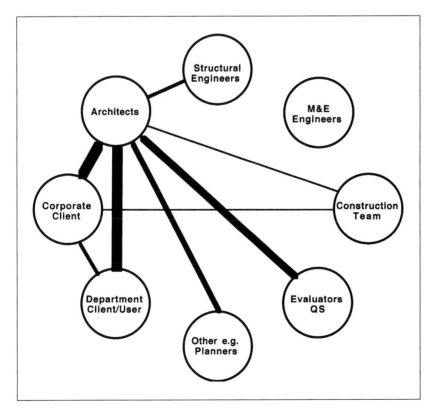

Figure 8.4: Diagram showing the strength of personal working relationships at York between 1962 and 1972.

- *continuity of key personnel.* The Bursar (Roger McMeeking), Architect (Sir Andrew Derbyshire RMJM), Project Architect (Bob Owston) and Builder (Shepherd Construction) being associated with projects on the campus from 1962–97, when Roger McMeeking retired.
- *continuous personal working relationships* between individuals and organisations. Throughout the 35-year period at York, the University Bursar as a client, developed a consistent relationship with a small group of building contractors, engineers and architects, all of whom have had roles in the creation of the York campus (Figure 8.4).

The 35-year history of design, development and construction at the University of York shows three distinct periods.

1 1962–72 Continuous Strategic Briefing – constructing

The first period was one of intense activity, characterised by dependence on formal planning and more transparent briefing with specific milestones and targets reflected in the building programme. Approximately 70 per cent of the current university building stock was built in the first 10 years. This period was characterised by:

- a high level of direct commitment by the Readership (Lord James the Vice Chancellor);
- a strong vision for the quality of academic and social environment shared by academics, the administration and consultants;
- a client/user focus with close integration of academic and building planning;
- an integrated team structure with short and simple lines of communication between client, design team and contractor;
- a continuous building programme that allowed feedback from one project to the next with a common design and construction team on site;
- a mode of construction and procurement (CLASP) which resulted in close working relationships between project designers, system development designers, the contractor and specialist component providers.

2 1972–92 Incremental development – consolidation

The second period was characterised by a drift away from strategic planning with an ad hoc approach to procurement. The building programme was small scale buildings, extensions and the use of temporary buildings to meet rapid growth. No attempt was made to revisit the original development plan, though Sir Andrew Derbyshire continued to sit on the Estates and Building committee as an adviser. Building decisions were made without a strategic framework, and briefs were prepared opportunistically as demand emerged. The result was small-scale schemes with high building costs, insufficient resources for design development and no continuity of commitment. Looking back over the programme, there was continuity of project team members, though this was the result of an unspoken understanding, rather than explicit agreement. Each project was a fresh start 'and a contract to be fought for'. Without a revitalised strategic framework, the building programme was responsive to individual departmental demands, small scale and incremental. The period was characterised by:

- an emphasis on oral briefing with discussion centred around cost limits and the schedule of accommodation;
- under resourcing and cut backs in government funding. Buildings were not considered to be central to the university's mission;
- strong personal relationships between user and architect, resulting in high user satisfaction.

Briefing procedures during the period reflected a drift away from strategic planning, to an ad hoc approach to procurement. Roger McMeeking attributes this change to 'collective uncertainty' with no clear shared vision for the future, or confidence in future demand, the result was an incremental response.

3   1992–1997 – re-establishment of an Estates Strategy

In the third period there was a redefinition of the strategic direction with the preparation of the Estates Strategy (1993–4). The briefing process is supported by a well researched and documented Estates Strategy, prepared for the Higher Education Funding Council, which sets out academic ambitions and a building strategy to achieve these aims. The strategy is backed by policy documents for transport planning, energy and landscape and a corporate strategy that reflects government targets for increasing student intakes of 18-year-olds (33 per cent of the population by year 2000) and mature and overseas students. The period has reflected an upturn in the floor area constructed and the beginning of a major programme of upgrading and adaptation for the 30-year-old residential stock.

The Estates Strategy provided a major opportunity for a new Vice Chancellor (Professor Ron Cooke) with Council to review the university's business and academic strategy. The plans were drawn up by Roger McMeeking, the Bursar, who left his day-to-day duties for six months to prepare the report, supported by Adrian Leaman (IoAAS), Sir Andrew Derbyshire (architect/planner), Sam Cassells (space planning), Hal Moggeridge (landscape), Janet O'Neill (planning) and with a steering group of the Vice Chancellor and Professor John Worthington (Director IoAAS). The physical resource strategy (Conclusions) (Figure 8.5) differed from the past in focusing on:

- adding value through a wider range of 'customer services' for a wider range of students;
- intensification of the use of existing buildings and sites. Capacity for over half a million square feet of space was identified on the existing campus by new building exteriors and adaptation;
- an integrated transport policy, following the Park and Ride initiatives of the City of York;
- a policy of space utilisation and energy changing to control demand and promote the efficient and responsible use of space and energy;
- development of generic building types, which can be adapted to alternative uses (the new 4000 m^2 Computer Science building is the first of the generic buildings;

Physical Resources Strategy – University of York 1995

1. Establish mechanisms for implementing strategic principles for the physical planning and management of Campus 1 at an institutional level, for example;
    – information, communication, transportation and access policies
    – energy and environmental policies
    – framework landscape zones and their funding
    – protected areas
    – recreation policy;
2. Agree and implement plans to house academic departments coherently, after consultation;
3. Establish the Campus 1 planning areas:
4. Agree medium to long-term area planning briefs with Campus 1 'stakeholders' – departments, colleges and students;
5. Implement the plans to develop Campus 2, through the King's Manor Resources Group;
6. Complete the plan and development brief for Campus 3, with full consultation via the statutory planning process;
7. Review and agree the future pattern, number and characteristics at colleges, through a body charged with regular oversight of their organisation, consulting widely with students;
8. Agree and implement new structures for facilities management, with local managers responding to Heads of Department/Provosts as clients, and to the University Bursar as the reporting line;
9. Prepare and implement a human resources strategy for facilities management;
10. Implement procurement, briefing and design policies for all projects described in the review, monitored by Estates & Buildings Committee:
11. Bring locally controlled teaching spaces into the central timetable, unless they are categorised as departmental resource, with their upkeep being a charge on the department concerned;
12. Integrate and regularly maintain the database prepared for the Estates Strategy project into existing management Information systems, and fully develop the Physical resources module of the MAC system (together with related modules);
13. Introduce facilities management software to match the supply of teaching spaces to demand, with a target utilisation of 50 per cent;
14. Keep all space under review, to minimise capital expenditure;
15. Prioritise expenditures between renewal/upgrading and new construction, through the college and catering committee and other appropriate bodies;
16. Prioritise capital projects within a rolling plan, with financial appraisals and re-appraisals, via Policy and Resources Committee:
17. Develop and implement existing and new income generating projects and cost reduction measures in all areas;
18. Implement maintenance plan;
19. Communicate the Physical Resources Strategy and objectives throughout the university;
20. Monitor progress of all aspects of this action plan, by further reviews in 1997/8 and every three years.

Figure 8.5: Physical resources strategy – the University of York, 1995.

- improved facilities management to support the university's academic objectives. Greater control on planning is diverted to department heads, with local area resource managers responsible for area briefs.

So far this period has been characterised by a move to a recognition of the university as a business enterprise. The briefing approach provides, through the Estates Strategy;

- a well-documented, explicit long-term approach for development against which individual projects can be assessed;

Indicative Information for an Area Brief

1.0   Academic/Social Mission defined by the focal 'street' running from the lake/Central Hall piazza in the south, to J. B. Morrel Library as the heart of the university and the focal point for university life and for outside conferences as well as a point of orientation for first time visitors.

2.0   Functions and Constituents defined by; the 280 residences, the dining and events space, snack bar, lecture and seminar space SCR and private dining; the Central Hall activities – examinations, degree ceremonies, concerts, lectures, films, theatre and exhibitions; the Language Centre activities – language/linguistics, Careers, counselling and the language teaching centre; the Computer Science and its 244 undergraduates, 70 postgraduates, 26 academics, 40 research assistants and 23 support staff; and Computing service as IT support for the whole University.

3.0   Capacity as defined by the proposed Vanbrugh additions such as piazza retail development, enlarged SCR and private dining, increased lecture space, Central Hall proposals for teaching and creation of seminar spaces in the 'green room' and relocation of Computer Science.

4.0   Zoning defined by Vanbrugh nucleus with distinct front doors for departments; enhancement of public areas (dining, bars, lecture theatres) and links to the retail concourse on the piazza of separate entrance to first floor SCR/GCR/private dining; upgrade to ensuite residences and new uses for space released by Computer Science.

5.0   Planning Criteria/Design Guidelines defined by a focus on lakeside views, development and intensification of north/south and east/west routes, creation of campus-wide focal point as a hub of activity; provision of quiet – green courtyards off the north/south axis and improvement of western entrances area separating services from people.

6.0   Milestones/Timetable defined by commissioning a detailed area master plan and establishment of expenditure priorities.

7.0   Management defined by required appointment of a full-time facilities manager responsible to the Provost and local resources group as clients, and to the Bursar as reporting line.

Figure 8.6: Indicative information on area brief.

- area briefs prepared, monitored and implemented locally with strategic support from the centre (Figure 8.6);
- an identifiable pre-project stage where options are assessed, financial viability evaluated and a thorough process of design team selection undertaken against a formal Strategic Brief (The Estates Strategy and area briefs);
- a process of requirements verification by the design team who prepared a Project Brief and design concept (Computer Science, Nicholas Hare Associates).

This period has been significant in briefing development, in its recognition of the need for a development framework which links the Corporate Plan and Policies to individual building briefs; and in the emphasis on facility management to improve business performance.

Findings on the process

The study reinforces the need to:

- adopt a continuous strategic briefing approach which establishes long-term academic/business goals against which immediate demands can be proposed and options assessed;
- distinguish between the strategic and operational. The strategy being the role of the Board, and the operational that of the Estates department;
- establish a structured and formalised (transparent) briefing framework that clearly articulates steps, milestones, expectations, information required and decision-making procedures;
- concentrate on innovating those items with the greatest return with a continuous building programme. The opportunity of learning through feedback, improved performance and reduction in costs, are to be found in identifying those key items where innovation could improve performance. Through maintenance, feedback such as a step change was made at York with the briefing of designers to move from flat to pitched roofs;
- clarify roles between types of client (Figure 8.7) and between procurer, user and provider within a framework that establishes the relevance of requisite skills, responsibilities and decision-making processes at each stage of the project (Figure 8.5). The briefing manager defines requirements and 'closes the loop' in terms of feedback. The designer adds value through synthesis and innovation. The project manager aids the client in monitoring and achieving the end product. The resource manager provides the day-to-day management of the building and the resources within;
- develop personal commitment; for example, the foundation of the University of York's initial success is generally recognised to have stemmed from Lord James' personal commitment and attention.

General lessons for success

From the University of York's experience, eight factors for successful briefing and building procurement can be identified.

1. *Strategic planning*
   The most vital factor for success is a template for consistently well-integrated projects. In organisations with major estates and continuous building projects, the masterplan or estates strategy can take on the function of the Strategic Brief, providing it is continuously reviewed and updated.

Figure 8.7: Three different client types.

Client types	Main Objective	Example
Paying Clients "Paymasters"	• Return on investment and best performance in terms of capital and operational costs	• Benchmarks and performance standards (like organisations or like sectors)
Facilities / Resource Managers "Resourcers"	• Meeting needs of Paying or User Clients	• Minimum complaints
User Clients "Users"	• Accommodating adequately their activities	• Rapid response to meet spatial needs

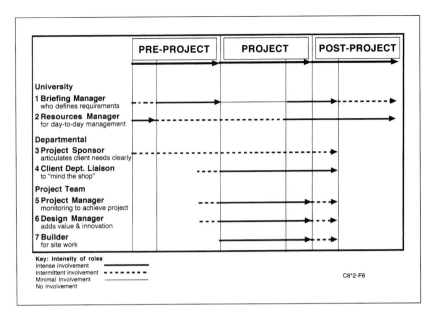

Figure 8.8: Clarifying responsibilities and requisite skills.

Figure 8.9: Levels of development and user strategies.

(Figure 8.9) presents the three types of information used at the University of York. The Strategic Plan, reviewed every five years, Policy documents, reviewed bi-annually and Procedures and Project Data arising from feedback from each project after evaluation and maintenance.

2. *A transparent framework*, which sets out expectations, procedures, and performance measures against which evaluation and improvements can be made. Figure 8.10 shows, from the university's experience, the value of a continuous, proactive briefing approach (1962–72 and 1992–present) against the reactive incremental approach with no clear framework.

3. *Clarity of roles*
   The clarification of roles goes hand-in-hand with empowered clients who are able to articulate needs clearly within the long-term strategic framework.

4. *Manageable buildings that absorb change*
   Manageable buildings fall into two categories:[1]
   Category 1   Simple, robust, with low costs-in-use and low impact. In the university, these represented approximately 85 per cent of the stock.

Figure 8.10: Approaches to briefing.

	PROACTIVE	REACTIVE
	Continuous Strategic Briefing Approach	Incremental Briefing Approach
1. Nature of decision-making systems	• Sequential and within a specified framework, consistent, logical	• Ill-structured, reactive
2. Requisite skills and abilities	• Defined, identified, planning	• Undefined, haphazard
3. Nature of information systems	• Structured, systematic, models and referenced	• Short-term, absence of templates, formats or models, less transparent
4. Nature of communication and relationships	• Defined, flexible, max involvement of senior management, close collaboration between team members	• Erratic, unclear, chaotic, limited team spirit
5. Sequence of necessary actions	• Prioritisation, programmed, sequential	• Periods of inactivity or non-action 'drip-feed'
6. Nature of the product	• Innovative, fulfilled potential	• Unfulfilled potential, short-term and limited, uninspired, often whimsical

Category 2   Complex, technically advanced, higher but affordable costs-in-use, manageable, with unavoidably greater environmental impact and perhaps a stronger image which reflects corporate aspirations.

5. *Monitoring and feedback*, by introducing quality improvement loops and greater customer-orientation. Until recently, York, like most other institutions, had a complete lack of formal feedback other than in an anecdotal-informed way. The reasons for any absence of feedback are reflected in the prevalent attitudes of:

   • every building being regarded as a 'one-off prototype' and the role of the Estates department being seen as 'supply side' and building focused;
   • the users being the 'enemy' ready to snipe at any mistake, resulting in a fear of exposure and being blamed for failure;
   • reluctance to commit resources to all defined paybacks when no mechanisms for effective 'knowledge management' exist.

   The recent interest in feedback mechanisms and continuous briefing at the University of York is a reflection of:

   • the recognition of the importance of the design brief on helping to second-guess how the finished building product will operate over time, when there is greater uncertainty about the future;
   • change management being a recognised need.

6. *Continuous review*, that tests assumptions and revisits hypotheses. The current focus is to provide a robust and transparent framework to test projects as they progress, and a focus on a continuity of process as opposed to relying on a continuity of individuals.

7. *Concentrating innovation on items with the greatest return*. Organisations with a continuous building programme have the opportunity to reflect on poor performance, repeat those items that have been successful, and find new solutions for those areas where they can achieve the greatest return.

Conclusion

The University of York as a case study is an accurate reflection of the practices and mind sets found in most institutional clients. The last five years of its Estates management history have seen a change in expectations and processes, with the re-establishment of a long-term strategic framework, a greater customer focus, and a recognition of the need for continuous briefing and feedback. The pointers exist for how quality and performance can be improved, and costs reduced by establishing a briefing process that standardises policies, processes, and details and learns from past experience.

Notes

1   This case study is a synopsis of the Engineering and Physical Sciences Research Council (EPSRC) Innovative Manufacturing Initiatives (IMI) research undertaken by John Worthington, Adrian Leaman, and Michael Phiri at the Institute of Advanced Architectural Studies (IoAAS), The University of York. This research is now continuing at the School of Architecture, University of Sheffield under Dr Michael Phiri.

   Worthington, Leaman, Phiri. 'Briefing a Continuous Building Programme: Factors for Success.' *35 years of Briefing & Design at the University of York* (IoAAS), Kings Manor, York 1998.

3   *Briefing through visualisation*

John Worthington

Briefing and design are inexorably enmeshed. At the simplest scale of building the house, the architect is both the problem seeker (brief maker) and problem solver[1] (designer). He takes a statement of need from the client, makes a sketch response, which then stimulates the client to identify the features which match expectations and adapts those aspects which don't match. This process of iteration continues to the point of building. Where the client and user are encompassed by one point of contact, design as briefing works well. However, in today's world most projects are complex with sometimes several clients, many layers of stakeholders and a myriad of users. Clearly establishing goals, determining needs and unambiguously stating the problem, is imperative to reduce risk and unnecessary expenditure. How then can the power of design as a synthesiser and visualiser be used without beginning the design process?

Architects have long recognised that 'the one who holds the pencil wields the power'. Diagrams and sketches can encapsulate complex ideas, focus discussion and speed up the process of understanding. The process of briefing is concerned with collecting the facts, establishing the issues and seeking the 'whole problem',[1] through synthesising the different perspectives and expectations into an organisational concept. Drawings and precedents of previous examples can be used as a "guinea pig" to test assumptions and identify these features which fit or are inappropriate. Three examples are explored of situations where images, diagrams and drawings are used in interactive client/user sessions to articulate the brief.

Workplace Envisioning™

Workplace Envisioning™[2] is a powerful interior planning briefing methodology developed by Steelcase Inc. in North America in association with DEGW. The development programme which began in 1990 provides interactive software that allows a group of different interest managers to determine simultaneously what kind of organisation they wish to be and the office environment needed. Using generic work settings, users are encouraged to take ownership of the design strategies which emerge, so speeding up user acceptance and the process of change.

The programme is spread over three workshops. Workshop One, for a cross-section of senior management, sets the parameters of the workplace strategy for the organisation now and in the future. Workshop Two is a series of events with groups of staff from similar functions. Its objectives are to create a model of the work processes and identify the use of office space over time. With an interactive software programme, it asks representatives of job functions to examine work content (tasks) and the time, place and mode in which each critical task is performed. The outcome of these responses are used to select appropriate work settings to support work activities now and in the future. Workshop Three focuses on headcount and financial data to create a brief for facility design. At the heart of this process is:

- the ability to get different interests in the same room, making simultaneous responses and decisions towards a common understanding;
- the use of a visualising framework that allows participants to see and respond to the impact of their perceptions;
- the involvement of a wide cross-section of client and user representatives in the problem definition and option appraisal stage.

The first workshop with senior management defines the character and workstyle of the organisation and examines the content of work, and the time, place and mode it is performed now, and how it might be in the future. A small group of participants (usually between six and eight) with a facilitator, can sit around a common computer or each have their own terminal linked to a large screen projector. The group is initially asked to reflect on the organisation's profile under ten dimensions, each of which is assessed on a ten-point scale. The strategic direction of the organisation is assessed by stating the relative value of each dimension to the success of the organisation in the past (last five years), today (as it is now) and future (within the life of the facility being designed). The ten dimensions and the bi-polar measures[3] cover the areas set out in the section below.

Structure

The formal (organisational chart) and informal structures recognised by people within the organisation.

Hierarchical v. flat	Hierarchical structure refers to vertical authority from top down; flat structure refers to operational authority shared horizontally across the organisation.
Centralised v. decentralised	Centralised structure implies decision making at the top of the hierarchy, decentralised.

Environment

The external context in which the organisation works, including such factors as business sector, types of market and government regulations.

Stable v. volatile	In an era of 'discontinuous' change, stability implies predictability whilst volatility implies uncertainty.
Short-term v. long-term horizon	Short-term horizon implies limited planning, rapid write-offs and responsiveness to stock holder pressures; long-term builds for the future.

Work processes

How the organisation does the work.

Linear v. non-linear | Linear and sequential refer to 'assembly line' operators. Non-linear includes parallel working and is useful in managing ambiguity.

Directive v. participative | Directive refers to top-down, traditional authority. Participative refers to bottom-up input and collaborative work.

Organisational style

The appearance, customs and expected behaviour of the organisation.

Formal v. informal | Refers to factors such as dress code, style of titles and acceptance of flexibility of behaviour.

Rigid v. flexible | Responsiveness of organisation to meet new challenges.

Spartan v. opulant | 'Lean and mean' compared with 'status and wealth'.

Traditional v. experimental | Traditional organisations stick with tried and tested ways of doing things until forced to change. Experimental organisation are constantly trying new things.

In Workshop One, additional information is collected on headcount, working hours, location of work, type of work (individual or collaborative) and the content of work now and in the future.

Problem seeking

In the mid 1960s, Caudill Rowlett & Scott, the Houston-based architectural practice, under the inspiration of Bill Caudill and supported by William Pena, established a methodology for programming (briefing) complex educational and health facilities. These techniques expanded their traditional architectural services to include pre-design briefing and building evaluation at the end. Problem-seeking[1] set out the principles and techniques for sound programming, a publication initially for their clients, in its later editions it became a wider publication for professionals.

Problem-seeking focused on a search for the whole problem, through close participation with clients and users. The process of programming recognised the need for analysis, objectivity and problem statements; however, developed by architects, it saw the value of conceptualising ideas through drawings and providing an integrative framework through visual charts which all could see. Pena sets out five stages in a brief:

- establishing goals;
- collecting facts;
- uncovering concepts;
- determining needs;
- stating the problem.

In searching for the 'whole problem' which encompasses function, form, economy and time, a series of workshops with users and the design team were arranged where a facilitator (the briefer) collects, organises and displays an array of information. Typically for a medium-sized project the process might be spread over a week, when the programming team comes to the client's existing premises. The first day would be taken up with set-up, kick-off and interviews which would go through to the end of day three. The fourth day was a six-hour work session, with a similar group testing the feasibility of options in the evening. The final day (Friday) is a final work session, wrap up and clean up. At the work sessions, three techniques were typically used to extract and communicate information. They are discussed in detail below.

Brown sheets. Literally large sheets of paper pinned up around the wall to graphically indicate space derived from project goals. The sheets provided a visual expression of the magnitude of numbers and sizes.

Analysis cards. Small 'address cards' that can be held in the hand, hold one idea, and be pinned up as an array for later scrutiny. The card is a 'method of graphically recording information intended to be displayed, discussed, directed, decided upon and sometimes discarded during the programming phase of a project'.

The key requirements are that the cards should:

- Be easily handled, sorted and displayed;
- Of the same size and proportion (e.g. 50×80 cm);
- Use visual language and few words;
- Be legible and producible by any member of the group.

Gaming cards. Abstract images and reference projects (precedents) that can be used to help lay peoples focus on likes and dislikes or position themselves in a hierarchy of alternatives.[4]

At the workshop the facilitator organises an array of information and displays into a comprehensible, visualisable format Figure 8.11. The chart, which can take one large wall, is a matrix 'information index' (Figure 8.12) showing the inter-relationship between considerations (function, form, economy and time) and steps (goals, facts, concepts, needs, problems). Analysis cards are placed within the appropriate square of the matrix (Figure 8.13). The outcome is a clear visual picture of the overall issues to be addressed, classified according to type of issue and stage in the process the information is relevant to.

CRS' original concepts have been absorbed, developed and applied in Europe by Gunter Henn[5] supported by a small group of able facilitators. They have used the same concept of the information index and analysis cards (Figure 8.14) to provide a format for focusing the briefing process. Henn's team recognised that the definition of tasks (briefing) and finding of solutions became separated with a schism between client/user and designer.

Figure 8.11: Organising an array of information into a comprehensible visual form.
Source: Pena, W., Parshall, S. and Kelly, K., Problem Seeking: An Architectural Primer, AIA Press 1987

Information Index

	Goals	Facts	Concepts	Needs	Problem
Function People Activities Relationships	Mission Maximum number Individual identity Interaction privacy Security Progression Encounters Information exchange	Statistical data Area parameters Manpower/workloads Value of potential loss Time-motion study Behavioural patterns Type/intensity	Service grouping People grouping Activity grouping Priority Separated flow Mixed flow Communication	Space requirements Parking requirements Outdoor space requirements Functional alternatives	Unique and important performance requirements which will shape building design
Form Site Environment Quality	Bias on site elements Sound structure Sociality Individuality Building quality level Spatial quality level	Site analysis Soil analysis Surroundings Building efficiency Equipment costs Area per unit	Enhancement Density Environmental controls Neighbours Orientation Accessibility Character	Site development costs Environmental influences on costs Building cost/S.F. Building efficiency Equipment costs	Major form considerations which will affect building design
Economy Initial Budget Operating Costs Lifecycle Costs	Extent of funds Cost effectiveness Maximum return Return on invetment Minimize operating costs Maintenance and operating costs Reduce life cycle costs	Cost parameters Maximum budget Time-use factors Market analysis Energy source-costs Activities and climax factors Economic data	Cost control Efficient allocation Multi-function Merchandising Energy conservation Cost control Cost control	Cost estimate analysis Energy budget (if reqd) Operating costs (if reqd) Life cycle costs (if reqd)	Attitude towards the initial budget and its influence on the fabric and geometry of the building
Time Past Present Future	Historic preservation Static/dynamic activities Change Growth Occupancy data Cost controlled growth	Significance Space parameters Activities Projections Durations Escalation factors	Adaptability Tolerance Convertibilty Expansibility Linear/concurrent scheduling Phasing	Time schedule Time/cost schedule	Implications of change growth on long-range performance

Figure 8.12: Extracts from the information index developed by CRS is a useful framework against which to ask questions and tease out information.
Source: Pena, W., Parshall, S. and Kelly, K, Problem Seeking: An Architectural Primer, AIA Press 1987

Figure 8.13: Analysis cards can be used to draw out information during briefing.
Source: John Worthington

The language of tasks was largely textual and numerical, whilst the language of solution development was visual, using sketches and models. Henn's aim has been to use qualified diagrams (concept visualisation card) which describe requirements in the graphic language of the solution). Henn and Henn use the workshop as an efficient and effective means of collecting and agreeing information, with a facilitator who is adept at visualising organisation ideas. The visualisation process is transparent, increases trust and supports the process of change. The client leads the process, the facilitator draws their goals and expectations.

Action planning[5]

At the same time in North America, as CRS were developing their problem-seeking workshops in recognition, as they stated, that 'our client's participation is so critical to the success of our projects', the American Institute of Architects (AIA) were launching a community programme of Urban Design Assistance Teams (UDATS). In 1967, the AIA launched its first UDAT at Rapid City, South Dakota, and by 1978 there were a range of programmes being organised through universities and local AIA chapters as Design Assistance Teams (DATS). In 1985, Richard Burton (ABK), with the RIBA, organised the first UK pilot event at St Mary's, Southampton, under the title of Community Urban Design Assistance Teams (CUDATS). In 1990 John Worthington, in his term as President of the Urban Design Group (UDG), championed the idea of action planning,[6] and the UDG co-ordinated an event at Wood Green, Haringey.

Since 1990 the concepts of participative planning have matured under a variety of guises, such as 'planning for real' devised by Dr Tony Gibson,[7] Community Planning weekends[8] and the RIBA Design Days where teams of architects and local people brainstorm design solutions to neighbourhood issues.[9]

The action planning event, undertaken over a two or three day period, is intense, and preceded by months of careful planning if it is to be a success. The driving force for the event should come from within the community and all past expectations should be shelved. The best teams are non-hierarchical, cross-disciplinary with the minimum of pre-conceptions. Action planning events facilitated by the UDG and Bitc[9] have consisted of an invited team composed of a mixture of designers and property experts with other interests. The format is a period of listening – short (10 minutes) presentations of a cross-section of issues and interests; looking, time to walk and absorb the site; and, through drawings and diagrams, dimensioning the problem and establishing visions. Action planning can achieve objectives through the intensity and focus that would be hard to achieve by other means. Through the use of discussion and visualisation it can create a shared vision and a plan for action. However, action planning is not a substitute for the statutory planning framework. It is a valuable participatory process to help communities envision opportunities, agree goals and set milestones for action.

Conclusions

The danger of jumping to design solutions before needs have been properly formulated is that thinking becomes 'strait-jacketed' and solutions may be proposed in response to inappropriate questions. However, design options and 'references' can be valuable means to elicit lay expectations and short circuit arduous talk. Like 'reverse engineering' in automobile manufacturing, where previous products are analysed to identify features that work, and those that can be discarded, 'reverse briefing' might be equally helpful. Begin with design and work backwards.

Notes

1   Pena, W., Parshall, S. and Kelly, K., *Problem Seeking: An architectural programming primer*, AIA Press, Washington 1987.
2   *Workplace Envisioning, Participant's Guide*, Steelcase Inc., Grand Rapids 1995.
3   Bi-polar measures developed for Steelcase by Philip Stone, an organisational psychologist from Harvard University.
4   DEGW produced a pack of 54 image cards, January 1999. The image cards are designed to help clients communicate issues related to culture and design. The cards can be arranged into themes such as management style, work process and corporate image to facilitate briefing.
5   Wates, N., *Action Planning: How to use planning weekends and urban design action teams to improve your environment*, The Prince of Wales' Institute of Architecture, London 1996.
6   *Urban Design Quarterly* No. 49, January 1994 and No. 58, April 1996. Special issues on action planning.
7   Dr Toby Gibson's original concept of local groups working with flexible cardboard models and priority cards is now promoted by the Neighbourhood Initiatives Foundation, *A practical handbook for 'planning for real' consultation exercises*, Telford 1995.
8   Developed by John Thompson and the Urban Villages Forum (Poundbury and Bishopsgate).
9   Wood Green UDAT, *Cities don't just happen*, London, Borough of Hackney 1990. Business in the Community Burgess Park, Southwark Bitc 1993.
    Platting, Miles. and Ancoats, A., *Case for Collaboration Bitc*, Miles Platting Community Enterprises, Manchester 1995.

4   *Briefing for adaptable use*

*Susan Stuebing, The Twynstra Group of
Management Consultants*

Developing a brief for an unknown site, an undeveloped programme, and an extremely limited time frame is a challenge. When the client is a leader in one of the largest corporate enterprises in the world, and says, 'I give you my trust', the pressure is doubled. A project which was described to the team as 'limitless' in its possibilities was quickly understood to have real constraints and was very difficult to realise. This case study will discuss how the briefing process contributed to the successful delivery of a world-class professional development centre, which also resulted in an innovative model for real estate management.

The problem

Shell International's LEAP Programme is a prestigious professional development programme for top Shell executives from throughout the global organisation. In late 1996, coupled with a culture shift within the organisation, it was decided that LEAP needed a physical home or centre. This centre was to be both state-of-the-art and symbolic to participants. The centre was to send a message of the significance of the programme and be, in some respects, provocative.

The centre was to be located in the Netherlands. The LEAP programme activities in the new home were still under development, and the requirements were not fully decided. The most firm information for the project was that the centre must be open and operating by October 1998.

Less than one year before the date for operation, the director of the LEAP programme engaged the Twynstra Group to undertake the project. The project included the identification of a site, the brief and project management of the turn-key development.

Within a very tight schedule, the brief needed to be developed in spite of the absence of a site. The brief needed to be developed in such a way that it could be easily adapted and interpreted once the site was identified. Within this context, the brief by definition was required to be flexible.

The result of the project was an innovative arrangement between a hotel company and the LEAP programme. Rather than purchase or build new, the LEAP Programme agreed to enter into a leasing arrangement, in which the newly-constructed hotel (Holiday Inn – Scandic Crown) would operate as a hotel during the weekends, and as a professional development centre during the week. This innovative approach required re-addressing the brief to seek overlaps between the hotel function and the professional development function. 'Switchable' and flexible elements needed to be built into the design of the centre.

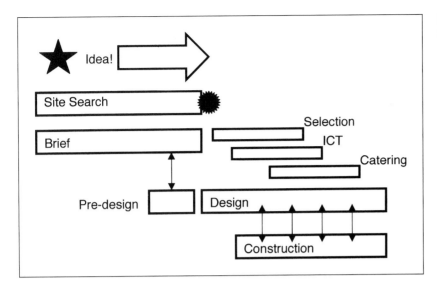

Figure 8.15: The project process.
Source: Twynstra Group

The brief

In this brief, 'flexibility' was the working process as well as a key requirement for the product. The result was a professional development centre for 60 to 80 participants with approximately 3500 net square metres of programme space and an additional 60–80 hotels rooms, support areas and recreational areas.

The brief was to set a tone for a fast track, demanding project to locate a suitable building and site, and to develop it into a world-class professional development centre. The resulting brief was broadly and visually described with graphics playing as large a role (if not greater) than descriptions and quantitative requirements. Its purpose was to form consensus with the client, who was developing his vision and had a very demanding agenda.

The brief included sections on the educational goals, building concept, building zones and IT scheme, as well as a section on catering and other operations. With these categories in mind, it should be clear that the brief was strategic and conceptual, speaking to the comprehensive vision of the building.

The final project would never have been delivered within the time constraints if the brief was not considered an interpretative document as opposed to a legal and binding one. In this way, the brief was to be a flexible document for a fast track and flexible project.

Self-fulfilling prophecy

In fact, the briefing process was not only the development of a document to construct or renovate a building, but the briefing process was a useful tool to test and clarify concepts for the overall Professional Development programme. Heavily relying on graphic images, photos and drawings, the briefing process both tested the clients concepts, and built a shared prophecy for the centre to come. The result was that this shared vision reinforced the acceptance of the final result as both client and consultant could clearly match the vision to the built environment.

The client and the managing partner for the project concurred that the resulting project met the descriptive brief by 90 per cent of their expectations. While many compromises had been made to realise the project, the participation in those decisions and the continuous re-adjustment and reflection on the intention of the brief, helped to contribute to this fulfilment.

Briefing process

The best method to develop the brief was a story-telling approach which was sometimes illustrated with architectural 'story-boards'. These discussions consisted of the client telling his vision or his story, and the project team telling the story back to the client with illustrations.

As the programme and its needs were still evolving, one method of developing a shared understanding was to run through 'walk throughs'. In this discussion, the briefing team 'walked' the client through the centre even though it had not been designed nor had a building even been selected. The walk-through allowed the details to begin to surface, and the client was quick to say which details were incorrect.

Ultimately the 'story' became four inter-related zones; The Activity Zone; Contemplative Zone; Social and Organisational Zone; and Service and Business Zone. These zones were not only different from one another in terms of space requirements, but also in terms of the ambience of the zone, its purpose, who would use the space, and the security required. Each zone was described in terms of use, size, adjacency and with schematic diagrams.

As the project required a 'design–build' approach, each of the zones was described in drawings in the brief. While a building had not yet been identified, much of the preliminary schematic design work was accomplished in advance and was in the brief. In the same way, the co-ordination between the professions began through the briefing process as well. Discussions with the information and communication technology professionals in the briefing process began the mapping out of a strategy for the design of the building.

As the client had a strong vision for what would make a successful centre, the briefing process was made easier. The client's vision stimulated the team's imagination with words such as 'empowerment', 'change' and 'leadership'. In this way, the team was motivated by the client to 'get it right' while key issues were itemised and agreed to by the client.

Consensus building

Briefs are often considered legal documents. While in this project, the brief was signed and approved as a formal document by the client, it served a perhaps more important role as a communication device. It was also an important tool in a stressful site selection process, and it served as a consensus building device. The brief also fast-tracked the design process.

The brief offers an almost artistic and architectural view which could be used for interpretation in the making of the building. The boundaries of the brief were a series of stress points which helped to make the client's intentions clear and to control the project which had little or no limitations other than to make the timetable.

Site search

At the same time as the brief was developed, a confidential and pressured search was underway to identify an appropriate site. The site search was very broad within a limited geographic area (to be within one hour from an international airport). Two possible scenarios were considered:

1. Find a site appropriate for a long term home for the centre;
2. Find a site which would be appropriate for a temporary location and continue to seek a permanent home for the centre.

The site could also potentially share with another organisation, requiring functional flexibility for the complex.

More than 48 sites were investigated. In the end, four sites were seriously considered. These included; a dilapidated castle (Middle Ages); an inner-city landmark building (twentieth century); a private boys' school; and a newly-constructed hotel (1997–8). Obviously this broad range of possibilities tested the flexibility of the brief.

With less then seven months until the centre was to open its first events, the hotel was chosen for a number of reasons. First, the hotel was assessed to require the least renovation. Secondly, the hotel met several criteria, including an excellent location in a remote National Forest that was also less than an hour from Schipol, Amsterdam's International Airport. Thirdly, and as important, the hotel offered many types of spaces which were described in the brief. These included a large circular dining room and a semi-circular dance room, and the required number of hotel rooms to house the participants in the programme. Perhaps less important, but also a contributing factor, was the fact that the hotel developers had constructed a small, nine-hole golf course which offered added value to meet the centre's brief for a 'reflection zone'.

The events which took place in negotiation for the hotel could not have been predicted by anyone working on the brief or the overall team. An agreement was reached for a mixed-use arrangement. The mixed-use could actually be phrased as 'switched-use', as the owner of the hotel and the client for the Learning Development centre agreed to switch the use of the building complex from professional development centre to hotel every weekend. This resulted in several benefits to the owner and to the client, including maintaining a staff year-round, additional client revenues, and the building of a long-term reputation for the hotel owner.

Realisation

With less than seven months to go, following the signing of the contract for the site, the brief took on a conceptual purpose during its realisation. Naturally, compromises were required to meet the deadline. However, the brief played an important role for the team to defend, maintaining the principles of the brief and to accept compromises.

Perhaps the largest compromise was driven by the requirement to be able to 'switch' the building from development centre to hotel. This aspect was completely unforeseen in the brief and required re-interpreting the brief to meet this requirement. Intriguing solutions to signage, lighting, access and even technology were positive results.

The increase of mobile and other non-fixed solutions made meeting the overall intention of the brief more difficult. While some of these solutions were argued against by members of the team, the compromises were nearly always argued for by the client.

The 'engagement arena' is the best example of how a vision described in the brief was interpreted and maintained in the realisation of the project. While the 'arena' was to be a full circular theatre with a long processioned approach, the realisation was a semi-circle with a surrounding processional arc. While the shape and organisation of the 'arena' had changed due to the limitation of the building footprint, the overall concept and theme of the space was maintained in the design. This result, and the results in other spaces such as the 'zen café' must be attributed to the architect.

Trusting relationships

In a situation like this, the personal commitment of the team worked as a form of quality assurance for the project, which became better understood by the client's phrase, 'I give you my trust'. With this phrase, the client assigned to each of the team members a professional duty to do their best. The status of the project underscored this assignment.

Nevertheless a tension between the budget (assigned by the partner in charge), the time-frame budget (more critical than the financial budget in many respects) and the integrity of the brief existed to the completion of the project. The defence and final equilibrium of these elements resulted in the successful project.

In particular, the architect, Terry Gunnery from DEGW, played a key role in quality assurance for the project. With a more conceptual brief, and in a fast-tracked project such as this, the quality of the project is highly reliant on the professional in charge as the client in this project clearly indicated.

The role of the brief was ultimately to set the stage for interpretation and evolution. It was also an important communication device to build consensus within the team and to build support for the project within the larger client organisation.

In retrospect, one could say that this is a fortunate story, and in fact it is. However, it is interesting to note that this is also a story about achieving something that, by definition, appeared impossible. Not only is the project a success, but it is also an interesting innovative model for others to consider.

5   *Briefing with the market in mind*

Bluewater: using research to define the brief

Alastair Blyth

Introduction

Many clients construct buildings within the context of an existing business. Bluewater, in Kent, is different. When the international developer Lend Lease arrived, there was no existing business, there was just a disused chalk quarry, some market potential for a retail centre and a planning consent for a scheme that had fallen prey to the recession of the early 1990s.

Lend Lease wanted to develop a new type of retail destination. To do that it needed to define the nature of the business by understanding the needs and values of the shoppers and retailers. In the beginning Lend Lease were not entirely sure what this new concept would consist of, let alone what the built artifact was to be that would serve it.

Lend Lease set out to define the brief for the business which would inform the buildings. It is a good example of the holistic nature of the briefing process which encompasses both organisation and buildings, and the interactions between the two.

Research was to form the bedrock of the briefing process; it would help define what Bluewater needed to be as a 'retail and leisure destination', and encapsulate the sense of place. However, the research did more than just define a business brand, it helped identify those elements that are critical in making the business work – for example car parking, store layouts and crèche facilities. The research also underpinned design decisions about major elements like the roof, as well as smaller, but no less important elements, like the balustrades.

The Lend Lease corporation is an Australian-based international property and financial services group with considerable retail and commercial experience. To successfully complete a construction project that would have and end value in excess of £1 bn and provide 1.5 million ft^2 (150 000 m^2) of retail space for 300 shops, the developer needed to create a unifying culture and a committed team. The research behind the positioning and branding of the business was crucial. What also became important was that the values and ethos of Bluewater would be reflected in the project team culture as it developed both business and building.

Defining the case for Bluewater

There are four key elements that are needed for a retail destination: the market, infrastructure, retailers and the retail 'enhancers' – those elements that give the destination a distinct point of difference from the competition. For Bluewater to work as a business, it would have to attract and retain potential shoppers who might find it as easy to travel to central London or go to other out-of-town retail centres.

Lend Lease, who had only recently set up an office in the UK, began working on the project in 1994. A previous developer had obtained planning consent for a retail centre in 1990, which had been shelved due to the recession.

Before deciding to develop the site, Lend Lease carried out preliminary research to identify the market. This confirmed that there was a market potential; however, the developer did not want to build just another 'shopping centre'. Lend Lease saw the opportunity to create the most dominant retail development in Europe, by establishing a new concept for shopping as an advance on traditional retail centres.

The initial strategy was to use the knowledge that had already been gained by the previous proposals. First actions were to bring in the letting agents and designers Benoy and with them came data about the retail market and the site. Lend Lease also canvassed the views of the retailers and city institutions about investment.

Lend Lease also began to assemble a 'core team' which consisted of a design representative, retail representative, and development and project management representative to create and champion the vision for Bluewater.

Research behind the brief

While the demographic research carried out to establish the viability of the site was useful in identifying the number of people, the catchment area, how far people would have to travel to Bluewater and their social status, earning and spending power, it gave no information on what values these people held and

Figure 8.16: Aerial photo of Bluewater.
Source: Lend Lease

how they made a decision to go shopping on any particular day. It was important to identify why people might decide to go to Bluewater as opposed to another shopping centre, and what other activities shopping at Bluewater might have to compete with.

Lend Lease found that while the more traditional market research companies could provide demographic data, they had little experience in providing the more qualitative information that was needed. It therefore approached an advertising agency whose experience was in putting together product advertising campaigns. However, the brief to this agency was to define what characteristics Bluewater would require to meet the needs of the people within one hour's drive. The reverse of the normal approach which is to take a known product and through research define the characteristics and catchment of the market.

Initial research used the Target Group Index (TGI), a quantitative research tool used by communications and marketing groups to establish brand values and attitudes. The TGI, a national and regularly updated database, gave a 'psychographic' profile of the principal catchment area and covered lifestyles, values, attitudes and social habits. It enabled the market to be defined in a way which represented life-style rather than social status. The data from this research was verified through a programme of in-depth focus groups throughout the development of the project. A range of techniques were used in these groups, which varied from displaying images to exploring metaphors as well as examining prototypes, and this enabled ideas to be tested and retested throughout the project. At all stages, members of the project teams also attended.

The focus groups were structured around the different cluster groups in the TGI. For example, one was described as the 'County Classic' who would be more interested in exclusive designer clothes and gourmet food shops. The others were defined as 'club executives,' 'young fashionables' and 'sporting 30s'. Whilst giving invaluable insights into the market, Lend Lease recognised that classifications like this can be dangerous if taken too literally because no one fits any particular group exactly.

The focus groups were an effective way of tackling intangible issues which are difficult to define empirically. For example, a balustrade detail had to be altered because it looked unsafe and a shiny floor finish changed due to perceptions of danger. Particular attention was paid to tactile elements by inviting people to see and touch materials, products and prototypes. The groups also were used to tease out issues of safety and security, and led to the concept of creating Bluewater as a 'safe house' with its own dedicated police station.

Most people could identify what they disliked but found it hard to pinpoint why they liked something. For example, people in one cluster group disliked a particular out-of-town shopping centre but liked a local town centre. However, they could not easily identify *why* they liked the town centre.

Although responding positively to a list of dislikes is difficult, the focus group research did enable the design team to see the project from different perspectives and enabled them to test the implications of their thinking. Design concepts were tested at further focus group meetings.

The research showed that the people spending the money are not always the ones who decide to shop. In a family it may be the children who decide to go to the shops while it is the parents who spend the money. This finding informed the idea that visitors should be thought of as guests rather than customers, and that Bluewater should concentrate on hospitality rather than merely customer service. It also suggested that while an area would need to attract a particular group of people it should not be offensive to others, so a grandmother should not feel uncomfortable shopping with a teenage grand-daughter.

The research and focus groups informed a number of different types of evolving 'brief'. Some examples are:

- car park brief (see Box);
- children's brief which covered facilities for children, such as crèches;
- elderly people's brief which covered mobility around the site and access to it;
- mood brief which covered the senses and how to blend light and sound;
- customer brief which covered issues of concern to customers generally, such as safety;
- retailers' brief which set out what was expected of the retail fit out and how this process would be managed by the Bluewater construction team.

DEFINING THE CAR PARK BRIEF

The research identified car parking as a critical issue which influenced shoppers' perceptions about the retail environment. To identify the major issues, Lend Lease decided to test shoppers' reactions to other car parks by video recording from inside their cars. The aim was to 'get into the minds of the shoppers as they used the car parks'.

Among the issues identified, safety was a key issue in terms of both actual safety risk and a person's perception of the risk which was often raised by 'squealing tyres', 'banging doors to fire escapes' and 'dull lighting'.

The customer brief for the car parking identified the following important issues:

* no ramps to come up within the structural frame because that is where people walk;
* improving design of lifts and stairs, and quality of access;
* walking up and down fire escape stairs;
* consistency of light levels, an avoidance of duct work hanging down;
* sprinkler pipes and duct work hanging down from ceilings is visually unpleasant;
* parking bay widths too small and often collided with columns making it difficult to park, as well as get in and out the car;
* queues in multi-storey car parks as well as 'spiralling' down the car park to get out.

The response to this brief was to locate the ramps and fire escape stairs at the edge of the structure. Wider parking bays were provided, cars are loaded into the car park from the front. To reduce the shoppers' perception that they are in a multi-storey car park, there are separate ramps on and off each level.

Figure 8.17: Entrance to decked car park.
Source: Lend Lease

Layout of Bluewater

The different clusters of shoppers who might go to Bluewater, and identified during the research, are reflected in the layout of the building.

The building has three distinctive shopping zones. The aim was to create areas reflecting three different styles, which would enable it to attract a wide mix of customers. The West side is for those attracted to designer names, while the East side is for every member of the family, and the South side is for those interested in contemporary culture. Each area consists of a retail zone and a 'village' with bars, cafés and other leisure activities. The West village is designed to reflect café society life with an eye for exclusivity. The East village is for a younger audience and includes playgrounds and crèches with family areas and restaurants. The South village has a media and entertainment centre with a multiplex cinema and spaces for fashion shows, concerts and exhibitions.

The building is surrounded by lakes and planted woodlands. The car parks are arranged so that each level of the multi-deck car parks are accessed via an individual ramp.

Using a culture to manage the project

The research and branding of Bluewater enabled the project team to create a Bluewater culture. This was an important mechanism for controlling the project and was an important lesson. On a project of this scale, one person cannot control every small detail. However, by creating the culture and sense of what the values are, it was possible to get staff buy-in so that those working on various aspects of the project would approach their tasks in the same way. The aim was to get the whole team, 400 designers and engineers, and 500 construction staff, to understand the context and values in the project. This was done through regular meetings, workshops and presentations with staff.

Critical success factors

The only way to tell whether a project has been a success is to define early on how that success will be judged and the sort of measures that will be used to judge it. The success of Bluewater will be judged against a range of measures, some quantitative, others qualitative. When defining the project and business the Bluewater team identified those areas critical to its success. They also realised that there would be different expectations of success from the different stakeholder interests in the project:

- Hermes 10 per cent.

Shareholder investment:

- Prudential invested 35 per cent;
- Limited Partnership 25 per cent;
- Lend Lease.

Other measures of stakeholder success are:

- customer-loyalty to Bluewater brand;
- community acceptance by local authorities;
- retailers can be measured against respective portfolios;
- employment – people wanting to be employed at Bluewater;
- legacy of people working on the project. For example, whether people have developed different ways of working which can be used elsewhere.

Other measures might include security and perhaps a reduction in the number of incidents, the growth in the number of shoppers and how far they have travelled, as well as interest shown by retailers not yet at Bluewater.

Conclusion

In most building projects the business has already been defined. Here was an opportunity to develop both together. The research enabled the developer to articulate a view of what the business should be, the type of place it should happen in and how to get there.

This was not a clean sheet of paper; there were already many constraints, primarily the location and site as well as the constraints of practicalities such as funding.

Notes

1   Construction management: Bluewater Construction Management team (Lend Lease Projects and Bovis).
2   Client: Lend Lease Global Investments.
3   Developer and project manager: Lend Lease Projects.
4   Concept design: Eric Kuhne and Associates.
5   Principal Architect: Benoy.

6   *Briefing with innovation in mind*

Notley Green Primary School

Alastair Blyth

Most projects offer the chance of innovation, although relatively few make it an up-front condition of the brief. Innovation is often seen as dangerous, it implies something new and untried, and therefore likely to go wrong. In its brief for a Primary School, Essex County Council (ECC) made innovation a principle component. It wanted to explore the notion of 'sustainability' and use the project to develop ideas that it might be able to adapt and use on later schools and other projects. The client was looking for both innovative technology and processes. Whether the 'idea transfer' has been wholly successful can only be judged several years down the line when other projects have been built. However, what Essex has been able to learn from is the process, which for the local authority has been innovative by:

- appointing a dedicated design team to include artists, all of whom start work on the project from the beginning;
- using the project as a path finder;
- using a competition as a way of selecting the team.

Design team competition

ECC teamed up with the Design Council in 1997 to organise a competition to find an innovative team to design a 180-place 'sustainable' primary school catering for children from 5 to 11 years old. ECC had already done considerable work on low energy and passive solar schools as well as inter-disciplinary team working. The Design Council, the UK's national authority on design, works with a range of organisations to develop new techniques and tools – which inspire action and debate on the effective use of good design. The Design Council had wanted to use a 'live example' as a model to produce a learning framework for use in teaching architects and other designers.

The competition brief required competitors to form an integrated team of architect, artist, engineer, educational expert, landscape design and cost consultant. Teams were offered a maximum of ten A4 pages on which to present – however they wished – a compelling argument as to why they should be chosen. From the 91 submissions, six were selected for interview. Interviews were an hour long and involved each team giving a short presentation followed by a question and answer session. The panel of interviewers was drawn from both inside and outside the County Council. They were interested in how well the team behaved like a team as well as commitment to the ethos of the project. The team that eventually won was led by architects Allford Hall Monaghan Morris.

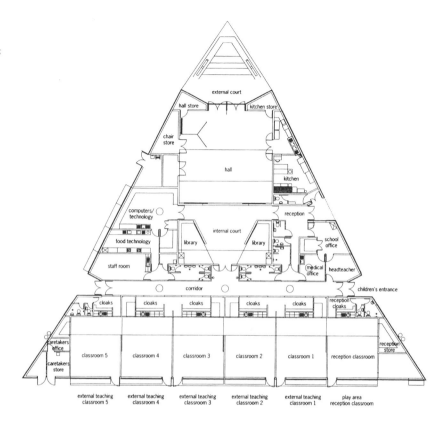

The brief

Essex has built over 500 schools and so knows a thing or two about them. Over the years it has developed a standard primary school briefing package which includes detailed room datasheets, and this is the information it gave to the design team as the brief. The building was to be 1080 m^2 and to be built to a budget of £1.2 million. It would be the first phase of what was envisaged as an eventual 360-place school. Whilst the team was not to design the second phase, it had to show that it was possible to add a second phase to its design. This would be the first of the County's primary schools to include a dedicated space for teaching technology. Otherwise, the school would have six class bases, a food technology base, a hall and administrative spaces for the staff. Externally, there would be soft and hard play areas. The aim was that the environment would also become a teaching tool.

The client made it clear that the design team could challenge the brief and that the standards set out in it was a body of knowledge based on its experience. Essex saw the notion of sustainability as being a logical progression from earlier projects involving low energy and passive solar design. It also wanted to explore what 'sustainability' meant for them in their context. The design team was therefore asked to explore implications of sustainability that could be replicated. However, the key constraint of the budget would remain, although some money would be found for some research by the team.

The school was to be built as part of the development of a new village at Great Notley where 2000 homes were being provided on a green field site.

Innovations

There were innovations at different levels of the project. Here innovation is taken to mean something that is new for the client or context rather than something that no one has done before.

In developing the model brief for the County's primary schools, the education officers had been liaising with the head teachers of the existing schools. This is a continuous process and, as in this case, can lead to changing requirements for schools.

Like many organisations, schools are having to respond to the impact of information and communications technology (ICT). This is both in terms of teaching children how to use computers but also as a means of delivering part of the education curriculum. A number of schools had developed dedicated class bases for teaching the subject and the feedback to the education client in the authority was that such class bases should be provided in the model brief. Following this consultation, the client questioned the use and value of other spaces such as the 'amenity area' provided by the current brief and decided that there would be a greater benefit in taking this allocation and reconfiguring some of the support spaces to provide a dedicated art and technology base. This enabled the client to keep to within its space budget but respond to a changing context. The school at Great Notley is the first new Essex school to have this facility built into it.

The running of a design team competition was, for the education client, an innovation, although in itself not a novel idea. Like many similar authorities in the UK, much of the design work is carried out by its own consultants. However, it can procure the design services for a small proportion of work from external consultants. But it tends to do this using separate appointments for each member of the team. The aim was to use external consultants who could provide a new perspective and challenge its current thinking.

Part of the design team appointment involved handing over the total fee to be subdivided as the team, rather than by the client, saw fit. The constraint was that the total fees to be paid by ECC would be the same as for any similar project. The aim was to enable the design team to make the decision about a fair split rather than basing it on a percentage of the construction cost.

The constituents of the team was unusual in so far as artists were included from the beginning. Often, if artists are to be involved at all, they would come in later to design a piece of 'art'. Here the idea was to get a more 'strategic' input into the early phases of the design. Artists would provide different perspectives on the design issues.

Not only were elements of the process innovative, but so too were elements of the design.

Partly in response to the shape of the site, but also in response to the need for energy efficiency and to make best use of a very tight budget, the building is a triangular shape. The main class bases are arranged along the southern side with the hall in the northern apex and administrative areas on the sides. At one stage during the design, an open courtyard had been placed in the centre of the building. Although this helped the natural ventilation strategy, the client was concerned that in the future it might be covered over by a head teacher looking for more classroom space. The design team turned this idea onto its head. Instead, they created an internal courtyard which can perform several functions. First it is part of the circulation route through the school, it could be used as an extension to the school hall space for some events and it could be used as an extra teaching space.

Construction

Developing the notion of sustainability within the constraints of a budget that the client has to work to, has meant balancing conflicting interests of site and cost with maximum energy efficiency and resource availability. The aim of the project is to demonstrate how far one can go, although Essex will use these ideas as a springboard for further development.

There were technical innovations too. The design team decided to use a timber framed breathing wall. Also, the timber has generally not been treated with preservatives following advice from the Timber Research and Development Association.

An initial audit of sustainable materials was carried out with materials being selected using criteria of low embodied energy, renewable resource and recycling, both in terms of materials used being made from recycled products but also their capability of being recycled. The products used include marmolium, recycled newspaper for insulating recycled plastic products for work surfaces, and recycled tyres for entrance mats.

Whilst the design team has tried to specify home-grown products, it has found that some materials needed to be sourced abroad. This will continue to happen until the UK market for sustainable products improves.

Much of the landscaping is to be treated as meadow with the contractor's work on site to be restricted to a small area so as to reduce site disturbance to the site. To reduce the amount of material carted off the site, the soil removed to make way for foundations will be used to re-grade other areas.

Technologies explored

The design team explored the use of archetypal 'sustainable' features but found them to be inappropriate in this context.

Three options for PV were studied using 70, 35 and 10 m^2 of panels. However, the payback for each was over 200 years. Also considerable areas of photovoltaic panels would be needed to make a real difference to the operating performance of the building. Whilst a computer could be run from 2 m^2 of PV panels, the system could generate this only for 1–2 hours per day in winter and 4–5 hours per day in summer.

The effective use of Biomass for space and water heating would need to be near a source of fuel to reduce the environmental impact of transport. No such source is near Great Notley, although there is potential for growing and harvesting willow on the site. However, the main drawback is the intensity of maintenance. The cost of employing someone to stoke the boiler daily was considered to be disproportionate to the energy saved.

Solar power for heating and water would come into its own during July and August just when the school's demand would be very low. The use of flat plate collectors and evacuated tube collectors were explored. However, the payback would be 30 years and this was considered excessive.

Three options for the use of a wind turbine were considered. Apart from cost, the appearance and noise generated by the turbine makes it difficult to use this technology near housing. A turbine could be sized to meet the winter consumption over 24 hours. A turbine with a rated output of 21.5 kW would be required. This would contribute 70 per cent to the annual demand for the school which is likely to be 33–34 000 kWh. However, the size of the plant (a 25 m high mast; 10 m diameter rotor; and associated battery bank with control house) would have significant planning implications. The capital cost of this would be £60 000.

The second option was for a turbine to meet a specific load, e.g. lighting. The capital cost would be £17 000 per unit.

The third option was to install a demonstration machine which would cost between £5–10 000, although it would only contribute 3–6 per cent contribution to the energy requirement of the building.

Finding the right head teacher

For it to stand a chance of success, the ethos of the sustainable school had to be accepted by the head teacher. To find the right head, ECC decided to involve the design team in the preparation of the advertisement and in putting together the pack that it would send out to respondents. Normally, the design team would not get involved in this type of administrative function. But ECC believes that there are benefits in doing this such as enabling the design team to feel that their role has been more than just to provide a building. Again, including different types of people in the recruitment process provided a different perspective although it was not possible to follow this through into the selection process itself.

Creating the environment for innovation

Being innovative within any large, diverse organisation is a challenge. The culture in such organisations tends to default to doing what it has done before, with individuals often being unable to shift the thinking of the whole. The creative nature of design is one way to challenge current thinking but there do seem to be certain ingredients that are crucial to the success of this.

The first key is a dedicated client. At Essex the client is a complex being. It is split between different departments of the organisation but, principally, there are two components. The education client who needs the building, and the property client who is responsible for managing the procurement. The complexity of the project was increased by the involvement of the developer of the village with whom there had to be much liaison over the site and services to it, as well as the design of the building. There was also much work to be done liaising with other local authority agencies such as the highways department. In addition, it was important that a client representative 'held the vision' and was able to persuade others inside and outside to follow it.

Being clear at the beginning about what was wanted in terms of innovation was essential. Rather than restrict the design team to the client's own preconceptions about what sustainability was, it was left open to the design team to explore it within the context of the local authority.

To get everyone to 'buy into the vision' meant extensive consultation. There are several valuable lessons reinforced by this project that are worth reflection. Consultation takes time and unless it is made a priority in a project, especially one with a tight budget, it may be relegated. The design team and client spent a good deal of time in not just attending consultation meetings but also on preparing for them. The amount of consultation required, especially with the local community, and the developer, may have been underestimated by the design team. This has led to some concern about the amount of resources being committed to it.

Consultation must begin before committing a design to paper, however tentative, and it should make life easier in negotiations with planners and developers, which is why they were involved in this particular project in setting a planning brief prior to the design team being commissioned. There is the worry for designers, however, that they will be forced down a particular route before they have had the chance to test other solutions.

Consultation is not just presentation, it is also about listening, so that people feel involved in the development of the idea. For many designers, the difficulty may be that carrying out consultation in the abstract, and perhaps with non-designers, is less attractive and possibly more threatening than their more normal form of presentation to clients. It may not be easy but this project has proved that increased consultation can be worthwhile, although there are probably still a number of others who feel that they too should have been consulted. Lessons have to be learned, however, about the level and timings of such consultations and who to involve.

To carry out the necessary research to establish the value of other forms of technology meant that extra money had to be found. ECC was able to offer money from another budget. However, this leads to the broader question of whether an 'innovative' project should receive considerable extra funds. The client would argue that it wanted a project that would give ideas that it could adapt for other projects and that, for it to be able to do this; the budgetry constraint must be similar, otherwise it could never afford to use the ideas elsewhere. The design team argues that to develop new ideas requires more investigative time and the benefit is that for future projects that work has been done and so does not need to be paid for in future. There are merits in both arguments. But this scheme does show how far one can get within the tight constraints of a public sector client.

Clearly, the model brief performs a useful role in that it summarises the client's experience. However, to enable any innovation to happen, as in this case, it was important to enable the team to challenge the brief. Model briefs can be very prescriptive, and with innovation one needs to get away from that to some extent.

Learning the lessons

For Essex the development of its schools programme relies on learning from experience. ECC intends to monitor the performance of the building during occupation and carry out a post occupancy evaluation in order to assess what ideas incorporated into the building can be used elsewhere. The design process is being written up by the Design Council in the form of a model which will be widely distributed around the design professions and construction industry.

Already the client is considering how to run a similar type of project for a future school with the intention of building on the lessons learned from this.

Conclusions

The creative design environment is an important element of the briefing process for developing innovation. However, innovation on most projects relates to the context and offers challenges to a client's way of thinking, which may be hard to resolve. Clearly, the client has to state clearly in the beginning where it is expecting the innovation to occur and what it hopes to get out of it. This not only focuses the project but enables others involved to buy into the ideas.

Notes

1   Client: Essex County Council.
2   Project monitoring: Design Council.
3   Architect: Allford Hall Monaghan Morris.
4   Structural Engineer: Atelier One.
5   Services Engineer: Atelier Ten.
6   Quantity Surveyor: The Cook and Butler Partnership.
7   Planning Supervisor: Appleyard and Trew.
8   Landscape Architect: Jonathon Watkins Landscapes.
9   Artists: Hartley and Kovats.
10 Contractor: Jackson Building Ltd.

7   *Briefing the narrative*

Christine Hanway

DEGW's exhibitions team present general conclusions for briefing exhibitions. Here they are drawing on their experience of both undertaking the concept and detailed design and implementation of the permanent Holocaust exhibition at the Imperial War Museum, London, and working with Daniel Libeskind on proposals to the Museum of Twentieth Century Conflict, Imperial War Museum of the North.

Introduction

The identity of a museum is defined through the exhibits the museum chooses to present. How a museum selects and displays these exhibits is intrinsic to its public voice, and the briefing process, therefore, can have an enormous influence on shaping a museum's image of itself.

Every step of briefing an exhibit, from the story to the final design, is based on a trust that develops through the briefing process between the client and the designer. The relationship between the two is mutually dependent, and it is imperative that this is recognised by both parties for the project to succeed on any level.

Briefing is an organic process and inherent in this is the idea that no briefing ever proceeds according to plan. When immersed in the briefing process, however, the main focus can easily become obscured and often lost. The designer's most critical role is to take on the responsibility of maintaining clarity in the project through confident, informed, and flexible briefing.

This case study explores the measures that flexible briefing can bring to the realities of the briefing process for a very specific and the most critical part of a museum – the exhibition making.

The story

Museums span a broad spectrum that includes art, science, natural history, sociology, and history. They each come with their own problems and complexities that require a rigorous briefing process in order to distil the greatest issues at hand. The common thread of all of them, however, is that they tell stories in space to reach their audience.

Designing an exhibit has its own particular complexities where communicating the story becomes the driving force behind all design decisions. Getting the story right is key, and requires an involved process of extraction, clarification, and distillation. As part of the briefing, the designer must enable the client to recognise the importance of the 'story' in determining the exhibit.

Fixing the story is highly dependent on the available space and, once again proper briefing becomes critical to the client's understanding of the given spatial constraints and how the story they want to tell might fit within the space. The better the client's understanding of the spatial aspect of an exhibit, the better they can do their own job in terms of culling and editing the story they want to tell.

Fixing the story and understanding the space, however, is only half the battle in the design of an exhibit. Communicating the story and pacing its delivery within the space is the second half of the battle. The designer has the difficult job of conveying to the client the complexities of integrating various modes of delivering the story – graphics, artefacts, AV, and computer interactives – to achieve the client's objective.

The project champion

Designing an exhibit is similar in many ways to creating a film – the articulation of an intellectual idea developed through a sophisticated production process. Both require a great deal of creativity and vision on the one hand, and a serious organisational and co-ordination effort on the other. In co-ordinating so many different and disparate pieces to make one whole, a project champion is a prerequisite. This is the person who claims ownership of the project. Determining who the actual project champion should be is not always obvious considering the regular conflict between creation and production.

Typically, the producer of a film is the film's project champion. This person is responsible for the film being finished on time and on budget. Closely linked to the producer is the director who has the creative responsibility for the film. Various aspects of the project champion role are often shared or split between the two. The relationship is worked out through the specific circumstances of a particular project. The key thing to note is that the director and producer are on the same team.

In exhibition making, if the museum or the client is the producer, the designer is the director. While the client may recognise their role in developing the vision, they have enlisted the expertise of the designer to make the vision come alive in three dimensions and have to, thus, share and entrust their vision to the designer. Determining the project champion is even less obvious in exhibition making, as the producer and the director are not on the same team. Instead, the client and designer have a contractual relationship that inhibits the more facile transference of the project champion role between producer and director that exists in film-making, and this can often result in a tense and tenuous relationship.

A mutually dependent relationship

Briefing, in its highest and most productive form, is based on a reciprocal relationship between the designer and the client, as the two become mutually dependent on each other. Neither can get very far in developing the project without the other. In the case of exhibitions, this mutual dependency is further exaggerated as the designer cannot even begin to second-guess the story the museum wants to tell. In hiring a designer for a building or interior space, the client hires a professional because he or she has experience in designing other buildings or spaces of the same nature. The client looks to the designer to create the story.

When a museum hires a designer to design an exhibit, they have hired a professional designer who has experience in design but not with their particular story. It is the client's responsibility to create the story.

However, like many organisations, museum clients are complex bodies which often need to resolve internal conflicts. A common organisational conflict in museums, which can impact greatly on the briefing process, is the one between the curatorial department and the production department.

On the curatorial side, the main priority is the accuracy of the story that is being told while on the production side, the priorities centre around practical issues: visitor turnout, communication, spatial concerns, wear and tear, ease of maintenance and accessibility, and ultimately budget.

The conflicts that arise between the two often present a dilemma. One arm of the client attempts to work toward budget and schedule but the other arm of the client is reluctant to commit to anything, prefers to keep its options open and wait for one more artefact that will tell the story better or one new discovery that will tell the story more accurately.

The conflict at large becomes one of resolving the different attitudes toward time and schedule, which ultimately impacts on the budget. From the point of view of construction and getting something built, a designer's schedule is filled with peaks and valleys. The designer is always working toward the next deadline, with the opening of the exhibit as the culminating peak and the final valley of finishing the job and walking away from it. To the museum, however, the opening of an exhibit is merely a blip on the continuum of what has probably been, and will continue to be, years of work on a certain subject matter. The significance of a deadline is not as vital to the museum.

Flexible briefing

Through briefing, the client and designer must come to an understanding and trust about each other's needs. The information passing and digesting between the two needs to be open minded and constructive. Designers must be aware of the problems or potential problems the process faces and must design and redesign their briefing strategies constantly and appropriately.

Getting the story right is difficult and futile if the operational issues are not resolved. Workshops are probably the most effective way for the client to recognise the potential conflicts within the organisation. If the project is without a champion, a workshop can highlight the problem and compel the client to find one. While workshops at the beginning of the project can help to overcome these problems, the client must be open and willing to go with the results.

If not, devising strategies to work within the internal conflicts of the organisation become an ongoing part of the briefing process. If a project champion is not found, it becomes even more difficult for the client to recognise the mutually dependent relationship. A very good example of this occurs when working out an approval process. As discussed previously, while the curator wants to retain ultimate flexibility, the head of production, ever mindful of budget and schedule, would like as many fixes as possible. A carefully designed approval process can give the curator the flexibility or adaptability he requires at the same time as giving the head of production the fixes in the project that he needs. This approval process must take into account the concept of 'last responsible moment'.

The production of an exhibit is the fusion of various processes of which the construction process is only one. The writing of the script, the design of the showcases, the production of the audio-visual, and the design and production of the graphics are all examples of the elements which combine to make one product. The construction process takes precedence, however, because it is the least flexible in terms of schedule and budget. The approval process must prioritise the decisions required from the client with regard to maintaining progress on the construction programme, and more importantly, the client must be made aware of how crucial his timely decisions are to the schedule and budget.

The key to briefing museums for exhibits, however, is the strategic use of models in each phase. A model is a universal tool when attempting to get people to understand space, especially the complexities involved with telling a story in space. The model's main function is to enable the approval process as it leaves so little open to interpretation.

The appropriate scale of the model for the various phases is an important consideration. During the concept design phase, a model at 1:100 is useful to determine the design strategy for creating the space to support the story. The level of detail at this stage is a very broad stroke with a general indication of key architectural elements like stairs, level changes, and materials.

After this is approved, a 1:50 model during scheme design allows everyone to agree on the key fixes of the story within the space. The model also becomes a helpful briefing tool for consultants, who are brought on at this stage, i.e., AV, graphics. The level of detail increases appropriately to indicate how the space further supports the story. At this point the designer and consultants work very closely with the client to determine the priorities within the story and how these priorities are to be articulated within the space. This is where the client first begins to have a feel for how much space there is to tell the story.

Finally, at the detail design phase, a 1:10 model is crucial to the client's understanding of his vision that is to be built. This is the model, which plots the entire exhibit in space: the story, the AV, the graphics, and the artefacts are all integrated into a 'gesamptkunstwerk'.

The detail indicated at this phase is the next best thing to getting it built. It is only through a model at this scale that the client can see and understand how something as subtle as a material change can change the entire nature of the space and character of the story. It is also only at this scale where the client can see how the story is fully integrated into the space and how the AV, graphics, text, showcases, and artefacts are woven together. And finally, on a purely functional level, this is the scale where the client can actually see how much physical space they have for the text and artefacts and enables them to proceed with their own editing process.

If one is to take the position that briefing carries on throughout the project, then the 1:10 scale model becomes a very helpful briefing tool for the

Figures 8.19, 8.20: Using different scaled models to refine the detail. Figure 8.19 scale is 1:100; Figure 8.20 scale is 1:10.
Source: Andrew Putler

next stage, construction – especially a design/build construction process. The model not only helps the contractor and quantity surveyor prepare their costings, but it is also an immense help to the contractor in preparing his rod drawings.

Conclusions

To design an exhibition is to design a total experience. As in all design, briefing is a critical and powerful tool if used effectively. The more you get right at the beginning, the more clear and focused the design is at the end. This is especially true in exhibitions where one wants the visitor to leave the exhibit with the story indelibly marked in his experience.

8   Briefing for the changing workplace

Using a process architecture to transform the work environment

Turid Horgen

Introduction

The nature of work is changing, due to technological innovation, global competition, and structural social and political change on a large scale. But this process of change is continuous and there is constant pressure on the workplace to undergo change and reinvent itself, but at the same time to continue to perform.

In this new and unfamiliar environment, workplace professionals, business managers, and end-users need to be able to handle uncertainty and anxiety in their effort to reshape the modern enterprise and improve the productivity of both human and workplace resources. The instability that is so characteristic of the modern organisation requires a combination of skills in design and change management.

Our research suggests that transforming the workplace supports the transformation of work itself. Engaging the people who hold the local knowledge of the work in a joint process of design inquiry will have a spill-over effect on the work practice and sometimes radically change the workplace culture. This interplay between the workplace and work processes is illustrated by a case study which looks at the transformation of research laboratories for Xerox R&D.

Process Architecture

The case study introduces an approach to creating workplaces, called 'Process Architecture', that facilitates the task of transforming stereotypical workplaces and outdated business strategies. The principles central to the framework of Process Architecture are:

1. The dynamically coherent workplace and the uneven development of workplace and work processes. Four interdependent dimensions of the work environment – spatial, organisational, technological, and financial – constitute the workplace. They exist in a dynamic relationship with one another: a change in one demands change in others (Figure 8.21).
2. The Design Game of powers, interests, and freedoms. Workplace-making is a political process and is carried out by people who hold interests in the product of design, and in its process as well. The setting for design becomes an arena of contention, and actors become players in win/lose games that come to be 'draped over' the existing structure of rules and roles.

Figure 8.21: Four interdependent dimensions of the work environment. A change in one demands a change in the other. *Excellence by Design*, Horgen, © 1999. Reprinted by permission of Wiley-Liss, Inc., a subsidiary of John Wiley & Sons, Inc.

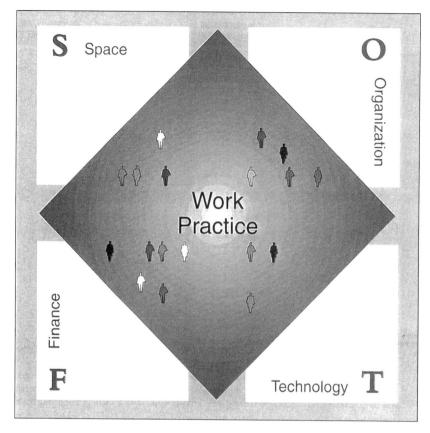

3. Transforming the workplace supports the transformation of work itself: mobilising people around workplace intervention entails developing the organisational capability for design inquiry, and facilitates shifts in the fundamental culture, enabling collaboration across competencies. This, in turn, may result in a more innovative work practice.

Process Architecture is the practice of deliberately designing and facilitating the process through which an organisation creates and manages its workplace – in real time, and adjusting or reinventing the process as needed – within these contexts of the Design Game and the multiple interacting dimensions of the work environment.[1]

The dynamically coherent workplace

Dynamic coherence is an evolving match between the changing work process and its workplace. It depends upon the evolving integration of the four principal interdependent dimensions of the workplace – spatial, organisational, financial, and technological. This relationship is represented in the SOFT diagram in Figure 8.21. When one dimension of that environment changes, there are implications for change in its other dimensions. And those changes in turn will require yet others. There is only a temporary match between workplace and the work that is going on. The uneven development of a dynamically coherent workplace is an aspect of the larger process of organisational development.

The Design Game

Design Games are endemic to workplace making. Workplace making involves many different stakeholders, individual or organisational, who partly co-operate, and partly interact in non-productive or even antagonistic ways, in order to produce what they see from their own point of view as their interest. The spaces and physical accoutrements of the workplace are coveted resources that inevitably provoke new antagonisms or provide new occasions for exhibiting old ones. The interaction between the players in the 'game' has a direct impact on the quality of the workplace, whether it is a workstation, a team workplace, a building, or a portfolio of buildings.

To think of a social activity such as market competition, war, or politics as a game, unfolding and evolving over time, is to conjure up a conceptual framework that makes it possible to analyse that activity, explain its evolution, understand the internal dynamics that link moves to outcomes, and predict the patterns of processes and outcomes that are likely to occur in any particular instance of play.

Process Architecture uses the metaphor of the game to explain, analyse, and anticipate the unfolding of any workplace making process. Thus, the game becomes a diagnostic tool that enables players – workers, managers, and owners, as well as professional consultants – to play their roles more productively, according to their own values and design intentions. This can be done whilst the game is in progress, or used retrospectively to help managers and stakeholders learn from past experience how the workplace making process succeeds or goes astray.

The actors in this game have a variety of agendas and conflicting ideas which they may not be ready or able to share but which, nevertheless, shape the workplace outcome. These actors hold different interests in the workplace, give priority to different values, dispose of different degrees of power and freedom, tools, and even speak different professional languages and express themselves through different media.

In the absence of a common language, or ways of bridging across languages, communication amongst the experts and between the expert and the user of each corner of the SOFT diagram tends to be limited and unreliable. Though these professionals work together on the same product – the future workplace – they hold different values and base their assessments of success on the verdicts on their own professions, which often conflict with the opinion of the people who will inhabit and use the place, or the ideal of cross-disciplinary collaboration.

In games, there are winners and losers, with some players getting more prizes than others, at others' expense. Accordingly, the players in the design game – for example, architects and contractors; contractors and subcontractors; owners and managers; facilities managers and users of the building – try to win and avoid losing, adopting unilateral strategies of play. In order to achieve their ends, they may seek to gain control of important decisions, manipulate budgets, or solicit the support of higher authorities for their own purposes. Or they may form coalitions with other players, enter into negotiation with their adversaries, or work out relationships of reciprocal exchange. Sometimes, powerful actors achieve their own goals at an unnecessary cost to the quality of the workplace as a whole. Not infrequently, the outcome of a win–lose design game takes the form of fragmented, compartmentalised buildings, or the projects that never got built.

Process Architecture places a high value on the active and collaborative involvement of building users, workplace practitioners, and other stakeholders. Under these conditions, the Design Game does not disappear. Rather, it takes on a new, in some ways more dynamic, but at the same time seemingly messy, style of play. Different perspectives inform and influence one another, leading to new directions and paths for discovery. Such a dynamic, collaborative process of workplace design requires open and reliable communication among the players, where conflicting values can be placed on the table, and confronted and shaped in new ways in an atmosphere conducive to their discussion and resolution.

The metaphor of the game used here has two meanings. First, it is an implicit game – the game of interests, freedoms, and powers, a game being played 'for keeps'. It is a social activity, in which multiple actors occupy defined roles, operating within a shared system of rules and within a conventionally defined context, seeking to achieve certain outcomes.

Second, it is explicit, transient games used as tools within the intervention process, for the sake of bringing to awareness different possible design solutions. These can take the form of role play, or alternatively can be played with cardboard tokens on a game board. The result of such games may be a set of conceptual diagrams for organisational design or spatial design.

Transforming workplace and work practice: the LX workplace experiment

The LX workplace experiment was a business-driven experiment, initiated by the upper management of Xerox R&D, in response to a corporate challenge to reduce time to market. The LX laboratory is among the leading laboratories in its field, and has become the benchmark for the research centre it is a part of, the Joseph C. Wilson Centre for Research and Technology in Webster, New York. As a result of the experiment, the LX laboratory has undergone a dramatic change in its work practice. The changes ranged from achieving a new team identity and a shared mission for the laboratory, to undertaking a commitment to generate the knowledge base for the company's twenty-first century marking technology.

Programming for the changing workplace is a social process. Over four days in August of 1994, the LX laboratory held facilitated workshops for one and a half hours every morning. All the members of the LX laboratory were asked to participate, and these four highly structured collaborative events were recorded and documented. The design process started out as a visit and walk through of the individual laboratories, and proceeded through users' sketches of their ideal workplace; and a cardboard game to structure the new organisational relationships.

The mode of inquiry included photographs, audio-taped conversations, communication maps, cardboard games, yellow trace paper, letter paper, and flip charts. Seeing the material or documents produced in such sessions as a means of making and maintaining social groups, not just as a means of delivering information, makes the records of the inquiry critical to the programming process. The documents from these seminal workshops became a crucial vehicle in mobilising the work group to assess its work process as well as its work environment, and for forming a workplace which had the capacity to transform the work processes in a radical way. The new workplace was created as a collective work process, where everybody could see and hear what another person suggested, and could comment on the material and documents developed and discuss it. The openness of the process also showed how a not-yet-understood problem can be worked on in an open and collegial manner, in which expertise on the work itself is combined with expertise on workplace design, and the participants gradually discover bits and pieces of knowledge about the work which bear critical importance to the new place to be built. The new workplace gradually shaped itself over the following year, through the processes of building and move-in, and by evaluating and reflecting on the changes in work practice and its possibilities.

Collaborative work style

A more profound result was that this style of collaboration in problem solving across disciplines became the new working style of the group in their own research and development work. The laboratory members discovered that the new workplace was much more conducive to working in teams, and looking at representation of data in public, using electronic documents as well as hand-written notes and white board drawings in their creative process. This way of working became natural both within the group and in meetings with vendors or possible business partners.

Discovering the nature of work

The mental image of what a laboratory 'should look like' is stronger than the understanding of how work is actually done. Therefore, the purpose of the intervention was to reveal the nature of work, the potential for change, and the hindrances to change, and to develop concepts for the new workplace. Like most innovations, the LX Common was first discovered, then designed. The findings from the workshops included: that work is not routine, no two days are the same; people would have different requirements for space when they work 'inside a situation' from when they move to 'the outside of the situation'; the need to be in the middle of the work; the need for the presence of data in the workplace and the need for multiple representation of data; and that in order to develop an environment for remote collaboration, it is critical to understand what is going on when someone works face-to-face, and that innovation work requires dialogue. These discoveries all became crucial elements in the evolving understanding of a new kind of R&D environment, unlike any others in the research centre.

In the LX experiment, the design events themselves took place in the very space the LX group would later inhabit. The setting migrated around in a large empty room, designated for part of the LX laboratory – a space whose partitions from its previous use were now removed. The previous plan of this space – the narrow corridor lined by office compartments, some closed offices, and cubicles – could vaguely be identified as a reminder of how things used to be built, as the footprint of the old wall was still dominant in the linoleum on the floor, with carpeted work areas on both sides. The experience became a direct experiment, at one-to-one scale, in how the breaking of the traditional corridor as a demarcation line between different functions could create a permanent meeting area as a bridge between lab work and office work.

What emerged through the four-day workshop was the idea of a space that challenges the prototypical conference room and also the traditional landscaped office. The new space was a meeting room without walls, built in an open expansion of the corridor, in the midst of central laboratories and office areas, and well-equipped with communication technology. Cubicles open to the public area replaced the individual offices. The opening up of the traditional corridor creates an open work and communication area that invites constant spill over from the adjacent laboratories, meeting rooms, and service areas. There is a certain informality and freedom in the spatial arrangement which lends itself to a style of collaborative inquiry rather than to formal presentations. The Common became the main workplace for solving day-to-day problems, the site of spontaneous meetings as well as scheduled ones; and through its conspicuous vitality it also functioned as a sales area for the laboratory's technology. The boundaries between the different activities and spaces are blurred, encouraging collaboration and communication. Two thirds of the laboratory lived in other buildings, but the LX common became the core of the LX work area – the place where the team was built – and the large scalloped table in the middle of the room was referred to as 'our family table'. The workplace becomes a permanent stage for collaborative design and learning, flexible enough to take into account the continuous new understanding of what the final product will be.

Departing from workplace stereotypes

An important challenge in the LX researchers' design process was for them to avoid replicating spaces they had known before. Old images of the workplace tend to persist, even when they do not match changing patterns of work and new technologies. Institutions as well as individuals tend to design space for old patterns of work: 'the way things have always been done'. People have images in their heads about how their workplace can be improved, but these images are often outdated, reflecting the familiar world of the existing workplace – the building, the work station or the equipment to which they have long since adapted. It is difficult for most people to visualise how work is changing, will change, or could change, and what attributes of physical and technological arrangements will support or interfere with that change.

Workplace making should help people break out of stereotypes and take a fresh look at their work environment. Process Architecture does this by making the work through which the organisation produces goods and services the prime focus of design inquiry. It explores the relationship between work and the environment within which work is done. Departing from the conventional images associated with certain workplaces (e.g., an office or a nursing station) helps people to challenge conventional approaches to work practice, enabling imaginative solutions.

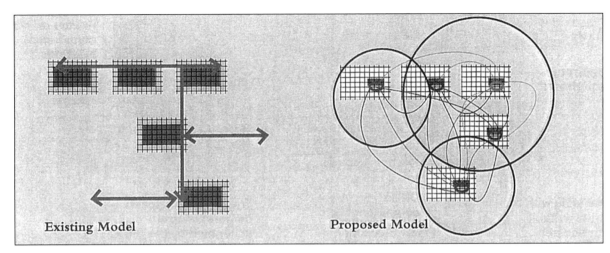

Figure 8.22: The campus model – buildings are linked by the infrastructure, a city grid of roads, utilities and services.
Excellence by Design, Horgen, © 1999. Reprinted by permission of Wiley-Liss, Inc., a subsidiary of John Wiley & Sons, Inc.

Figure 8.23: The New England town model with its multiple linkages. Overlapping towns and locations of commons within the existing grid.
Excellence by Design, Horgen, © 1999. Reprinted by permission of Wiley-Liss, Inc., a subsidiary of John Wiley & Sons, Inc.

Departing from stereotypes of place makes way for the development of leading ideas for workplace design – powerful images that guide the design process through all of its phases. These may be developed in ways that cut across projects and become adapted and refined in each new project. Using these ideas, participants illustrate what they want to produce even before they design it. In the LX case, the LARK consultants used 'the New England town with its common' to explain their idea for the Wilson Centre. This idea suggested 'boundaries' between towns as overlapping. The consultants could then identify and attack the contrast between volatile organisations and 'stiff' infrastructure, showing how it was possible to inhabit several laboratories – or

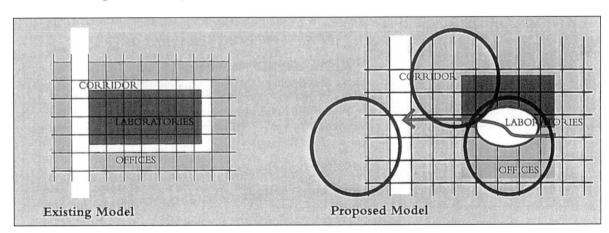

Figure 8.24: Traditional layout of a research building. Laboratories are located in the centre of the building with offices along the perimeter.
Excellence by Design, Horgen, © 1999. Reprinted by permission of Wiley-Liss, Inc., a subsidiary of John Wiley & Sons, Inc.

Figure 8.25: Virtual co-location. The laboratories are networked throughout the building. The corridor is transformed into an interactive workplace.
Excellence by Design, Horgen, © 1999. Reprinted by permission of Wiley-Liss, Inc., a subsidiary of John Wiley & Sons, Inc.

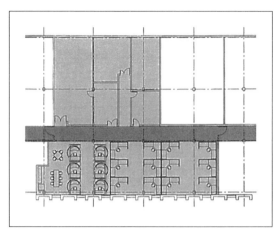

Figure 8.26: The original plan for the LX laboratories.
Excellence by Design, Horgen, © 1999. Reprinted by permission of Wiley-Liss, Inc., a subsidiary of John Wiley & Sons, Inc.

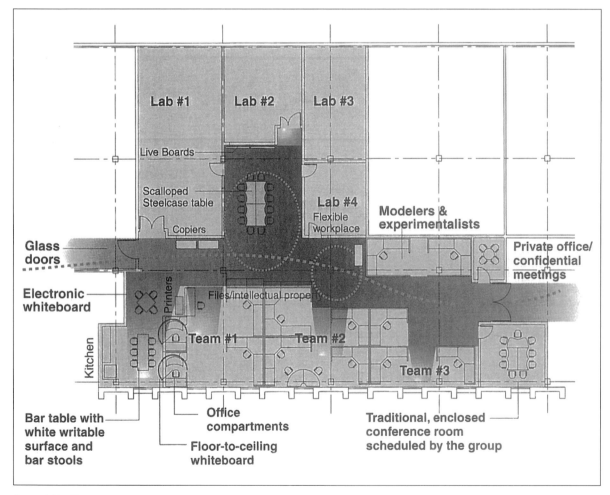

Figure 8.27: The new plan of the core of the LX work area.
Excellence by Design, Horgen, © 1999. Reprinted by permission of Wiley-Liss, Inc., a subsidiary of John Wiley & Sons, Inc.

'towns' – at once, suggesting that each of the competency centres or laboratories could be focused around one Common, with shared communication among the Commons.

Conclusion

Process Architecture recognises the need to change and adapt to an unstable environment, in a way which involves all people of any level of the organisation who have knowledge about the work to be performed. Engaging the stakeholders in a collaborative process of inventing the new workplace will open up options not yet seen and can transform the workplace as well as the institutional processes of workplace making. It is applicable in the design and redesign of all forms of enterprise-factories, service centres, offices, laboratories, schools, and health care institutions.

Experiencing the concepts and practise of Process Architecture has the promise of enabling the participants to transform their work practice. Engaging in the invention of the new workplace helps the participants to imagine what to do in other situations of change, and recognise new strategies for action.

Notes

1   Horgen, T. H., Joroff, M. W., Porter, W. L., Schön, D. A., *Excellence by Design – Transformation of Workplace and Work Practice*, Wiley & Sons, New York, N. Y. 1998.
2   Process Design, in Information and Process Integration in Enterprises: Rethinking Documents, Kluwer Academic Publishers, Norwell, MA.

9   Strategic briefing for a global organisation

Partnering with clients to manage change for continuous learning

Despina Katsikakis

Context

Developing a Strategic Brief and tools for managing the space requirements for a global services organisation with over 100 000 people and average growth of 30–35 per cent per annum is a real challenge. The case study shows how partnering with a client in the briefing process can develop methods and tools to unite real estate with the core business and provide a framework to manage constant change.

The starting point of such an exercise is that such a global business will be undergoing constant change to the services delivered and work processes undertaken as well as a redefinition of its corporate culture of structure. Therefore, the real challenge is to recognise jointly with the client that a Strategic Brief cannot be mistaken for a prescriptive set of solutions. The briefing process will need to be constantly evolving with the lessons from each project fed back into the process, followed by the setting of appropriate benchmarks.

This approach establishes two criteria. Firstly, that the briefing process is multi-layered and continuously changing. Secondly, that in order to achieve such a process the client and consultant need to partner in a journey of joint exploration and discovery. The client must be willing to openly assess and analyse the components of the business that can be affected by space and commit to not only explore new concepts that will facilitate change through linking the business to space but, most importantly, measure the effectiveness of any solution and undertake the appropriate change; therefore committing to continuous learning.

The consultant brings the wider experience of similar organisations, global pressures, differing cultural work characteristics as well as local legislative regulations. Most importantly, the consultant is the facilitator for making the connection between business issues and physical space. The strategic briefer can develop processes and tools to support the setting out of a new approach as well as feedback the learning into appropriate benchmarks which will enable long-term real estate management solutions to support constantly evolving business change.

The problem

In 1992 Andersen Worldwide, which incorporated Arthur Andersen and Andersen Consulting, needed a strategy to enable all partners worldwide to manage the partnership's real estate by maximising value and minimising strain on financial resources. While a set of universal standards would appear to offer an ideal solution, the experience of many global organisations suggested otherwise. The world is full of different codes, regulations, cultures and practices, making a universal approach impractical. Andersen were concerned to provide a strategic approach, that would help local partners maximise valuable resources and improve staff productivity, whilst reflecting local regulations, expectations and requirements.

The framework

To create a framework with the right level of buy-in from the business, the briefing process was set up and co-ordinated by a steering group consisting of managing partners representing different geographical areas, the Andersen Real Estate Management team (as owners of the framework) and DEGW as the external consultants. The steering group was chaired by the Chief Financial Officer of the Worldwide organisation. The result was the Global Real Estate Management Strategy (GREMS) which was geared to local decision making within each geographic area. The strategy aimed to support local decisions with guidance gleaned from many years of experience in providing office space planning services to offices around the world (i.e. benchmarks). It provided the information the local offices needed to maximise the effectiveness of real estate by tapping into information about business needs, as well as a real understanding of the necessary decisions and timelines.

There are three components (documents and software packages) which support the framework:

- managing partners' overview – reflecting the importance of balancing local expectations with an understanding that the choice of the appropriate building and office layout can be a powerful tool in positioning the company with clients and motivating staff;
- facilities guide – set out with milestones for product delivery and guidance on steps to be taken to achieve effective space use and staff acceptance;
- real estate toolbox – easy to apply methodologies that can be used by local offices to assess space use, forecast requirements and identify current staff demands and space and time utilisation.

Managing partners' overview

It is the responsibility of the managing partners to implement change and to ensure that the critical factors from all elements are taken into account. History suggests that place is the most frequently ignored element in the business case. The intention of the managing partners' overview is to demonstrate that buildings matter. Building costs are second only to salaries and they transmit powerful messages to clients and personnel alike.

Business decisions can therefore be linked to design decisions. Consequently, facilities costs are related to business advantage. To ensure maximum effectiveness, there is a very strong link between the business plan and facility plan, and GREMS enables the local managing partner to use a framework for creating a business case for facilities.

The managing partners' overview is an aspirational sixteen-page document that, as stated in the Chief Executive's introduction, provides 'advice that will challenge our traditional ways of thinking. We must not let ourselves down by ignoring it. We owe our clients and our worldwide organisation more than that.' The document presents the need for continuous change and change management, proposes a concept for the control of space and time, leading to effective utilisation and gives advice on building selection.

The overview sets out the scope of the framework strategy and highlights the key links between business planning and facility planning. It is the basic information tool for positioning the partnership's new approach to real estate across all locations.

In 1996, four years after the Global Real Estate Management System (GREMS) was developed, Andersen Worldwide moved into a new headquarters building in Chicago. Under the direction of John Lewis, the Chief Financial Officer, the offices became a shining example of how change could be achieved through support and real drive from the top of the organisation. The scheme, as John Lewis pointed out, was 'not simply a matter of cutting costs' but reflected the 'need to interact naturally and spontaneously with clients'. The space per person was reduced by 30 per cent from the old offices, whilst at the same time the amount of space for collaboration work went from 4–30 per cent. The Chicago office inspired a mood for change and became a benchmark for others to follow.

The office facilities guide

The guide is intended for the individual responsible for planning and running space-related projects on a day-to-day basis and their advisers. It ensures that issues are addressed which have most impact on the end result, particularly in terms of cost and business flexibility. This is done by defining specific criteria under each stage of the project.

The hundred page guide is divided into two parts. Part one sets out management issues in planning for the effective use of space, with guidance on methods of improving space intensification, measuring usage and satisfying facility needs. In addition, the sequence of managing the process is set out from identifying needs to post occupancy evaluation. Part two provides detailed guidance on technical preferences, with critical dimensions and specification.

Building projects are often slow and mostly long-term. Most of the information required to make the right decisions is about the future. Therefore, key decision makers need to be involved in forecasting long-term personnel projections as well as concepts relating to the development of new services which will impact on the way facilities are used.

Planning for a new facility also opens the door to new ways of working. Innovation at the workplace is occurring across Andersen Worldwide with various degrees of success, and the internal real estate management team can provide best practice benchmarks to support immediate and long-term needs. To ensure the best integration of the facility issues with the business planning, the management team should begin working on any real estate project two to three years prior to requiring space.

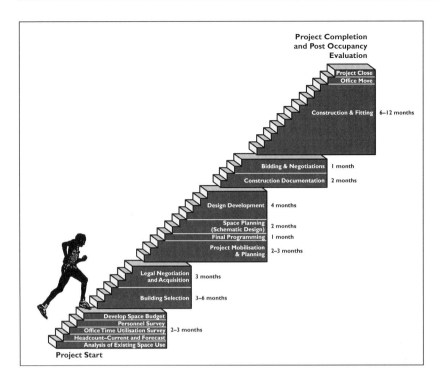

Figure 8.28: Intensification of use. Different capacities can be achieved by using different sharing patterns.
Source: DEGW for Andersen Consulting

The decisions about space should include the dimension of time. The combination of space and time usage provides a management tool to reduce the future cost of space and challenge traditional thinking. Research indicates that most professionals are likely to spend only 30 per cent of their time at allocated workstations. Given a choice of either having a large personal office or less space but freedom to work to a flexible schedule that satisfies both work and personal needs, most professionals opt for a flexible schedule.

It is not necessarily a flexible schedule outside the office that is required for innovation of space use to be appropriate. Work in the office itself is often very mobile and can be helped by the provision of a number of different work settings appropriate to the work processes being undertaken. Control of both space and time can lead to dramatic utilisation effectiveness.

Figure 8.29 demonstrates how, using various space allocations, a number of space-use scenarios were developed across the whole range of sharing patterns for a Reference Unit. The results are shown graphically in two ways. The people bar chart shows the changing capacity of a fixed building as the organisation grows and intensifies its use. The pie charts indicate the reduction in space needed if the organisation remains fixed in number but intensifies its use.

The evidence of this work is that truly effective use of space arises when the time-sharing opportunities are implemented and the right application can reduce business planning issues.

One of the most important issues for the Worldwide Organisation was that time sharing solutions should provide an ability for the use of space to be tuned through time. The result was a more stable requirement for space, achieved by changing the sharing ratios and providing a longer life to existing space. In right-sizing situations it can remove the need to move a new location or take on further floors of existing buildings.

Figure 8.29: The GREMS process from analysing existing space use and need to project completion.
Source: DEGW for Andersen Consulting

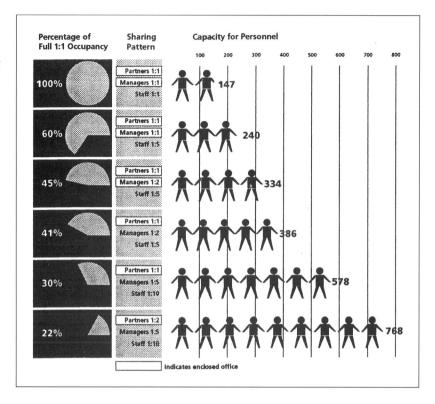

Real estate toolbox

A number of specialised tools have been developed to support the process of a major refurbishment or relocation project. While each tool is self-contained, the integrative result of using the different tools also contributed.

The analysis of the need for more or less space requires data to be available. The toolbox provides tools within four prime areas of investigation:

- analysis of existing space use;
- headcount – current and forecast;
- time utilisation;
- employee survey.

A clear understanding of the way space is currently used is an essential ingredient of planning. Where change is to take place, it is important to be able to quantify the current position. The tools enable an audit of current space use through a combination of visual surveys and analysis of plans and layouts, providing a consistent approach globally. A surprising number of decisions about offices are based upon management opinions of what personnel at all levels think. The surveys remove uncertainty and provide a valuable base from which to measure change.

Furthermore, the use of the same questionnaires and data collection tools around the world provide a unique set of data for comparing and benchmarking change over time.

GREMS – a method not a solution

There is no boilerplate solution for the use of office space when new space planning is under consideration. Aside from the obvious cultural differences across different geographical areas, each business unit represents unique requirements. Imaginative concepts and ideas, together with key data about the local operation, can lead to the development of a solution tailored to the business' needs. Early in the process, a user group representing the future occupants is set up. The role of this group is to contribute and disseminate information and to be drawn into the decision making process so that the solutions proposed are developed from both 'top-down' and 'bottom-up' perspectives.

Typical tools include those for:

- facility planning (e.g. headcount forecasts, personnel surveys, space budget);
- acquiring a new facility (e.g. economic analysis, legal requirements checklist);
- design and construction (e.g. questions for selection interview, generic contracts, statement of requirement, move checklist, post occupancy evaluation).

Experience at Andersen and other clients has shown that successful projects are led by a visionary partner who demonstrates that there is a better way of using facilities and supports innovative, effective space-use solutions.

The world-wide application of GREMS since 1992 has enabled Andersen to experiment with a variety of solutions. Many of these challenged conventional ideas of space-use by introducing concepts of space-use intensification based on the data collected from the various GREMS tools.

The original development of the tools is maintained through the commitment to always undertake post-occupancy evaluation of the facilities implemented, and through linking the data collected by the tools pre-project to the development of the business case for the project. The framework of GREMS must be viewed as the underlying platform against which project-related strategic and detailed briefs are generated.

Why a framework?

The implementation of a global framework that links real estate to business decisions enables global organisations to:

- increase business effectiveness through linking their real estate decisions to the business;
- control the quantity and quality of real estate across a variety of cultural and legislative boundaries;
- develop benchmarks and establish best practices;
- stimulate design and innovation against a tried and tested set of principles;
- support continuous business change.

However, the framework and its tools must always be continuously reviewed and revised as the business conditions change and continuous learning is implemented.

Ensuring success

In order for a global framework to succeed, it requires the following:

- a champion at board level;
- data on improved business effectiveness in relation to real estate;
- top-down commitment to supporting better working practices across the organisation;
- a process which ensures the involvement and contribution of personnel at all levels;
- the collection of data about the type of space provided and the utilisation of space and time;
- a detailed understanding of the job tasks and work processes involved;
- a commitment to change management;
- a commitment to measuring success of implementation and inspiration;
- a commitment to continuous learning;
- a direct link between the framework and its tools to business case development and day-to-day decisions.

The success of new solutions for the use of space will depend upon the way they have been developed. The needs of the personnel should drive the solution, *not* the reverse. There is strong evidence to show that people will work comfortably in a smaller, undedicated space, providing the overall office infrastructure supports their job tasks and responsibilities better than the traditional model.

It is critical that GREMS is understood to provide a Strategic Brief which is further developed into operational and detailed Project Briefs by using the data and learning from the worldwide experience.

CHRONOLOGY OF ONGOING LEARNING

1992 Development of GREMS   Strategic framework defining process and tools to enable new projects and measure ongoing success of existing projects.

1994–Present   Local Project Briefs developed and implemented, testing new planning concepts in various geographic areas and extensive database development by Andersen Real Estate Management group.

*1996–8   Andersen Worldwide Headquarters in Chicago (1100 people relocation) Project Brief: major cultural and change management process involving 80 per cent of population.

This project was a catalyst in the validation of the GREMS framework and tools, and in demonstrating the necessary link from a strategic framework (GREMS) to an operational Project Brief and a continuous feedback process through reapplication of the briefing tools in post-occupancy evaluation.

1997–Present   Review of best practices and development of revised framework and tools to support business change for Andersen Consulting.

THE BASIS FOR GLOBAL GUIDELINES

The nature of guidelines can be somewhat elusive, everyone seems to know what they want and yet no one can quite describe the product. A brief history is informative and particularly relevant to placing the concept behind current guidelines in their true perspective.

In the 1920s, corporate standards for the procurement, development and occupation of buildings began as natural extensions of company policy. Developed where repetition occurs, they define from past experience the best way of achieving a given goal; they aimed to ensure conformity across the company. The purpose was to save time and money.

By the 1980s standards came under increasing pressure, growth was the order of the day, and whilst big was still beautiful, the management style was becoming more democratic and the hierarchies were flattening. Consequently, grade structures followed suit. Standards and democracy are not comfortable bedfellows. Rather than standards the new material was called 'guidelines'.

The development of corporate guidelines progressed through the 1980s and, by the beginning of the 1990s, these were recognised as the most realistic way of supporting the business goals of the company. However, guidelines had varying degrees of success in organisations, some working quite well and others never really making the mark they should have done.

Most design guidelines are developed to control the excesses of external designers and engineers, and written either directly for them or to be transmitted through an internal project manager to them. Frequently the nature of these 'technical' guidelines are either too prescriptive or patronising, and from the standpoint of the chosen designer immediately places them in a 'box' that minimises their creativity. Interestingly, design guides are nearly always written by designers themselves being either part of the in-house property team or a valued consultant designer who 'knows and understands' the company.

The development of guidelines in the current environment owes as much to PR and communications as it does to understanding the content. There are likely to be a number of parts to the guidelines package, the first being an overview for the decision maker. The overview should:

* talk the language of the decision maker;
* be in a format which they will utilise (brochure, video, etc.);
* identify how the guidelines can help them achieve their goals in both the short- and long-term;
* indicate the important links between organisations and facilities;
* set out some key performance indicators which will become highly visible across the corporation;
* describe the few critical areas that they need to influence to ensure the most optimum solution.

The presentation of such material needs to be quite different from conventional guidelines and should be much more concise, enabling a busy person to absorb the key points quickly. More than anything else they must explain why certain decisions they make will affect their 'bottom line'. The challenge is to capture their imagination and to provide a mechanism for influencing change.

Source: Tony Thomson, DEGW

9 Model Briefs

Introduction

Five generic types of brief are analysed in this chapter:

- an **Urban Brief**. The briefing process established for buildings is equally as relevant for urban areas;
- a **Strategic Brief** which sets out the goals, objectives and case for a project based on an organisation's needs;
- a **Project Brief** which operationalises the Strategic Brief into building requirements;
- a **Fit-out Brief** which defines in building terms the client's requirements for internal building spaces;
- a **Furniture Brief** which defines the furniture attributes to meet the requirements of the fit-out brief.

Each section of this chapter sets out some key issues for each type of brief and uses case study examples which are annotated. More detail on the content of each brief are set out in Chapter 6, 'Communicating Expectations'.

Urban Brief

The urban masterplan is equivalent to the Strategic Brief but at an urban rather than building scale. It clearly states the mission, objectives, priorities and gives measures of success.

Urban Briefs seek to understand the particular needs of an urban area. It sets it in a regional context, addressing a range of stakeholder interests.

The development of a successful Urban Brief depends on gathering information about a wide range of issues and expectations from a variety of sources and then synthesising it into a coherent picture. The objective of the Urban Brief is to:

- identify the range of stakeholders and their expectations;
- set out the conditions, constraints and opportunities of the site;
- test alternative uses, and design strategies to meet the different expectations;
- focus on an achievable vision by presenting precedents of best practice from local examples and abroad;
- establish goals, objectives and a plan of action.

The Urban Brief is an opportunity for all parties to agree a vision and clear objectives for the area, before beginning detailed urban design studies. Precedent and generic design are powerful tools to help assess options and dimension the appropriate design response.

The example below is from work undertaken by DEGW for the City of Utrecht in the Netherlands. The brief was for two geographically separate but interlinked sites at the central station UCP (Utrecht Centrum Project) and on the periphery (Papendorp). Each site accommodates over 350 000 m^2 of mixed use development. The final recommendation (Two sites, one city) identified the synergy between the two sites and a development strategy for each.

The approach in reaching a development brief was to:

- interview the relevant stakeholders and external development partners, and identify the possible needs of business and the community in the picture;
- draw on experience of global business expectations, match these to local practice, and propose trends in space use and building form that may need to be accommodated;
- propose a development model of uses and floor area allocation for each site;
- test the opportunities and dimensions of the site against relevant precedents;
- work closely with the appointed Urban Designer and project managers.[1]

The selected issues are:

- the mission statement;
- Statement of Objectives;
- precedent;
- managing the process;
- accounting for growth and change.

Commentary	Example

Mission statement

The vision is set out as a series of bullet points. The first statement is the mission, followed by specific goals that define 'a distinctive quality environment'.

The successful development of Papendorp as a new business location will depend upon achieving a distinctive quality environment based on a clear understanding of the needs of likely users.

The development concept is based on a series of specific goals:

* to establish a new type of 'place' in the Netherlands, both for working and living;
* to plan for integrated development with mixed working and living appropriate to a city quarter with an emphasis on sustainability;
* to provide for a range of environments and building types to meet various requirements including new types of business accommodation;
* to allow for a people-friendly environment which also allows for the convenience of car usage.

Objectives

Set out what the development has to achieve. The objectives encompass how the development will be marketed, built and managed. These objectives are backed up by proposed actions setting out what should be done in response to the brief.

The development should:

* focus on firms requiring a flexibility in the variety of functions they undertake, the speed of growth and change and staff profiles;
* establish a comprehensive development approach, where in addition to individual plots for large users, selected developers are attracted to promote comprehensive site development plans;
* prepare overall guidelines for Park management and business services.

Proposed action:
* aim for comprehensive development areas with flexibility of plot development within common landscaped environment and amenities;
* ensure each phase feels complete;
* create distinct and identifiable areas within the development;
* allow development flexibility within strong design guidelines.

Commentary   Example

Precedent

*Precedent is a useful way of achieving a
shared understanding between the client
and readership of the brief. It can
demonstrate the desired qualities of the
building and urban fabric – for example,
density, spatial cohesion. Here examples
of other developments have been
superimposed on each site. The aim is to
present realistic alternatives for
development by placing relevant
examples on the site to the same scale.*

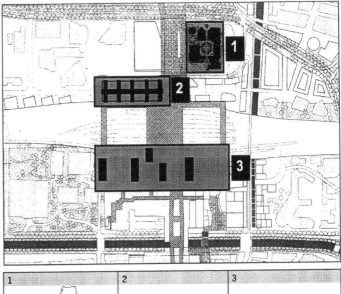

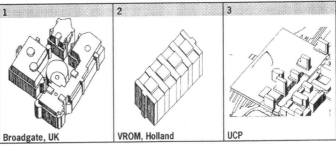

Broadgate, UK   VROM, Holland   UCP

Managing the process

*Here the brief sets out the general
management framework. Each project
will be the responsibility of individual
developers. However, what is important
to the municipal client is the co-ordination.*

*The management criteria are more
general than perhaps in a project-specific
brief.*

*In effect some of these statements are
mini-briefs for different elements of the
'management process' (e.g. the design
review committee).*

* The preparation of site-specific briefs, especially for key locations,
  which reflect and secure the implementation of the overall objective
  and guidelines set in the master plan. In parallel, they can evaluate the
  particular condition and opportunities of each site and define the
  compatibility parameters between individual buildings.
* The appointment of a design review committee to review all
  development proposals according to master plan and guideline
  documentation.

Commentary	Example

Briefing the area management process as well as the physical product

This brief is not only written for the municipality itself. Like building briefs it is also briefing the organisation and therefore suggests what the municipality's role should be.

Studies carried out during the briefing process through research, interviews and workshops identify how people and organisations see Utrecht and its context within the region.

The ongoing role of the municipality should be to act as the 'clearing house' for organisations looking to take on new space in Utrecht. The municipality should assess the needs and working practices of the organisation concerned and suggest whether new building in the UCP site or Papendorp, or indeed refurbished space in existing buildings, would be most appropriate for their immediate and longer term requirements.

Accounting for growth and change

Any brief needs to allow for growth and change, none more so than an Urban Brief. The dynamics of urban life and the time that it takes for buildings to be developed adds to the complexity. Here the brief points out that one response to change is not just modification but possible changes in strategy.

To reflect the potentially long period of implementation, in special circumstances, the committee will need to consider modification, waivers or even changes of strategy to adapt to changes in circumstances.

Strategic Brief

The aim of the Strategic Brief is to set out the objectives of the project based on the organisation's needs. The essential task is to ensure that the design objectives coincide with the corporate objectives. To minimise misunderstanding the Strategic Brief must clearly and unambiguously set out the organisation's priorities and aims. This brief will define the essential requirements of the building, and communicate these to the design team to provide a robust structure for the subsequent phases of design development.

An example is worked through below based on Prospect Park, British Airways' new headquarters at Waterside, Heathrow.[2]

The new building was to be an expression of the airline's business goals and objectives. The briefing team studied in detail every department that was to be housed in the building. They looked at work processes, how people used their time and spaces, as well as gaining an understanding of the organisation's business objectives and culture.

The selected issues are:

- the mission statement – which expresses the reason for undertaking the project;
- statement of objectives which sets out how the 'mission' will be accomplished;
- measures to enable the result to be evaluated. Both building and business measures are used in the brief, here we look at the business measures;
- priorities. This brief distils both business and design priorities, identifying those issues most important to the client;
- change and growth;
- decision framework. A successful project demands a clear decision making framework.

Commentary	Example

Mission statement

A vision is intended to capture the thrust of both the building and the business project.

The need for the building is related to the company's mission statement – and reminds the project team what the business is about.

'By bringing together our key business staff under one roof, the CBC represents much more than a traditional headquarters office. Rather, it is a highly integrated unit responsible not only for strategic decisions but also for "hands on" management of an international business.'

Business objectives

Set out what the Combined Business Centre (CBC) building aims to enable the user to do. These objectives can be used to continuously test the design development, through defined business measures which enable the client to determine whether they have got what they wanted

* Co-locate business functions to enable staff to work effectively together and create synergy;
* Improve links between business groups and the operational airline at Heathrow and beyond;
* Encourage hands-on management and face-to-face contact;
* Enable new forms of synergy.

Business measures

This statement tells the designers how the result will be measured in business terms. Some of them are quantifiable measures, for example the number of interactions, others are qualitative measures such as staff loyalty. This example shows how briefing for the organisation is as important as briefing for the building.

The yield of its building to be maximised to push the synergy of the organisation. This will be achieved by measuring the performance of the building against management goals. The Organisational Brief for the new building should include such measures as:
* speed of response;
* optimal mixing of staff;
* numbers of interactions;
* face-to-face contact time;
* effective working time;
* reduced stress, so maximising health and well-being;
* staff loyalty and levels of corporate commitment.

Business priorities

An effective brief clearly sets out the client's priorities. This sets out what is important to the client and what it wants the design team to concentrate on.

The senior and middle managers must be integrated both horizontally and vertically (within and across the departments). Senior managers must have direct access to their colleagues in other central business and professional departments. This togetherness is vital to the sharing of information.

Commentary   Example

Design priorities

*Having used the metaphor of a village
to establish a vocabulary for translating
the business objectives into building
terms, tables such the one opposite are
used to define the priorities relating to
elements of the metaphor: village, lanes,
streets and neighbourhoods. In each table
a set of design issues are examined
using three different focuses:*
* *corporate objectives to be achieved by
the design;*
* *commitments: what has already been
decided;*
* *opportunities: issues needing resolution,
an assessment of the design so far and
opportunities for the design team.*

*The statements in this table are written as
objectives, the intention being to use the
design process to identify how they will be
achieved.*

DESIGN	CORPORATE REQUIREMENTS	COMMITMENTS	OPPORTUNITIES
Access and movement	Reinforce intimate relationship between CBC and Heathrow Airport operations	Prospect park selected as most suitable available site	One site to **integrate** core business staff for BA. One main visitor entrance – highly visible. Separate staff entrances to houses. A **cohesive** design must bind together a complex organisation while maintaining identity of its parts. Focus on relationship of entrance to **street**.
Security		Fully secure BA site within Prospect Park, sensitive handling of boundary to public.	Ensure road access can cope with risks of external threats, e.g. alternative routes. Provide a layered system of security appropriate to different levels: site, village, street, houses.
Image	CBC as heart of BA's global business strategy. Enhance site within Green Belt. Image of site not exclusive to BA	Provide park and amenities for use by Hillingdon residents. Site and buildings can be demised to others	A **welcoming**, not exclusive image, a place where BA staff come to work together. A place using interaction, shared **knowledge** and **intelligent** technologies to create **synergy.**
Space	Provide office space, amenities and parking for 2,500 staff.	Parking arranged separately by buildings. Each house to have own visitors' car park.	The village in the park provides an orientation for the user to both a quiet reflective landscape (parkside) and towards a busy heart of activity (streetside).

Change and growth

*The future of the building is an
important consideration in a rapidly
changing industry. Not only did the client
need a building that enabled it to operate
in a particular kind of way, but also one
that represented a good investment.
Practically, this might mean one where
all or part of it could be used by another
organisation.*

*The Strategic Brief is for both the
organisation and business. Here it
addresses how change within the
organisation will be handled.*

*The bullet point list defines how the
client will measure whether the building
meets the 'long-term commercial
property investment' objective.*

The achievement of the mission demands constant cultural change as an
essential feature of management; the airline must 'be able to handle
change proactively'. A 'hands on' approach to management is adopted.
Managers must have face-to-face contact with the people and to the
things they manage.

The CBC must not only be designed to support the innovative and
changing patterns of work of the business functions of the airline, but
must also be institutionally acceptable as a major long-term commercial
property investment.

This means that it must perform in the market for high quality business
parks. Individual buildings must be:
* appropriately sized and specified for the market;
* capable of individual demise to other (non-BA) users;
* sub-divisible on a half-floor basis;
* independently serviceable and accessible;
* maintain their own identity.

Commentary	Example

Decision framework

*Diagrams and tables can be used
to set out responsibilities. The
purpose is to identify where decisions
should be made and by who.*

Principal Responsibilities

1. Executive client
   * establish policy – business vision;
   * delegation of executive authority;
   * business decisions, design reviews and approvals;
   * final arbiter on issues/disputes.
2. Occupier's Management Group
   * determine occupancy brief;
   * review and approve briefs from specialists;
   * review and comment on design concepts;
   * manage detailed planning and implementation of occupancy through user representatives;
   * resolve issues between different occupants – establish priority.
3. PM team
   * manage project delivery from inception to completion – time, cost, quality;
   * manage briefing and approvals processes;
   * manage external approvals and public relations.
4. Design team
   * design and production information for BA buildings, parkland, community facilities, traffic management;
   * inspection of construction as appropriate.

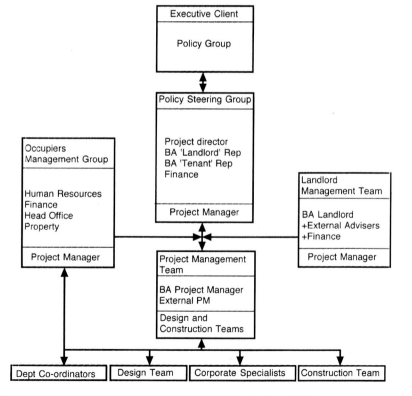

Project Brief

The appropriate procurement route having been agreed and the design team selected, the Project Brief is prepared by the team, working closely with the project sponsor and user to validate the original Strategic Brief.

The Project Brief aims to:

- understand the building and cost implications of the Strategic Brief aspirations;
- test the reality of client and user expectations;
- present requirements in the terminology of construction with goals and measures.

The new building for the Computer Science Department at the University of York (Figure 9.1a, b, c) designed by Nicholas Hare Architects, was initiated with a Strategic Brief prepared jointly by the Department of Computer Science and the Bursar's Department. The design team was selected through competitive interview and response to the aspirations of the brief.

The Strategic Brief contained a three-page summary setting the mission, expectations and requirements for location, site, content, quality, character, configuration, adaptability, environmental services, information technology, fit-out, budget, management of access and security and timetable.

The mission for the new building was to:

stimulate the imagination of the department's researchers, correspond to the enthusiasm of the department's students, signal to the visitor that the department has a sense of purpose and intellectual distinction, create a sense of belonging in those who work in the building and reflect the best of British design and craftsmanship.

On appointment, Nicholas Hare Architects and their co-professionals, Price & Myers (structural), Hoare Lea & Partners (environmental engineering) and Gleeds (costs) worked closely with the staff of the department in reviewing requirements, preparing a detailed space budget and verifying the expectations of the Strategic Brief. Fortnightly meetings were held over an intensive three-month period with design requirements being captured as minutes of meetings and workshop notes.

During this period, the expressed requirements of the individual work groups were moderated through consideration by the head of department, and the central university officers. For instance, a decision was taken that generally only researchers who also did individual teaching would have separate offices. At the same time, the outline design evolved through the development and simplification of alternatives. For instance, the planning grid was changed from 1.5 m × 1.5 m to 1.2 m × 1.2 m in order to allow a more compact and economical building through the use of deeper but narrower offices.

Two key presentations were made by the design team: first to the whole department, and the second to the Development Subcommittee of the university. These confirmed the fundamental points of the proposed design, and allowed the concept scheme design document to be assembled. The Project Brief was encapsulated as drawings and a report within the concept scheme design presentation.

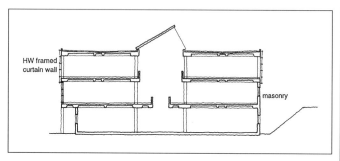

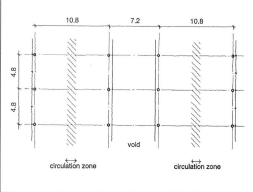

Figure 9.1: a. The Computer Science building (Photo); b. Section through building. c. Part plan showing grid.
Source: Nicholas Hare Architects

Commentary	Example

Site planning

The written commentary is a combination of a description of proposals, statement of unresolved issues and pointers to future opportunities.

1. Building disposition;
2. expansion;
3. access;
4. landscape.

1. 'The Western end of the building will be dug into the higher ground which will slope sharply down to the ground floor entrance of the building on the south side, where it is intended to create a relatively flat lawn extending almost as far as the Library.'
2. '… allow the expansion of the Computer Science Department in a block perpendicular to the main building at the Western end. The extended building would form an enclosing L-shape creating a sheltered lawn between itself and the library.'
3. 'At ground floor level the external wall of the new building is cut back to form a colonnade leading to the principal undergraduate and pedestrian entrance.'
4. 'The building has been sited to provide a simple sheltered lawn on the south side which will be further protected to the west by a sloping bank planed with two rows of trees.'

Internal arrangements

Provides a description of the accommodation required, functional relationships and its disposition.

The concept report:

1. sets capacity of fixed areas;
2. specifies demands for security and access;
3. presents layout options.

1. 'Two hardware laboratories each designed to accommodate 48 students and separated by workshop one which will also serve as the preparation room for both laboratories.'
2. '… the main stair which is separated from the lobby by a glazed screen which can be secured at night to allow 24 hour undergraduate access to the software laboratories without prejudicing the security of the department as a whole.'
3. 'A sum has been included in the cost plan to provide cellular offices to all staff members. The location of individual research teams and their associate office will be determined at detail design stage.'

Detailed schedule of accommodation and areas (Figure 9.2).

Building envelope

The description of the concept design proposals specifies requirements for:

1. cleaning and maintenance;
2. durability;
3. security.

1. '… access to all areas of roof via the internal escape stair. The internal glazing and the longitudinal extract duct which runs the length of the rooflight may be reached via the same stair.'
2. 'The hardwood will be suitable for self weathering externally without protective treatment; iroko is one suitable species, which weathers to a silver-grey.'
3. 'Opening windows except at ground floor level where security measures dictate that the windows should be fitted with restrictors to limit the size of aperture.'

Schedule of Areas

Ground Floor Plan	**m²**
Hardware Laboratory 1	146
Hardware Laboratory 2	143
Software Laboratory 1	148
Software Laboratory 2	148
Store	4
Workshop 1	96
Workshop 2	44
Workshop 3	38
Software Technicians	14
Store	10
Darkroom	10
Computer Room	30
Ground floor total of net usable area	**831**

First Floor Plan	
Department Office/Reception	27
Laboratory Superintendent	10
Superintendent's Secretary	10
Filing/Archive	23
Head of Department	27
Departmental Secretary	13
Common Room	96
Kitchen	14
Seminar Room	101
Library	33
MSC Laboratory	100
MSC Terminals	49
Research Areas (measured as open plan area 10.8 m deep)	614
First floor total net usable area	**1117**

Second Floor Plan	
Research area (Measured as open plan area)	1289
Second floor total net usable area	**1289**
Total net usable area	**3237**
Total gross internal area	**4204**

Figure 9.2: Schedule of areas

Commentary	Example

Environmental design

The description is aspirational, referring to external publications for acceptable criteria.

1. External criteria;
2. environmental effect of building fabric.

1. 'It is the University's policy to apply BREEAM criteria to all new buildings whilst not actually seeking an independent assessment.

    The design team have undertaken a provisional assessment which indicated that the building design could be developed at the Detail Design stage to meet the 28 point target set by the University which would be equivalent to a "Very Good" rating by BREEAM. Because the building occupies a green field site and is necessarily located close to the Library building, it is unlikely than an "Excellent" score could be achieved.'

2. '… good levels of insulation, the use of building thermal mass to limit summertime temperatures and the maximum use of controlled daylighting. The systems have also been designed to allow the future introduction of heat recovery.

    These measures also have significant impact on the resulting internal environment for the occupants. The intent of the design is to provide a fresh and comfortable environment with good natural light using simple but efficient systems. The use of air conditioning has been avoided in all areas except the central computer room.'

Fit-out Brief

The Fit-out Brief for a building project may be a separate or integral part of a Project Brief. Although often, in commercial projects, a fit-out is treated as a separate project from producing the structure and envelope of the building, in some situations there may be no other project than a 'fit-out' since the structure, envelope and cores already exist.

The aim of the Fit-out Brief is to define in building terms the client's requirements for the internal building spaces. It responds to the Strategic Brief by setting out the aims of the design and gives detailed information on the dimensions of spaces and elements to be provided.

The Fit-out Brief may use design concept sketches to verify the client's aspirations, and establish requirements. Intangible factors such as quality and image can be ascertained by showing examples, and using these images to prescribe requirements.

The Fit-out Brief, in addition to establishing built responses, may also be concerned to agree a space planning strategy that will inform the physical fit-out.

An example is worked through below based on a project for Capital One Financial Corporation.[3] The client is a US company which has recently established a base in the UK. It has set up an operations centre in an old printworks in Nottingham.

The selected issues are:

- Aim of the design which restates the objectives in building terms;
- Growth and change in response to the Strategic Brief;
- Environmental qualities;
- Measures showing how the building will be evaluated;
- Design priorities which respond to the client's needs and expectations.

Commentary	Example

Aim of the design

This is a rapidly growing business and the statement on the aim of the design shows the response to growth and how the design must meet the client's need to have one operations centre.

The brief is to provide an operations centre for an integrated business in the former Boots Printworks in Nottingham, bringing together several business areas committed to the shared task of delivering products to customers.

Phase One will accommodate:

* data centre requirements on the ground floor. The area is given over for a communications room, UPS and a standby generator.
* business centre requirements on the second floor. The net internal area provided is 25 000 ft^2 (2320 m^2). It meets the headcount requirements, with an additional 'squeeze' factor for staff and their support space requirements.

Growth and change

An organisation can change not only in size but configuration. There can also be fluctuations in the sizes of teams or departments. The building has to be able to accommodate short-term growth.

The brief sets out how this is included and, in practical terms, how elements, for example the partitions, allow the building to respond to these demands.

The layout of workstations allows for teams to reconfigure with ease and incorporates a 'squeeze factor' to accommodate short-duration growth immediately prior to further planned expansion.

The layout allows groups to reconfigure with ease. Growth is accommodated by enabling professionals to extend into operations area if necessary.

Demountable propietary partitions/walls where applicable. Demountable: allow for approximately 30 per cent of the open plan are to be occupied by enclosed offices.

Environmental qualities

This statement addresses the question of what the environment will be like and how this will be achieved.

The interior will be a varied, stimulating environment. This is provided by the use of a mixture of forms at differing scales, so creating a variety of views around the workplace and from individual desks. This is required to balance the very strong factory aesthetic and the necessary orthogonal desk layout.

'We have developed two principal formal elements:

* the orthogonal frame and panel "screen" or "box" which we use of the anti-glare screens and smaller enclosed spaces;
* the curved embracing form which we have used for the assembly spaces – Reception, Soft Training and the suite of large Meeting Rooms. These two forms represent the duality in the culture of Capital One.'

Commentary	Example

Measures

Some measures are quantifiable, others are more qualitative and are a matter of judgement.

Certain types of measure are difficult to appreciate in real terms. Sound transmission is measured in decibels (dB) However, it is important to ensure that there is a common understanding about what such measures mean in practical terms. This can be achieved by identifying examples of rooms reaching these sound reduction levels within similar office contexts.

* Enclosures from office to office (including ceiling and floor voids) to achieve 43 db mean level 250 hz–4 khz separation in the field;
* a design to accommodate line of sight between all team work stations;
* a raised floor ideally providing 300 mm minimum void below.

No part of the sub-floor or surrounding walls must show readings of more than 75 per cent RH (relative humidity) when tested for moisture content using an accurately calibrated hygrometer in accordance with BS 8201, Appendix A. Sub-floor temperature must be maintained above 5 °C.

Design priorities

The design priorities remind the design team what the client's priorities are. In this brief, they are set out for each specific type of space. They are a response to the client's priorities set out in the Strategic Brief, and are a valuable inclusion in this brief because they enable the client and user to verify the design team's understanding.

Design priorities – Reception

Both receptions seek to respond to the needs of Capital One's primary customer (potential and successful recruits) and other visitors.

Security procedures should not unduly impede the flow of personnel entering and leaving the building.

The impression created should not be ostentatious. It is open, efficient and contemporary in character.

The environment created must allow for maximum flexibility.

Way-finding should be an important consideration in the overall configuration

Furniture Brief

The Furniture Brief needs to capture the requirements for furniture items that are needed within an organisation to enable their business to function successfully. Rather like the urban masterplan, which deals with requirements on a 'macro' scale, the Furniture Brief is a response to requirements on a 'micro' scale.

The brief must define the needs of today and the future to ensure that the project can develop and a comprehensive solution can be achieved. The definition is not an isolated one however, and it usually manifests itself as part of a larger strategic response. As the information regarding the organisation is extracted, a process of validation and verification takes place, not only relative to hard, tangible elements such as furniture but also to 'softer' organisational issues. It is important to recognise the relationship between these issues; from the information obtained to create the brief, a 'generic' concept design can be developed for comment – that is 'non-manufacturer specific'.

The example below of a Furniture Brief from a large property investment company illustrates this important relationship with the Strategic Brief. The following are extracts taken from the Strategic Space Management Study. This is the first response back to the organisation after interviews and workshops.

The selected issues regarding furniture briefing are:

- mission statement;
- project objectives;
- planning strategy;
- product strategy;
- performance specification;
- milestones or decision making framework.

Commentary	Example

Mission statement

The mission statement gives the project team an understanding of the client's overall aim. The mission statement in this case strongly suggests that the organisation wants to change and the project team objectives can be drawn from this.

Combining old with new to lead the organisation into the twenty-first century with a cutting edge design solution that will foster better communication and collaboration.

Project objectives

The objectives set out what the project aims to achieve; the project team are provided with a basic understanding of the likely direction. At this point the objectives refer to the overall project strategy and from this we can begin to draw out the beginnings of the Furniture Brief.

* Move a highly cellular organisation into open plan with the required support network;
* capture the essence of 'nomadic' environments;[a]
* provide an interior design and furniture solution that will not date over the next 10 years;
* form the catalyst for more efficient, collaborative working practice.

Planning strategy

Endorsement of the planning strategy is important to the success of the project, particularly in terms of the programme. By stating the project team's understanding of the strategy at an early stage, the client is given the opportunity to react. The planning strategy sets out the early principles by which the furniture specification can be established.

During our discussions with the Steering Committee, it became apparent that an 'open plan' solution would be preferred. There is likely to be some resistance to this approach. However the potential benefits will be considerable. When images of other environments were shown to the committee, ideas associated with the modern, 'nomadic' environment were liked. The opposite was the case with the more traditional approach to open plan working – serried ranks of desks and a sea of faces was not a popular choice.

The key principles for providing a 'nomadic' environment are:
* organic, fluid planning;
* provision of control on immediate space (no 'fixed' work stations);
* movement within the space;
* a movement away from the 'corporate' feel.

Commentary	Example

Product strategy

The Product Strategy is the next level of endorsement required. It involves a higher level of investigation into the actual type of furniture product(s) required to meet the planning strategy and overall client objectives. Obtaining client approval of the 'generic' route helps to ensure a robust and fair product evaluation process.

In order to achieve a 'nomadic' environment we considered a 'generic' desking concept that has an opportunity of evolving as the business does. By using 'intelligent' furniture elements that have minimal component inventories there are many opportunities to change and develop space. The furniture market place however, is a complex one, with many different 'generic' solutions available. It is very important to clearly define the solution that best fits the organisation prior to exploring the market.

For this reason we have developed a series of space standards that are 'generic desking concepts' that reflect the varying tasks within the organisation.

Performance specification

The performance specification is an independent document developed throughout the briefing process. It is a culmination of all of the stages preceding it and is a detailed 'generic' description of the furniture types required.

The evaluation of products is by an agreed framework of quantitative and qualitative measures.

Quantitative

* *The main static element to be 2000 mm long and 800 mm deep providing a generous work surface;*
* *3 compartment cable management to rear axis to allow simple delivery of services at any point along the table.*

Qualitative

* *Crisp, clean appearance to match building aesthetic;*
* *desking to be certified to: BS 4875: Part 5: 1985(1995) Methods for determination of strength of tables and trolleys.*

All tiers within the organisation will utilise the 'standard' desk configuration described below. The standard offering will be supplemented by additional elements depending on task.

* The main static element to be 2000 mm long and 800 mm deep providing a generous work surface;
* the leg frames should be non-handed and not hinder the user;
* 3 compartment cable management to rear axis to allow simple delivery of services at any point along the table;
* attached to the main static element is a square 800 mm × 800 mm 'flexible' element that will allow the user 'control' of the work environment;
* crisp, clean appearance to match building aesthetic;
* desking to be certified to:
  − BS 4875: Part 5: 1985(1995) Methods for determination of strength of tables and trolleys;
  − BS 4875: Part 6: 1985(1995) Methods for determination of stability of tables and trolleys;
  − BS 5459: Part 1: 1977(1998) Specification for performance requirements and tests for office furniture: desks and tables;
  − BS 5940: Part 1: 1980(1997) Specification for design and dimensions of office workstations, desks, tables and chairs;
  − BS 6396: 1995 Specification for electrical systems in office furniture and office screens;
  − BS 7179: Part 5: 1990(1996) Specifications for VDT workstations.
* all materials to be from sustainable sources.

Commentary	Example
Milestones or decision making framework	
The decision making framework needs to be established at the project outset. It will ultimately choose the furniture products and therefore needs to have been party to all preceding briefing stages. For 'fast-track' projects, it is critical that the decision makers are available at the key milestone points.	For any project to operate successfully it is very important to establish exactly who will make the decisions that will effect the outcome. The timing of these decisions will relate to the project programme. The following are typical milestones: * agreement of the brief; * agreement of the 'generic' route; * agreement of the budget; * agreement of all scoring criteria; * agreement of product options.

[a] The nomadic environment is one that supports highly mobile knowledge workers with a variety of different activity settings.

Notes

1   The Urban design master plan for UCP was co-ordinated by Reek Bakker, with overall co-ordination of the development process by Twinstra Gudde. OMA were the urban designers for Papendorp with project co-ordination by the Leidsche Rijn area team. The brief for the Utrecht Central Project was prepared by Andrew Harrison, and for Papendorp by Lora Nicolaou, under the direction of John Worthington.

2   DEGW prepared a Strategic Brief for British Airways' new combined business centre at Prospect Park, Heathrow.

3   The Project Brief for the new building for the Computer Science Department at the University of York was prepared by Nicholas Hare Architects, their co-professionals on the team included Price & Myers (structural engineering), Hoare Lea & Partners (environmental engineering) and Gleeds (cost management).

4   The fit-out for the Capital One Financial Corporation in Nottingham was carried out by DEGW.

5   This example of a Furniture Brief was prepared by Peter Crouch of DEGW.

Part Three
The process in practice

Briefing is a continuous process, informing, challenging and inspiring the project team at every stage of the project.

Chapter 10 sets out the steps from pre-project to post-completion evaluation, highlights the activities to be considered in the process and provides checklists of questions the client should consider when reaching key decision points in the process.

As an inspiration for those considering a role as design brief managers within client bodies, or external consultancies, we have included at the end of this section the curriculum for the Design Brief Management Masters Course initiated at the Institute of Advanced Architectural Studies at the University of York and now continuing at the University of Sheffield.

Achieving success in briefing

In the largest and most complex projects, each stage may be formalised to ensure agreement, with a team of client personnel as well as external consultants dedicated to developing the content and spirit of the brief. In small projects, briefing documentation may be prepared and 'championed' by the client supported by his consultants, with the minimum of formal documentation and decision making points. However, even in the smallest project, expectations should be explicit with clear agreement points where proposals are reviewed against objectives.

10 Process primer

PRE-PROJECT STAGE

Statement of need

A concise statement which defines in operational and business terms the need or opportunity. It is the starting point for development of the Strategic Brief.

The Statement of need should state the problem not present a solution.

KEY ACTIVITIES
- Prepare Statement of need

WHO IS INVOLVED
Senior manager

Statement of need

Key points
- Clearly state corporate mission and business objectives;
- identify triggers for change;
- place need in a historic context, e.g. pattern of growth and change;
- identify sites/buildings and business resources available;
- identify comparable best practice.

Agreement and action

Agreement that there is a problem to be addressed, to carry out option appraisal and commit funding and resources for this.

KEY ACTIVITIES
- Client organisation's board agrees to initiate study;
- board identifies project sponsor;
- project sponsor appoints business case team;
- appoint client adviser.

WHO IS INVOLVED
Organisation's senior management team.

Assessment of needs

Assess the needs and resources of the organisation and generate options for meeting the need.

At this stage there is no presumption that the solution to the need will be a property based project. Options which are distinctively different must be considered, including 'do nothing'. The options may well include what turn out to be a set of projects.

The options appraisal should set out the needs and options open to the service, and include their relative benefits, drawbacks and risks.

Assessment of options

Testing options to meet requirements against available resources.
- Business options, e.g.:
  - change pattern of work;
  - improve use of technology;
  - re-allocate resources;
  - rent space on another site.
- Constructions options, e.g.:
  - new facility;
  - adapt existing facility;
  - build on another site.

KEY ACTIVITIES
- Risk assessment;
- appraisal against business strategy;
- analysis of client needs and resources available (including buildings affected – potential planning permissions);
- initial discussions with stakeholders which should include users of the building.

WHO IS INVOLVED
- Senior manager (project champion);
- business case team.

Statement of need	Agreement and Action	Assess-ment of Needs	Assess-ment of Options	Agreement and action	Strategic Brief	Action	Team

Agreement and action

Evaluation workshop, to establish that the project(s) represent value for money and provide the optimum solution for the department's need as well as the corporate need.
- Agree option to build;
- agree budget;
- agree procurement strategy;
- prepare Strategic Brief.

KEY ACTIVITIES
- Confirm that options have been identified;
- agree which option to pursue;
- identify budget problems and agree overall budget;
- identify timetable;
- agree procurement strategy;
- submissions for funding;
- sign-off;
- present chosen option;
- value management exercise;
- carry out a risk assessment;
- explore objectives.

OUTPUTS
The output from this workshop should provide the basis for the development of the Strategic Brief. The outputs should be:
- weighted objectives;
- programme.

WHO IS INVOLVED
- Project champion;
- project manager;
- stakeholders, including users;
- Project Board.

Strategic Brief

It is the essence of the project and the gauge by which the rest of the project development process is measured.
- State clearly the department's objectives and priorities;
- place these objectives within context;
- organisation structure and relationships;
- location;
- global cost;
- statements on size and capacity;
- building quality;
- human qualities;
- procurement process;
- timeframe;
- milestones.

KEY ACTIVITIES
- Check and clarify user needs;
- check and clarify service needs and standards;
- prepare the brief;
- prepare the Project Plan.

WHO IS INVOLVED
- Project champion.

Agreement and action

Meeting to formally agree the Strategic Brief before it can be passed on to the project team.

KEY ACTIVITIES
- Confirm that the Strategic Brief has taken account of all stakeholders' views and that a budget and timescale has been agreed;
- confirm that a value management and risk assessment exercise has taken place;
- to review plans for future activity;
- sign-off;
- select list of potential project teams;
- seek responses from project team;
- appoint project team.

WHO IS INVOLVED
- Project champion;
- project manager;
- key stakeholders including users.

PROJECT STAGE

Validation

The design team tests its understanding of the project and Strategic Brief. It is an opportunity for the design team to establish that all assumptions have been clarified. It can be undertaken through interviews with the client and users to gain a further understanding of the project as well as surveys of the site or existing building.

KEY ACTIVITIES
- Explore opportunities, constraints and costs arising from the Strategic Brief;
- confirm to the client an understanding of the Strategic Brief;
- agree any changes to the Strategic Brief and confirm;
- consider design options and develop concepts;
- define which risks are limited and high;
- prepare elemental costs;
- prepare concept scheme design;
- apply for outline planning consent.

WHO IS INVOLVED
Design team.

Draft Project Brief

The aim of this brief is to convert the organisational terms of the Strategic Brief into building terms fixing functional relationships, giving initial indications of sizes, areas and volumes, including planning and structural grids, principal building systems, and proposed elevations. It gives initial sizes and quantities to elements and gives an outline budget.

KEY POINTS
- Validation process should explore the opportunities, constraints and costs arising from the design proposals;
- give initial indications of size and quantities;
- give an outline elemental budget;
- clearly set out what is expected at next stage.

WHO IS INVOLVED
Design team.

EVALUATION

A workshop at which the design direction is reviewed. This evaluation is an opportunity for the client to review and approve the direction of the design and assure themselves that the objectives of the Strategic Brief are being met. It also provides an opportunity to test the design using value management techniques. It could last half a day or one day depending on the size of the project. The session should be facilitated by an experienced facilitator outside the project. Further work on the Draft Project Brief and concept design may be required after this meeting before sign-off.

KEY ACTIVITIES
- Present proposals – design team;
- value management/engineering;
- risk assessment;
- test the proposals against the Strategic Brief;
- prepare a report of the conclusions.

WHO IS INVOLVED
- Project board;
- project champion;
- project manager;
- stakeholders including users;
- design team.

Validation	Draft Project Brief	Evaluation	Testing Opportunities	Project Brief	Evaluation

Testing the opportunities

Process of interactive, iterative communication and meetings between members of the design team. The design team will finalise room layouts, finishes, colours, etc. The extent to which fixtures and fittings are included in the design will be defined in the brief and the design must either be fully developed or the requirement for future installation carefully considered and allowed for.

KEY ACTIVITIES
- Develop the concept, design strategies and requirements;
- decide which elements are limited risk and which are innovative and high risk;
- prepare elemental costs;
- apply for planning consent;
- prepare concept scheme design;
- value management exercise;
- develop detailed brief;
- develop scheme design;
- develop outline specification;
- develop performance brief for elements of building.

WHO IS INVOLVED
Design team.

Project Brief

This brief includes the scheme design and should cover:
- the aim of the design;
- location of site, information on planning approvals and other detailed permissions agreed;
- dimensions of spaces and elements to be provided;
- cost plan;
- performance specifications for environmental systems and services;
- proposals for maintenance;
- key milestones and targets;
- performance measures.

KEY ACTIVITIES
- Prepare scheme design;
- confirm cost plan;
- assess risks;
- compare with Strategic Brief;
- prepare schedule of accommodation.

KEY POINTS
- Identify risks;
- assess quality;
- define the measures for success;
- fix as much of the design as possible.

WHO IS INVOLVED
Design team.

EVALUATION

A workshop at which the design is fixed and agreed by all client stakeholders so that production documents and construction can proceed.

The evaluation is an opportunity for the client to review and approve the design and assure themselves that the objectives of the Strategic Brief are being met. Once this evaluation is complete the design should be fixed with no more changes. It could last half a day or one day depending on the size of the project. This workshop should be facilitated by an experienced facilitator outside the project.

KEY ACTIVITIES
- Present proposals;
- carry out a value engineering exercise;
- assess risks;
- test against the Strategic Brief;
- sign-off if possible or hold a formal agreement meeting following this workshop.

WHO IS INVOLVED
- Project board;
- project champion;
- project manager;
- stakeholders including users;
- design team.

POST-PROJECT STAGE

Commissioning building

- Adjust the building to the need;
- test building systems against stated performance criteria.

Evaluation of process

Evaluation of:
- performance and communication between and within team members: client, design and construction teams;
- how well contractual procedures worked;
- shortfalls in programme.

Evaluation of product and process

KEY POINTS
- Compare the process and facility against the business objectives in Strategic Brief and with Statement of need;
- clearly set out findings of evaluation in objective manner;
- clearly set out objectives of post-occupancy evaluation.

KEY ACTIVITIES
- Interviews;
- facilitated post-project evaluation workshop.

OUTPUT
A report which identifies the types of problem encountered during the process and how they might be overcome in the future. Clearly states the performance against the expectations set out in the Strategic Brief.

WHO IS INVOLVED
- Client team including the project board, project champion, project manager;
- consultant team;
- contractors;
- facilitator for the workshop.

Commission-ing Building	Evaluation of process	Monitoring	Post-completion evaluation	Feedback	

Monitoring during use of building

- Space performance;
- records of feedback, e.g.:
  - responses of people
  - complaints
  - maintenance feedback.
- measures:
  - energy use
  - cost in use.

KEY ACTIVITIES

- Collect information on energy bills; water consumption, etc.;
- record feedback, e.g., user/staff responses, complaints, maintenance.

WHO IS INVOLVED

- Manager of the building.

Post-completion evaluation

- Assess building performance;
- assess client/user satisfaction;
- assess building usage;
- local community and organisation's market.

KEY ACTIVITIES

- Interviews;
- workshops/focus groups;
- analysis of energy data, etc.;
- questionnaire circulation;
- analysis of questionnaire responses;
- preparation of report.

OUTPUT

- Written document;
- generic conclusions to public domain;
- detail conclusions fed back to long-term building programme or best practice guide;
- agreement to scheme design and Project Brief by project sponsor;
- agreement to scheme design and Project Brief by project sponsor.

FEEDBACK
Post-occupancy survey report

This report should:

- set out the purpose of the study;
- describe the building and its main function;
- summarise the conclusions on building performance and give reasons for good or poor performance;
- include detailed reports on survey data;
- include detailed reports on space survey, building capacity and comparison with design targets;
- give details on lessons learned; and,
- give major points for action.

Checklist of questions to address during a project

Questions to be asked when assessing needs

Organisation

* What are the organisation's objectives?
* What are the organisation's policies, procedures and methods?
* Can the relationship between the departments in the organisation be described?
* What changes in markets, technology, and staff skills, may influence the number and type of staff and equipment required in the future?
* How does the organisation approve development projects and authorise the finance for them?
* What are the distinctive features of the organisation's culture?
* How does the organisation wish to present itself to the public, customers and staff?
* What attributes does the organisation value most highly?

Buildings

* How suitable for its business are the organisation's buildings?
* How much usable space is there, and what are the quality of environmental conditions?
* What opportunities are there for improving utilisation and environmental quality?
* What are the current conditions of the buildings?
* How do the standards which the organisation sets for its buildings compare with best practice?
* How does the way in which the organisation runs and manages its buildings compare with best practice?
* What is the most significant improvement that can be made within the next 5 years in sites, buildings and internal layouts

Questions to be asked in establishing the Strategic Brief

* Can the main benefits to the organisation that will be provided by the new buildings be described?
* What is the business case for the new buildings?
* Why can't the existing buildings be used?
* What is the increased efficiency that will result from operating in the new buildings?
* What are the main risks involved in the proposed approach?
* What are the most difficult practical and technical issues to be resolved in the design and construction of the new buildings?
* How does the proposed approach compare with comparable operations in the UK and abroad?
* What procurement route will best suit the organisation's needs and why?
* What roles are required in the design and production team and when should they be appointed?

* How quickly could the new buildings be produced?
* How and by whom are decisions on quality and timing made?
* How will the success of the project be judged?

Questions to be asked in establishing the Draft Project Brief

* What additional information is needed to prepare concept designs and how will it be obtained?
* What performance standards will be provided in the new building?
* What flexibility in use will be provided in the new building?
* What quality standards will be provided in the new facility?
* What safety provisions will be incorporated in the new facilities?
* Does the project team understand the priorities in respect of quality, time and cost?
* What are the risks that the cost will exceed the budget?
* What are the risks that the project will be handed over late?
* What are the main areas of possible construction problems and how they will be managed?
* What are the construction safety risks?
* What procurement route will best meet my needs?
* How will the success of the project be judged?
* How will the design help the organisation achieve business objectives?
* How will the design serve to support organisation's policies, procedures and methods, and work of divisions and departments?
* How will the design serve to support communication throughout the organisation?
* How will the design serve to support the flow of information through the organisation?
* How will the design support the flow of materials and products through the organisation?
* How will the new facility work for customers/users/visitors?

Questions to be asked in establishing the Project Brief

* What progress has been made towards meeting the success criteria for the project?
* What performance standards will be provided for each of the elements and systems that form the new facilities?
* What quality standards will be provided for each of the elements and systems that form the new facilities?
* What safety requirements have been incorporated into elements and systems that form the new facilities?
* How easy will the elements and systems be to maintain, keep clean and replace?
* What are the risks that costs will exceed budget?
* What are the mechanisms for controlling and monitoring change?
* How and when is the success of each element and system in meeting the defined performance requirements measured?

- What are the risks that the facility will be handed over late?
- What other risks are there?
- What is the likelihood of defects in new buildings?

Questions to be asked at post-completion stage

- Is the building being used as intended?
- Have the stated business goals for the project been met?
- Does the project meet the measurable performance criteria cited in earlier briefs, such as:
    - capacity;
    - operating costs;
    - environmental standards;
    - spatial efficiency;
    - image?
- Has the building adapted to changing needs?

- Did the building meet the cost and time targets?
- Does the facilities management system match the project concept?
- How does the use of space compare with the planning concept?
- Where are the points of friction (snagging list) – failures?
- How satisfied are the users?
- Will information be fed back into the:
    - construction industry – knowledge base of construction professionals (professional body of knowledge); and,
    - client's future building programme – experienced client?
- Has the post-completion included evaluation of:
    - project organisation and procedures;
    - building performance;
    - client/user satisfaction;
    - building use?

11 Design brief management

The Design Brief Management Masters course was begun at the Institute of Advanced Architectural Studies (IoAAS) of the University of York in 1995. The part-time, two years, workplace-focused course was designed for mid-career professionals who were already working as professional briefing or design managers in large client organisations, or consultants within the design, construction or property sectors.

The curriculum below was prepared by course co-ordinator Adrian Leaman, in association with IoAAS Director Professor John Worthington. The background reading list prepared by John Worthington has developed since the inception of the course, and is currently provided for the Design Brief Management Masters course at the University of Sheffield.[1]

Curriculum

The course has five specialist module courses underpinned by three management modules. Each of the five specialist modules are part of a total quality cycle from inception to completion, including feedback. The brief is based on strategic principles which underpin all aspects of the briefing-design-use-feedback cycle. These are gained from a detailed understanding of systems and use, with a balanced judgement on likely futures of organisations and buildings. The five elements: *Briefing, Use, Futures, Systems* and *Principles* make up the demand side of the building and construction equation. The supply side – how the brief is turned into a building – is not a taught component, although participants' everyday work will encompass this aspect. Underpinning these are the management modules: *Financial Management, Strategic Management* and *Managing Change*.

The course modules are:

- *Financial management.* This looks at the strategic and tactical views of finance. The allocation of, management and funding of resources within an organisation.
- *Strategic management.* Considers the long-term issues to be managed within an organisation.
- *Managing change.* Looks at creating and sustaining the necessary climate for growth within an organisation.
- *Briefing.* This examines the basis of briefing methods and techniques, and

their application. It considers how needs are investigated and expressed from a client and user's perspective.

- *Use.* This examines the factual basis of needs and requirements from a management and occupant perspective, but also includes an overview of design principles for usability.
- *Futures.* This course interprets technical, social and environmental change as it may affect buildings and their future uses. It looks at decision making in the face of uncertainty and futuristic design, and management visions.
- *Systems.* This course covers in more detail the methods and techniques introduced in the *Use* module. It outlines analytical methods which are considered usable, practical and give meaningful results.
- *Principles.* This module elaborates on the strategic principles which underpin all aspects of the briefing-design-use feedback cycle. It places design, procurement and use of buildings within the wider framework, examining how buildings work. It also examines major ethical and public interest considerations as well as the underlying philosophical tenets.

Further reading

Inspirational reading

Allinson, K., *The Wild Card of Design: A Perspective on Architecture in a Project Management Environment*, Butterworth, Oxford 1993.

Argyle, M., *The Psychology of Interpersonal Behaviour*, Penguin Books, Baltimore 1967.

Brand, S., *How Buildings Learn*, Orion, London 1994.

Davis, S. and Davidson, W., *20–20 Vision: Transform Your Business Today to Succeed in Tomorrow's Economy*, Business Books Limited, London 1991.

Gray, C., Hughes, W. and Bennet, J., *The Successful Management of Design*, Department of Construction Management and Engineering, University of Reading 1993.

Kidder, T., *The Soul of a New Machine*, Allen Lane, London 1982.

Lawson, B., *How Designers Think*, Butterworth Architecture, London 1980.

Norman, D. A., *The Psychology of Everyday Things*, Basic Books 1988.

Wolstenholme, E., *System Enquiry: A Systems Dynamics Approach*, John Wiley, Chichester 1990.

Zeisel, J., *Inquiry by Design*, Cambridge University Press, Cambridge 1981.

Blackmore, C., *The Client's Tale*, RIBA Publications, London 1990.

Briefing

Construction Industry Board, *Briefing the Team*, Thomas Telford, London 1997.

Duerk, D., *Architectural Programming: Information Management for Design*, Van Norstrand Reinhold, New York 1993.

Hubbard, B., *The Theory of Practice: Architecture in Three Discourses*, MIT Press, Cambridge, Mass. 1995.

Latham, M., *Constructing the Team*, HMSO, London 1994.

Lawson, B., *How Designers Think*, Butterworth, Oxford 1990.

Markus, T., *Building Performance*, Halstead Press, New York 1972.

Pena, W., Parshall, S. and Kelly, K., *Problem Seeking: An Architectural Programming Primer*, AIA Press, Washington DC 1987.

Preiser, W., *Programming the Built Environment*, Van Norstrand Reinhold, New York 1985.

Prieser, W., *Building Evaluation*, Plenum Press, New York 1989.

Zeisel, J., *Inquiry by Design: Tools for Environment-behavior Research*, Cambridge University Press, Cambridge 1981.

Use

Argyle, M., *The Psychology of Interpersonal Behaviour*, Penguin Books, London 1967.

Baird, G. *et al.*, *Building Evaluation Technologies*, McGraw Hill, New York 1996.

Becker, F., *Workplace Strategies and Organisational Performance*, Premise and Facilities Management 1993.

Becker, F., *The Total Workplace Facilities Management and the Elastic Organisation*, Van Norstrand Reinhold, New York 1990.

Becker, F. and Steel, F., *Workplace by Design*, Jossey-Bass, San Francisco 1995.

Bentley, I. *et al.*, *Responsive Environments: A Manual for Designers*, Architectural Press, London 1985.

Brambillo, R. and Losgo, G., *For Pedestrians Only*, Whitney Library of Design, New York 1977.

Broadbent, G., *Design in Architecture — Architecture and the Human Sciences*, John Wiley, New York 1973.

Canter, D. and Lee, T., *Psychology and the Built Environment*, Architectural Press, London 1974.

Deasy, C., *Designing Places for People*, Whitney Library of Design, New York 1996.

Duffy F., Laing, A. and Crisp, V., *The Responsible Workplace*, Butterworth-Heinemann, Oxford 1993.

Eley, J. and Marmot, A., *Understanding Offices*, Penguin Books, London 1995.

Eley, P. and Worthington, J., *Industrial Rehabilitation*, Architectural Press, London 1984.

Girouard, M., *Cities & People*, Yale University Press, London 1985.

Gutman, R. (ed.), *People and Buildings*, Basic Books, New York 1972.

Hall, E., *The Silent Language*, Doubleday, New York 1959.

Hall, E., *The Hidden Dimension*, Doubleday, New York 1966.

Harbraken, N., *Supports: An Alternative to Mass Housing*, Architectural Press, London 1972.

Harrison, A., Loe, E. and Read, J., *Intelligent Buildings in South East Asia*, E & FN Spon, London 1998.

Hillier, B. and Hanson, J., *The Social Logic of Space*, Cambridge University Press 1984.

Jacobs, A., *Great Streets*, MIT Press (Paperback), Boston 1995.

Kahn, V. and Sheridan, L., *Housing Quality: A Practical Guide for Tenants and their Representatives*, Joseph Rowntree, York 1996.

Kaplan, R. and Norton, D., *The Balanced Scorecard*, Harvard Business School Press, Boston 1996.

King, A. (ed.), *Buildings and Society*, Routledge and Kegan Paul, London 1980.

Kroll, L., *An Architecture of Complexity*, MIT Press 1987.

Leaman, A., *Buildings in the Age of Paradox*, Institute of Advanced Architectural Studies, The University of York, York 1995.

Lynch, K., *The Image of the City*, Harvard University Press 1960.

Markus, T., *Buildings and Power*, Routledge, London and New York 1993.

Mitchell, W. (ed.), *Environmental Design: Research and Practice*, Proceedings of EDRA 3/AR8 Conference, University of California, LA 1972.

Newman, O., *Defensible Space: Crime Prevention Through Urban Design*, Macmillan, New York 1972.

Nielson, J., *Usability Engineering*, Academic Press 1993.

Norman, D., *The Psychology of Everyday Things*, Basic Books 1998.

OES Building Bulletin 64, *Adaptable Facilities in Further Education for Business and Office Studies*, HMSO, London 1986.

Rapaport, A., *House Form and Culture*, Prentice Hall, New Jersey 1967.

Rudofsky, B., *Streets for People*, Doubleday, New York 1969.

Sommer, R., *Personal Space: The Behavioural Basis of Design*, Prentice Hall, New Jersey 1969.

Spedding, A. (ed.), *Handbook of Facilities Management*, CIOB Longman Scientific and Technical 1994.

Steele, F., *The Sense of Place*, Van Norstrand Reinhold, New York 1981.

Woods Shadrack, *The Man in the Street*, Pelican Books, Baltimore 1975.

Worthington, J., *Reinventing the Workplace*, Butterworth-Heinemann, Oxford 1997.

Worthington, J. and Konja, A., *Fitting out the Workplace*, Architectural Press, London 1988.

Young, M., *The Metronomic Society: Natural Rhythms and Human Society*, Thames and Hudson, London 1998.

Futures

Design for Change: The Architecture of DEGW, Watermark/Birkhauser, Basel 1997.

Ackoff, Broholm, Snow, *Revitalising Western Economics*, Jossey-Bass, London 1984.

Adams, J., *Risk*, UCL Press, London 1995.

Allen, J. and Massey, D., *The Economy in Question*, Sage Publications, Open University 1998.

Bernstein, P., *Against the Gods: The Remarkable Story of Risk*, John Wiley, New York 1996.

Binney, G. and Williams, C., *Leaning into the Future: Changing the Way People Change Organisations*, Nicholas Breazley, London 1997.

Brand, S., *The Media Lab*, Penguin Books, London 1988.

Cairncross, F., *The Death of Distance*, Orion Business Books, London 1997.

Cairncross, F., *Courtesy the Earth*, The Economist Business Books, London 1991.

Davidson and Malone, *The Virtual Corporation*, Harper Business, New York 1993.

Davis and Meyer, *Blur: The Speed of Change in the Connected Economy*, Capstone, Oxford 1998.

Edington, G., *Property Management – A Customer Focused Approach*, Macmillan, London 1997.

Edvinsson and Malone, *Intellectual Capital*, Piatkus, London 1997.

Garratt, B., *The Learning Organisation*, Fontana Paperback, London 1987.

Hall, P., *London 2002*, Unwin Hyman, London 1989.

Hamel and Prahaled, *Competing for the Future*, Harvard Business School Press, Boston 1994.

Hammer, M. and Champny, J., *Re-engineering the Corporation – A Manifesto for Business Revolution*, Harper Business, New York 1994.

Handy, C., *The Empty Raincoat*, Random House Hutchinson, London 1994.

Hutton, W., *The State We're In*, Vintage, London 1996.

Kermally, S., *Management Ideas in Brief*, Butterworth-Heineman, Oxford 1997.

Kock, R. and Godden, I., *Managing without Management*, Nicholas Breazley, London 1997.

McRae, H., *The World in 2020: Power Culture and Prosperity – A View for the Future*, Harper Collins, London 1995.

Ormerod, P., *The Death of Economics*, Faber & Faber, London 1995.

Ormerod, P., *Butterfly Economics*, Faber & Faber, London 1998.

Plant, R., *Managing Change and Making it Stick*, Fontana 1989.

Rheingold, H., *The Virtual Community*, Harper, New York 1994.

RIBA, *Strategic Study of the Profession Part 1 & 2*, RIBA Publications, London 1992.

Ringland, G., *Scenario Planning: Managing for the Future*, John Wiley, New York 1998.

Scott Morton, M. (ed.), *The Corporation of the 1990s*, Oxford University Press, Oxford 1991.

Seymour, J., *Changing Lifestyle*, Victor Gollancz, London 1991.

Sherden, W., *The Fortune Sellers*, John Wiley, New York 1998.

Sprent, P., *Taking Risks: The Science of Uncertainty*, Penguin Books, London 1998.

Stewart, T., *Intellectual Capital: The New Wealth of Organisations*, Nicholas Breazley, London 1997.

Van der Heijden, K., *Scenarios: The Art of Strategic Conversation*, John Wiley, New York 1997.

Systems

Argyris, C., *Understanding Organisational Behaviour*, Tavistock, London 1966.

Argyris, C. and Schon, D., *Organisational Learning: A Theory of Action Perspective*, Addison Wesley, Boston 1978.

Brand, S., *How Buildings Learn*, Viking 1994.

Checkland, P., *Systems Thinking – Systems Practice*, John Wiley, Chichester 1981.

Ferguson, F., *Architecture: Cities and the Systems Approach*, George Braziller, New York 1975.

Kelly, K., *Out of Control*, Addison Wesley, Boston 1994.

Leaman, A., *Buildings in the Age of Paradox*, Institute of Advanced Architectural Studies, The University of York, York 1996.

Peters, T., *Thriving on Chaos: Handbook for a Management Revolution*, ????? 1989.

Rothschild, M., *Bionomics*, Futura, London 1992.

Senge, P., *The Fifth Discipline*, Doubleday, New York 1990.

Principles

Abbott, A., *The System of Professions*, University of Chicago Press 1988.

Allinson, K., *The Wild Card of Design*, Butterworth Architecture, Oxford 1993.

Allinson, K., *Getting There by Design*, Architectural Press, Oxford 1997.

Arie de Geus, *The Living Company; Growth Learning and Longevity in Business*, Nicholas Breazley, London 1997.

Collins and Porras, *Built to Last: Successful Habits of Visionary Companies*, HarperCollins, New York 1994.

Evans, R. and Russell, P., *The Creative Manager*, Jossey-Bass 1992.

Gutman, R., *Architectural Practice: A Critical Review*, Princeton Architectural Press 1988.

Harvard Business Review, *On Knowledge Management*, Harvard Business School Press, Boston 1998.

Katzenbach, J. and Smith, D., *The Wisdom of Teams*, McGraw-Hill, London 1993.

Kaye, D., *Game Change: The Impact of Information Technology on Corporate Strategies and Structures*, Heinemann 1989.

Kelly, K., *New Rules for the New Economy: 10 Radical Strategies for a Connected World*, Viking Penguin, London 1998.

Maister, D., *Managing the Professional Service Firm*, Free Press 1993.

Maister, D., *True Professionalism: The Courage to Care About Your People, Your Clients and Your Career*, The Free Press, New York 1997.

Michelthwaite, J., *The Witch Doctors*, Butterworth-Heinemann, London 1996.

Raelin, J., *The Clash of Cultures*, Harvard Business School Press, Boston 1985.

Schon, D., *The Reflective Practitioner*, Jossey-Bass 1987.

Scott Mark, *The Intellect Industry*, John Wiley, Chichester 1998.

Womack, P. and Jones, D., *Lean Thinking: Banish Waste and Create Wealth in Your Corporation*, Touchstone, London 1997.

Additional reading on communication and teamwork

Adair, J., *Effective Teambuilding*, Gower Publishing, Aldershot 1986.

Baden-Hellard, R., *Project Partnering*, Thomas Telford Publications, London 1995.

Belbin, R. M., *Management Teams*, Butterworth-Heinemann Ltd, Oxford 1993.

Belbin, R. M., *Team Roles at Work*, Butterworth-Heinemann Ltd, Oxford 1994.

Emmitt, S., *Architectural Management in Practice*, Addison Wesley Longman, Harlow 1999.

Handy, C., *Understanding Organisations*, Penguin Books, Middlesex 1993.

Handy, C., *Gods of Management*, Arrow Books, London 1991.

Janner, G., *Janner on Chairing*, Gower Publishing, Aldershot 1989.

Langmuir, E., *Mountaincraft and Leadership*, The Scottish Sports Council, Edinburgh 1984.

Robinson, D., *Getting the Best out of People*, Kogan-Page, London 1988.

Woodcock, M., *Team Development Manual*, Gower Publishing, Aldershot 1989.

Index